The Netherlands

Australia

Germany

Ireland

Austria

Spain

Switzerland

Luxembourg

Canada

Mexico

United Kingdom

United States

New Zealand

Portugal

Finland

International Consumer Protection

The Center for International Legal Studies

The Center for International Legal Studies is a non-profit research and publications institute established and operating under Austrian law and with its international headquarters in Salzburg, Austria.

The Center has operated since 1976 in Salzburg, and it has had a close cooperation with the Faculty of Law of the University of Salzburg, the Austro-American Institute in Vienna, and numerous other universities and educational institutions in Europe and the United States.

International Consumer Protection

VOLUME 1

PUBLISHED UNDER THE AUSPICES OF
THE CENTER FOR INTERNATIONAL LEGAL STUDIES

Edited by

Dennis Campbell
Center for International Legal Studies,
Salzburg, Austria

Springer-Science+Business Media, B.V.

A C.I.P. Catalogue record for this book is available from the Library of Congress.

ISBN 978-0-7923-3390-6
ISBN 978-94-017-4869-8 (eBook)
DOI 10.1007/978-94-017-4869-8

Printed on acid-free paper

Reference List of Contributors and Law Firms

AUSTRALIA:	Graeme Johnson Freehill Hollingdale & Page MLC Centre 19 Martin Place Sydney NSW 2000 Australia Tel: (02) 225 5000 Fax: (02) 233 6430
AUSTRIA:	Elisabeth Stern Grohs-Hofer-Reiner Freyung 6/11 (Schottenhof) 1010 Vienna Austria Tel: 533 87 26-0 Fax: 533 87 28 34
BELGIUM:	Jules Stuyck and Chantal Goemans Katholieke Universiteit Leuven Faculteit Rechtsgeleerdheid Tiensestraat 41 3000 Leuven Belgium Tel: (016) 28 52 06 / 28 52 14 Fax: (016) 28 53 14
CANADA:	Dale B. Pope Singleton Urquhart MacDonald 1200-1125 Howe Street Vancouver, B. C. V6Z 2K8 Canada Tel: (604) 682 7474 Fax: (604) 682 1283

DENMARK:

Susanne Borch
Advokat
H.E. Teglersvej 9
2920 Charlottenlund
Denmark
Tel: 31 63 23 83
Fax: 33 12 18 79

FINLAND:

Taina Tuohino
Heikki Haapaniemi Ky
Mannerheimintie 14 B
P.O. Box 232
00101 Helsinki
Finland
Tel: 358 0 177 613
Fax: 358 0 653 873

MEXICO:

Juan Francisco Torres Landa R.
and Ramón Bravo Herrera
Barrera Siqueiros y Torres Landa, S.C.
Sinaloa 153, Colonia Roma
Delegacion Cuauhtemoc
06700 Mexico, D.F.
Mexico
Tel: 553-007
Fax: 553 8379

NETHERLANDS:

Peter Klik
Erasmus University Rotterdam
Faculty of Law
P.O. Box 1738
3000 DR Rotterdam
The Netherlands
Tel: 010 408 11 11
Fax: 010 452 02 04

SPAIN:	Jordi Faus Santasusana Jausàs & Terricabras Lleó XIII, 23 08022 Barcelona Spain Tel: 212 61 54 Fax: 418 21 99
UNITED KINGDOM:	Lynn West Norton Rose Blackfriars House PO Box 570 19 New Bridge Street London EC4V 6DH England Tel: 071 283 2434 Fax: 071 588 1181/410 0891
UNITED STATES:	John Letchinger and Donald Flayton Wildman, Harrold, Allen & Dixon 225 West Wacker Drive Chicago, Illinois USA 60606-1229 Tel: (312) 201 2000 Fax: (312) 201 2555

Table of Contents

Volume 1

Australia

Austria

Section 3
Testing

Section 4
Advertising

Section 5
Standard Terms (Adhesive Contracts)

Section 6
Reasonable Pricing and Price Controls

Belgium

Canada

Volume 2

Denmark

Finland

The Netherlands

Spain

United Kingdom

United States

Australia

Graeme Johnson
Freehill Hollingdale & Page
Sydney, NSW, Australia

Australia

Australia

Section 1

Introduction

1.1 Australia's System of Government

Australia has a federal system of government. There is a Federal Constitution which allocates specific powers to the central government (the "Commonwealth"), leaving the residue to the states. Some powers are exercisable by the Commonwealth concurrently with the states, but state legislation which is inconsistent with Commonwealth legislation is invalid.[1]

This chapter will review the Commonwealth consumer protection laws and those of the two most populous Australian states, New South Wales and Victoria. The other states, Queensland, Tasmania, South Australia, and Western Australia, have their own particular consumer protection laws which are not considered here. The two internal Australian Territories, the Australian Capital Territory and the Northern Territory, also have their own legislative regimes, which are not addressed here.

1.2 Sources of Power

There are a number of heads of Commonwealth legislative power [2] that are relevant to consumer protection. They include:

(1) Trade and commerce with other countries and among the states; (*placitum* (i));
(2) Postal, telegraphic, telephonic, and other like services (*placitum* (v));
(3) Banking, other than state banking (*placitum* (viii));
(4) Insurance, other than state insurance (*placitum* (xvi));

---

1 Constitution, Section 109.
2 Constitution, Section 51.

(5) Foreign corporations and trading or financial corporations formed with the limits of the Commonwealth (*placitum* (xx)); and
(6) External affairs (*placitum* (xxviii)).

It may seem odd that the "external affairs" power is considered relevant to consumer protection, but this head of power has been given an expansive interpretation by Australia's High Court. The Commonwealth can use the power when Australia in good faith enters into an international agreement, whatever the subject matter of the agreement.[1]

The Commonwealth government has exercised its powers to legislate quite comprehensively, and with effect throughout Australia, for the control of consumer protection and restrictive trade practices. However, because there is no head of power given to the Commonwealth over "consumer protection", the states retain considerable residual control and have their own significant laws.

The Commonwealth and the states can pass mutual legislation. They have cooperated in introducing uniform Australian legislation in some fields. Examples include Australia's Corporations Law, the model Food Acts, the Therapeutic Goods Act, and the Mutual Recognition legislation.

1.3 Judicial System

Australia's judicial system is based on the English Common Law model, as distinct from the European civil system. The litigation process is adversarial rather than inquisitorial. There are federal and state courts with separate areas of jurisdiction, although, at the Superior Court level, the state Supreme Courts and Federal Courts of Australia can (to a large degree) exercise each other's jurisdictions.[2]

A system of statutory tribunals also has been created, most notably the Federal Administrative Appeals Tribunal which has enumerated jurisdiction to review decisions under Commonwealth enactments. In the consumer law field, the states have created consumer or commercial tribunals to deal with minor consumer disputes.

---

1 *The Commonwealth* vs. *Tasmania* (1983) 46 ALR 625.
2 Jurisdiction of Courts (Cross-Vesting) Acts.

Section 2

Consumer Protection in Australia

2.1 Development of Consumer Protection

The consumer movement in Australia began in the 1960s, paralleling the growth of the movement in the United States. Before then, Australia's consumer protection legislation consisted largely of the various state Sale of Goods Acts, which implied terms in sale of goods contracts. Through the 1970s and 1980s, there was great legislative impetus, initially at the Commonwealth level but followed by the states.

In 1974, the Commonwealth introduced the Trade Practices Act. The Act sought, as comprehensively as the Commonwealth's powers allowed, to deal with restrictive trade practices,[1] consumer protection,[2] and liability of manufacturers and importers of defective goods.[3]

> "The general purpose and scope of . . . (Part IV) can be described by saying that it contains provisions which proscribe and regulate agreements and conduct and which are aimed at procuring and maintaining competition in trade and commerce."[4]

Part V of the Act deals with:

(1) Unfair consumer practices;
(2) Product safety and product information;
(3) Conditions and warranties in consumer transactions; and
(4) Actions against manufacturers and importers of goods by consumers.

Part V contains a general proscription, Section 52, which states simply that:

---

1 Trade Practices Act, Part IV.
2 Trade Practices Act, Part V.
3 Trade Practices Act, Part VA.
4 *Refrigerated Express Lines (Australia) Pty. Ltd.* vs. *Australian Meat & Livestock Corporation* (1980) 44 FLR 445 at p. 460, per Deane J.

> "A corporation shall not, in trade or commerce, engage in conduct that is misleading or deceptive or is likely to mislead or deceive."

This provision has generated an enormous amount of litigation. Much of this litigation is between corporations protecting their commercial activities. Often, this indirectly assists consumers.

The 1980s saw significant legislative movement at the state level. In 1985 and 1987, respectively, Victoria and New South Wales introduced Fair Tradings Acts, which to a large extent are modelled on Part V of the Commonwealth Trade Practices Act. In particular, each of those Acts contains a provision equivalent to Section 52 of the Trade Practices Act, but extending the proscription to conduct by natural persons.[1]

In the 1980s, New South Wales and Victoria also introduced uniform credit legislation. This legislation[2] is described below.

2.2 Private Law, Self-Regulation, Administrative Law

2.2.1 In General

Traditionally, the emphasis in Australia was on the private law enforcement by consumers of their legislative and contractual rights. However, during the 1970s and 1980s, a number of statutory bodies were created to assist consumers. These include the Trade Practices Commission at Commonwealth level and various consumer claims tribunals in the states.

Various trades and professions are regulated under state law by licensing schemes.

Following the economic crash of the late 1980s, it was speculated by many that government reaction to the frauds perpetrated and the economic harm caused to individuals and institutions would be to increase the powers of the corporate regulators.

While to some degree that has happened, in the area of consumer protection there has been a trend, albeit limited, toward greater emphasis on self-regulation and empowerment of consumers rather than the use of penalties and quasi-criminal sanctions.

---

1 New South Wales, Section 42; Victoria, Section 11.

2 New South Wales, Credit Act 1984, Credit (Administration Act) 1984, and Credit (Finance Brokers) Act 1984; Victoria, Credit Act 1984, Credit (Administration) Act 1984, and Credit Reporting Act 1978.

2.2.2 *Self-Regulation*

In 1989, the major Australian banks created the Banking Industry Ombudsman to deal with minor disputes between banks and their consumers. This was done by the incorporation of a company limited by guarantee, the Australian Banking Industry Ombudsman Limited. The members of the company are banks. The Ombudsman considers disputes relating to the provision of banking services.

The Ombudsman facilitates the settlement of disputes. He or she may make recommendations. If a recommendation is accepted by an applicant, but not by a bank, the Ombudsman has power to award a sum not exceeding Aus. $100,000 against the bank. If the applicant agrees to accept the award, the bank is bound to pay the sum because of certain undertakings given by the bank.

In New South Wales, the Department of Consumer Affairs is authorized by the Fair Trading Act to assist industry bodies to develop codes of practice, mandatory and voluntary.[1] In 1992 and 1993, the New South Wales Department of Consumer Affairs developed, endorsed, and launched the revised Entertainment Industry Code of Fair Practice and the Domestic Whitegoods Service Industry Advisory Code of Practice. Codes of practice, if approved by the Minister, may receive statutory support.[2]

Federally, the Broadcasting Services Act 1992 has required codes of self-regulation in the interests of consumers of broadcasts.[3]

A number of hearings are held from time to time by state and federal governments into specific industry sectors. These, among other things, consider the issue of further self-regulation.[4]

2.2.3 *Administrative Law*

Various forms of price control regulation exist in Australia, in both federal and state legislation. In particular, the Prices Surveillance Authority, established by the federal government under the Prices Surveillance Act 1983, embodies a scheme of price surveillance.

---

1 Fair Trading Act 1987 (New South Wales), Part 7.

2 Fair Trading Act 1987 (New South Wales), Section 75(1).

3 Broadcasting Services Act 1992, Part 9, and in particular Section 123.

4 *See*, for example, the Industrial Commission Issues Paper into the Petroleum Industry in Australia (May 1993).

There is a wide variety of legislation at state and federal level which prescribes standards for such things as the marking of goods[1] and the uniformity in weights and measures.[2] The Mutual Recognition Act 1992 has been passed by Commonwealth and state parliaments. It simplifies compliance with those standards. Under Section 9 of the Mutual Recognition Act, once locally produced or imported goods can lawfully be sold in one state, they may be sold in a second state without the need to comply with the second state's requirements as to:

(1) Standard of the goods themselves;
(2) Presentation;
(3) Inspection;
(4) Local production; and
(5) Any other requirement that would prevent or restrict the sale of goods.

The legislation is comprehensively expressed, and there are only a few exceptions to the mutual recognition principle.

Finally, from time to time, governments establish special commissions of inquiry when there is a perception that consumers have been treated unfairly. For example, in New South Wales, such an inquiry has been set up under the Home Fund Commission Act 1993 to investigate home loans made to borrowers, in a scheme established by the state government.

2.3 Primary Interest Groups

The Australian Consumers Association (ACA) was formed in 1959. It is an independent, non-profit organization formed to inform and protect consumers. The ACA is a body with a membership of 160,000, and it publishes a monthly consumer magazine.

The ACA and other consumer associations are affiliated with the Australian Federation of Consumer Organizations (AFCO), formed in 1974.

The AFCO is the leading council of the Australian consumer movement. It represents the views of consumers to the federal government through representation on major government bodies, such as the Economic

---

1 Commerce (Trade Descriptions) Act 1905 (Cth).
2 National Measurement Act 1960 (Cth).

Planning and Advisory Council and the National Health and Medical Research Council, and to other relevant organizations, such as the Standards Association of Australia and industry. It is affiliated with the International Organization of Consumer Unions.

All Australian states have enacted legislation establishing machinery to advise the government on the formulation of consumer protection policy and legislation and to receive consumer complaints and give advice to consumers. The Commonwealth government established the National Consumer Affairs Advisory Council in 1986 to advise it on matters of importance to consumers.

The Medical Consumers Association of New South Wales was formed in 1976 as a public voice for the client in medical and health services. Its aim is to disseminate information about health services, to further consumer education in the health field, and to advise and direct those with complaints against doctors and health services on the most appropriate course of action.

The Australian Shareholders Association was formed in 1968 with the aim of protecting and advancing the interests of investors in shares, debentures, options, unit trusts, insurance and superannuation bonds, and all financial products.

There are many other associations which comment on all aspects of policy including consumer issues.

For example, the Law Council of Australia is a national organization of the Australian legal profession, made up of the Law Societies and Bar Associations in the states and territories and of individual lawyers. It works for the improvement of the law and of the administration of justice as well as for better legal services.

The Business Council of Australia is a council of the chief executives of Australia's eighty largest corporations. The Council's aim is to establish common positions on the major policy questions confronting Australia.

The Retailers Council of Australia was formed in 1991 to represent major retailers on national, political, economic, and industrial issues.

2.4 Administrative Bodies and Public Law Structure

As discussed above, the power to regulate consumer affairs is divided between the Commonwealth and each of the states and territories.

The principal Commonwealth legislation governing consumer affairs is the Trade Practices Act. The Trade Practices Commission is established under that Act and is the authority responsible for enforcing the Act. The

Trade Practices Commission is subject to the directions of the relevant minister in the performance of its functions and the exercise of its powers.[1] The Trade Practices Commission has a number of functions, including:

(1) Making available to interested persons information with respect to the Commission's statutory functions and powers;
(2) Receiving references from the Minister to examine critically and report on consumer protection laws that are within the Commonwealth's sphere of legislative competence;
(3) Conducting research into matters affecting consumer interests;
(4) Providing information to the public relating to consumer interests; and
(5) Making consumers aware of rights and obligations arising out of consumer laws.

The Commission also is required to report to the Minister.[2]

In New South Wales, there is a Commissioner for Consumer Affairs.[3] In Victoria, the functions are carried out by the Secretary to the Department of Justice.[4]

The functions of the Commissioner for Consumer Affairs in New South Wales and the Department of Justice in Victoria include those to:

(1) Advise persons in relation to the provisions of the legislation and to take action for remedying infringements;
(2) Make available to consumers general information with respect to the legislation and matters affecting the interests of consumers;
(3) Receive complaints from persons on matters relating to the supply of goods or services, or the acquisition of interests in land;
(4) Investigate complaints; and
(5) Make known for the guidance of consumers and persons dealing with consumers, the rights and obligations arising under the laws relating to the interests of consumers.[5]

---

1 Trade Practices Act, Section 29(1) and (2).

2 Trade Practices Act, Section 101.

3 Fair Trading Act 1987 (New South Wales), Part 2, Division 1.

4 Administrative Arrangements (Order Number 114) 1992, made pursuant to the Administrative Arrangements Act 1983 (Victoria).

5 New South Wales, Section 9(1); Victoria Ministry of Consumer Affairs Act 1973, Section 8; Consumer Affairs Act 1972, Section 8.

The Commissioner in New South Wales is required to examine and report on the laws in force, and other matters relating to the interests of consumers. For that purpose, the Commissioner may conduct research and make investigations.[1]

There are a number of government bodies designed to provide advice on matters relating to consumer interests. For example, the Federal Bureau of Consumer Affairs ensures that consumer protection legislation and other mechanisms operate effectively for the Australian community. The Bureau promotes such things as the safety of consumer products and uniform packaging and labelling laws and practices. It also develops and implements consumer education and information projects.

The Australian Consumers' Council provides advice on matters of national consumer interests to the Minister responsible for consumer affairs. The Commonwealth-State Consumer Products Advisory Committee advises Commonwealth and State Ministers for Consumer Affairs on the introduction of mandatory consumer product safety standards and information standards, as well as advising on the need to ban or otherwise control the supply of hazardous products.

The Ministerial Council on Consumer Affairs administers, discusses, and develops uniform approaches (including uniform legislation) to consumer affairs matters of mutual interest. It comprises Ministers responsible for consumer affairs from the Commonwealth, states and territories, and New Zealand.

In New South Wales, the Client Services Division of the Department of Consumer Affairs operates a network of twenty service centers which provide the following consumer services:

(1) Advice on fair trading issues;
(2) Mediation of market place disputes;
(3) Advice and assistance in lodging Consumer Claims Tribunal and Building Disputes Tribunal application;
(4) Consumer education; and
(5) A computerized record system of financial interests in secondhand motor vehicles (the Register of Encumbered Vehicles).

---

1 Trade Practices Act, Section 9(2).

2.5 Market Regulatory Systems

2.5.1 Privatization

During the 1980s and 1990s, the federal and state governments have been privatizing state instrumentalities. They also have introduced private competitors into what formerly were exclusive government provinces.

For example, the Commonwealth now holds only fifty-one per cent of the previously 100 per cent-owned Commonwealth Bank. A further example is the telecommunications industry. Since late 1991, a private operator, Optus, has competed with the Commonwealth-owned Australian and Overseas Telecommunications Corporation (AOTC)[1] in the telecommunications field. Optus is permitted to compete with AOTC in international and long-distance markets through a requirement that AOTC provide Optus with access to the existing network.

2.5.2 Telecommunications

A statutory authority, AUSTEL, is responsible for the economic and technical regulation of the Australian telecommunications industry, including, in particular, the promotion of fair and efficient market conduct within the industry.[2]

One function of AUSTEL is to ensure that the provisions of the Telecommunications Act are carried out with due regard for the public interest and to protect consumers from practices of carriers and persons involved in the supply of telecommunication services.[3] AUSTEL receives and investigates consumer complaints, including complaints regarding charges for telecommunications services. In appropriate cases, AUSTEL refers consumer complaints to the Ombudsman or the Trade Practices Commission.

The Ombudsman is created under the Ombudsman Act 1974 (Cth) and investigates allegations of maladministration in Commonwealth departments and instrumentalities. For example, complaints which allege ineffective administration against AOTC are, in general, dealt with by the Commonwealth Ombudsman's Office.

---

1 *See* Australia and Overseas Telecommunications Act 1991.
2 Telecommunications Act 1991.
3 Telecommunications Act 1991, Section 38.

AUSTEL already has referred a number of complaints to the Trade Practices Commission, including allegations of:

(1) Predatory pricing;
(2) Refusals to deal;
(3) Misleading conduct; and
(4) Unconscionable conduct.[1]

AUSTEL has the responsibility for administering price cap and price control arrangements.

2.5.3 Government Activity

There are a number of government monopolies or major government activity in areas, including those relating to electricity, gas, water, post, ports, airports, transport infrastructure (rail and shipping), and agricultural products.[2]

For example, there is a government monopoly in the supply of water and the provision of sewerage and drainage services. In New South Wales, the Water Board is a statutory body established under the Water Board Act 1987. The general functions of the Water Board are to:

(1) Manage water and related resources;
(2) Provide and operate systems and services for impounding, conserving, and supplying water for sewerage and drainage and for the disposal of trade wastewater; and
(3) Generate revenue by levying and recovering charges, fees, and capital contributions.[3]

The Water Board is divided into several semi-autonomous regions. Each region has a detailed set of standards that spell out the quality of service to the customer. These standards include environmental as well as operational considerations.

---

1 Australian Telecommunications Authority Annual Report, 1991/1992, p. 23.

2 Trade Practices Commission submission to the National Competition Policy Review, April 1993; and Economic Planning and Advisory Council "Competition and Economic Efficiency", Background Paper Number 19, June 1992.

3 Water Board Act 1987, Section 12(1).

In Victoria, similar functions are carried out by more than one hundred separate regional water authorities established under the Water Act 1989 and the Water (Rural Water Corporation) Act 1992.

There has been recent reform in some areas of government monopolies, notably the creation of a National Rail Corporation. Until recently, railways operated by the Commonwealth government were managed and operated by the Australian National Railways Commission. That body was established on 3 July 1975 and operates under the Australian National Railways Commission Act 1983. The main function of the Commission is to provide railway services for the carriage of passengers and goods.[1]

Recently, the National Rail Corporation was established under the National Rail Corporation (Agreement) Act 1992 after an agreement was reached between the Commonwealth and four states, including New South Wales and Victoria. The aim of the agreement was to achieve micro-economic reform in the Australian rail industry. The primary function of the National Rail Corporation is to conduct national interstate rail freight operations on a strictly commercial basis. The National Railway Corporation is subject to the Trade Practices Act 1974.

Despite these recent developments, some markets, most notably a number of agricultural products, remain heavily regulated by government.[2] The Australian dairy industry, and in particular milk for fresh milk consumption, is an example. In its Report Number 14 of 26 September 1991, the Industry Commission identified the following government interventions said to result in "inefficient resource use and increased consumer prices for fresh milk and dairy products":

(1) Regulated farm gate prices for market milk in all states; and
(2) Pooled proceeds from market and manufacturing milk, or supply quotas for market milk;
(3) Regulated processing and distribution of market milk in most states, including set price margins for processors, distributors, retailers, and vendors;
(4) Regulated retail prices for market milk in all states except Western Australia;
(5) Restricted interstate trade in market milk between some states;
(6) A levy on all milk production which is used to subsidize exports of dairy products, thereby increasing the domestic prices of those products;

---

1 Australian National Railways Commission Act 1983, Section 5a.
2 Marketing of Primary Production Act 1983 (New South Wales).

(7) A tariff quota which restricts the imports of cheese;
(8) Commonwealth government underwriting of export returns on certain bulk dairy products; and
(9) Export controls enforced by a Commonwealth statutory body.

In New South Wales, dairy industry regulation is administered by the New South Wales Dairy Corporation, a statutory body constituted in 1985 under the Dairy Industry Act 1979. All milk produced in New South Wales is vested in the Dairy Corporation. Prices for market milk are determined by the Dairy Corporation.

Supply quotas are used to ensure adequate market milk supplies throughout the year. Processing, wholesale, and vending margins are set by the Dairy Corporation. There are individual vendor monopolies.

Maximum retail prices apply for plain milk and many other types of milk. These prices are set by the Dairy Corporation.

The equivalent body in Victoria is the Victorian Dairy Industry Authority, established under the Dairy Industry Act 1984.

The Dairy Industry Authority has power to vest all milk produced in Victoria, and it determines the price of milk using a system of benchmarking, ensuring that adequate supplies of market milk are available. The Dairy Industry Authority purchases all market milk from licensed factories.

At the Commonwealth level, a number of levies are imposed on the milk content of dairy products.[1] The Commonwealth marketing arrangements are administered by the Australia Dairy Corporation.[2]

The Australian Wheat Board is a statutory marketing authority, established pursuant to federal[3] and state[4] legislation. The Australian Wheat Board has the sole license to export wheat from Australia. Its objectives include maximizing the net returns to Australian wheat growers who sell wheat to the Australian Wheat Board and participating in the market for grain and grain products. The functions of the Wheat Board are to:

(1) Export wheat from Australia;
(2) Trade in wheat;
(3) Make arrangements for the growing of wheat for the above purposes;

---

1 Dairy Produce Levy (Number 1) Act 1986 and Dairy Produce Levy (Number 2) Act 1986.
2 Dairy Produce Act 1986.
3 Wheat Marketing Act 1989.
4 Wheat Marketing Act 1989 (Victoria); Wheat Marketing Act 1989 (New South Wales).

(4) Promote, fund, or undertake research into matters relating to the marketing of wheat; and
(5) Provide advice and make recommendations to the Minister with respect to matters relating to the marketing of wheat.[1]

The Australian Meat and Livestock Corporation Act 1977 (Cth) establishes the Australian Meat and Livestock Corporation. Among the Meat and Livestock Corporation's functions are to improve the:

(1) Quality of Australian meat and livestock;
(2) Methods of production, storage, transport, and marketing of Australian meat; and
(3) Methods of production, transport, and marketing of Australian livestock.[2]

The Meat and Livestock Corporation has the prime responsibility of marketing Australian meat and livestock in Australia and overseas. It is funded entirely by industry levies. One of its roles is to educate and provide information to consumers.

Finally, there is substantial regulation by the Commonwealth government of letter services in Australia. The Australian Postal Corporation Act 1989 gives to Australia Post the exclusive right to carry "letters" within Australia and between Australia and places overseas.[3] Section 30 of the Act then specifically excepts some articles from the reserved service, for example, letters weighing more than 500 grams and letters carried where payment is at least ten times that charged by Australia Post for a standard postal article by ordinary post (for domestic carriage) or by air for an article weighing twenty grams (for international carriage).

Australia Post is exempt in respect of its letter service from the provisions of the Trade Practices Act.

A number of letter services are notifiable under the Prices Surveillance Act 1983. The Prices Surveillance Authority has conducted a number of enquires into Australia Post prices and charges. The Prices Surveillance Authority examines the cost of providing services and an adequate rate of return on assets in considering whether to approve an increase in the price of reserved services. Apart from the

1 Wheat Marketing Act, Section 6(1).
2 Meat and Livestock Corporation Act 1977 (Cth), Section 8(3).
3 Australian Postal Corporation Act 1989, Section 29.

reserved services, there is competition, e.g., parcel services (business and houshold), city courier services, contract carriers, electronic transfer of information, and others.

2.5.4 Competition Policy

In August 1993, an independent committee of inquiry presented a report on national competition policy to the Australian governments.[1] The Hilmer Report recommended implementation of a national competition policy for Australia.

The committee considered competition policy in terms of the following elements:

(1) Limiting anti-competitive conduct of firms;
(2) Reforming regulation which unjustifiably restricts competition;
(3) Reforming the structure of public monopolies to facilitate competition;
(4) Providing third-party access to certain facilities that are essential for competition;
(5) Restraining monopoly pricing behavior; and
(6) Fostering competitive neutrality between government and private businesses when they compete.[2]

1 Known as the "Hilmer Report", after its chairman, Professor Frederick G. Hilmer.
2 Hilmer Report, p. xvii.

Section 3

Consumer Product and Service Standards

3.1 Source of Rule

3.1.1 Commonwealth and State Legislation

Mandatory consumer product and service standards are created under a variety of Commonwealth and state legislation. Consumer product and service standards deal with product safety or product information. Product safety standards set down minimum safety standards, while product information standards require sellers to provide certain information about a product. In addition to the mandatory standards, there are a large number of other standards with which compliance is not mandatory. A failure to meet these standards, however, may be relevant in some circumstances, for example, in an action for negligence.

Numerous standards concerning products and services are published by the Standards Association of Australia, an independent, non-profit organization. The principal function of the Standards Association is to prepare and publish Australian standards for a range of products and processes and to promote their adoption.

Standards take the form of specifications for materials and products, codes of sound or safe practice, methods of testing, nomenclature, and other matters. The standards are not law unless referred to by legislation. If a standard has not been prescribed as mandatory, it may have evidentiary significance in civil proceedings, such as in an action for negligence, in establishing what constitutes reasonable safety standards.

3.1.2 Consumer Protection Legislation

At the Commonwealth level, Parts V and VA of the Trade Practices Act contain a general regime for consumer protection. Division 1 of Part V prohibits misleading or deceptive conduct in trade or commerce and certain specific kinds of false or misleading representations about price, quality, grade, nature, manufacturing process, characteristics, suitability, or quantity of goods. Packaging and labelling of products is part of their promotion, and marketing will be governed by these provisions.

Division 1A of Part V of the Trade Practices Act concerns product safety and product information and provides for:

(1) The publication of warning notices by the government in relation to goods under investigation as possibly dangerous;
(2) The banning of goods which do not comply with prescribed product safety standards;
(3) The banning or compulsory recall of unsafe goods;
(4) Compliance with consumer product information standards; and
(5) Notification to the government of voluntary recalls.

Division 1A applies to goods supplied after 1 July 1986, but it does not apply to food or drinks supplied after 2 July 1988. Division 1A is expressed in general terms, leaving specific action to be implemented by regulations or other executive action. This is in contrast to the state regulatory schemes, which tend to apply to specific classes of goods and services.

Part VA of the Trade Practices Act deals with defective goods supplied after 9 July 1992. It creates statutory rights of action against a "manufacturer" in favor of persons suffering injury, loss, or damage caused by defective goods. The basis of liability is that the goods in question have a "defect" due to which injury, loss, or damage occurred.

The consumer protection provisions of the Trade Practices Act only affect the supply of goods by a corporation. The Trade Practices Act does not apply to partnerships or individuals unconnected with a company because of constitutional limits on the Commonwealth government's legislative powers. All states and territories, however, have legislation which contains provisions similar to Part V of the Trade Practices Act and which applies to individuals and partnerships.[1]

In addition, there is a variety of other state legislation dealing with safety and information standards that applies concurrently with the Commonwealth provisions. Where the provisions are inconsistent, the Commonwealth provision prevails. The states have legislated specifically in such areas as foods, drugs, poisons, protection from injury (particularly electrical injury), information about textiles, footwear, and furniture, information about agricultural products and chemicals, packaging and labelling, and weights and measures.

1 Fair Trading Act 1987 (New South Wales), Consumer Affairs Act 1972 (Victoria), and the Fair Trading Act 1985 (Victoria).

3.1.3 Causes of Action

Where a consumer suffers injury, loss, or damage due to a defective product, he or she may have a remedy at Common Law or pursuant to various additional statutes. If the consumer has entered a contract with a manufacturer or supplier, the consumer may sue for breach of one or more express or implied terms of that contract. If he or she can prove that the manufacturer or supplier owed a duty of care which was breached, then the consumer may succeed in a tort action based on the negligence of the manufacturer or supplier. A failure to meet mandatory or other product safety or product information standards may be relevant to these actions.

In addition, the consumer may have rights against the manufacturer or supplier under Commonwealth and state sale of goods, health and safety, or environmental legislation.

3.1.4 Relationship between Commonwealth and State and Territory Regimes

On 11 May 1992, the state, territory, and Commonwealth heads of government established a scheme for the implementation of mutual recognition principles. The principal aim of mutual recognition is to remove artificial barriers to interstate trade in goods and mobility of labor caused by regulatory differences among states and territories. The agreement empowered the Commonwealth to pass the Mutual Recognition Act 1992 to give effect to the principles of mutual recognition by overriding any state or territory laws inconsistent with these principles.

The agreement also required all state and territory governments to pass legislation enabling the enactment of legislation for the recognition of regulatory standards adopted in Australia regarding goods and occupations applying uniformly throughout Australia.

Mutual recognition legislation has been passed in New South Wales[1] and in Victoria.[2] Part 2 of the mutual recognition legislation deals with goods produced in or imported into a state ("the first state") and their sale in another state ("the second state"). Where the goods may be lawfully sold in the first state, they may be sold in the second state without the need to comply with certain requirements, including:

---

1 Mutual Recognition (New South Wales) Act 1992.

2 Mutual Recognition (Victoria) Act 1993.

(1) Standards of the second state relating to the goods themselves, i.e., production, composition, quality, or performance;
(2) Standards of the second state relating to the way the goods are presented, i.e., packaging, labelling, date stamping, or age;
(3) Requirements that the goods be inspected, passed, or similarly dealt with in or for the purposes of the second state;
(4) Requirements that any step in the production of the goods not occur outside the second state; and
(5) Any other requirements that can or do prevent or restrict the sale of goods in the second state.

However, certain laws must still be complied with, including laws which regulate the manner of sale of goods or the manner in which sellers conduct their business in the second state, and laws directed at matters affecting the health and safety of persons within the second state or environmental pollution matters. In addition, certain goods are not affected by Part 2 and are listed as permanent exemptions.

3.2 Scope and Application of Rule

3.2.1 Trade Practices Act 1974 (Cth)

Division 1A of Part V of the Trade Practices Act concerns "product safety and product information". Under Division 1A, standards may be prescribed in two ways:

(1) New standards may be prescribed by regulation;[1] or
(2) Existing standards may be adopted either with or without alteration.[2]

Under Section 65C(2) of the Trade Practices Act, regulations may be proclaimed prescribing a consumer product safety standard in respect of particular goods where the standard is reasonably necessary to prevent or reduce the risk of injury to any person. The standard may cover such matters as:

---

1 Trade Practices Act, Section 65C(2).
2 Trade Practices Act, Section 65E.

(1) Performance, composition, contents, methods of manufacture, or processing, design, construction, finishing, or packaging of the goods;
(2) Testing of the goods during, or after the completion of, manufacture or processing; and
(3) The form and content of markings, warnings, or instructions to accompany the goods.

A number of product safety standards were prescribed by the Trade Practices (Consumer Product Safety Standards) Regulations for the purposes of the now repealed Section 62 of the Trade Practices Act. These standards continue in force despite the repeal of Section 62. Further standards have since been introduced by regulation, pursuant to Section 65C of the Trade Practices Act.

Similarly, Section 65D(2) of the Trade Practices Act provides that regulations may be made prescribing consumer product information standards in respect of particular goods. Such standards must be reasonably necessary to give persons using the goods information as to the quantity, quality, nature, or value of goods. The standards may specify requirements as to:

(1) The disclosure of information relating to the performance, such as composition, contents, methods of manufacture or processing, design, construction, finishing, or packaging of the goods; and
(2) The form and manner in which that information is to be disclosed on or with the goods.

Mandatory standards have been introduced by regulations to the Trade Practices Act in relation to a variety of goods, including candles, airpots, balloon-blowing kits, bean bags, elastic luggage straps, and cosmetic labelling.

As an alternative to promulgating new standards by regulation, the Minister has power to declare, by notice published in the *Gazette*, that an existing standard is a consumer product standard for the purposes of Section 65C or a consumer information standard for the purposes of Section 65D.[1] Such standards are often those published by the Standards

---

1 Trade Practices Act, Section 65E(1).

Association of Australia. The Minister does not have power to declare standards that are inconsistent with standards prescribed by regulations.[1]

Mandatory consumer safety standards have been introduced by *Gazette* Notice in respect of a variety of goods, including children's night clothes, portable fire extinguishers, motor vehicle child restraints, reflectors for pedal bicycles, pedal bicycles, helmets for motor cyclists and pedal cyclists, sunglasses, jacks, and some types of children's toys.

Consumer product information standards have been introduced by *Gazette* notice for care labelling for clothes, household textiles, furnishings, piece goods, and yarns.

3.2.2 New South Wales

Part 3 of the Fair Trading Act, which is entitled "Safe Design and Construction of Goods", deals with product safety in New South Wales.

Division 1 of Part 3 of the Act provides for the imposition by regulation of product safety standards for specified kind of goods, for the purpose of preventing or reducing risk of personal injury.[2] A product safety standard can consist of requirements as to:

(1) Performance, composition, contents, methods of manufacture or processing, design, construction, finishing, or packaging of the goods;
(2) Testing of goods during, or after the completion of, manufacture or processing;
(3) Form and content of markings, warnings, or instructions to accompany the goods or to be placed on a vending machine for the goods or on a display stand or sign adjacent to the goods; and
(4) Equipment or accessories to be supplied with the goods.

Product safety standards have been made pursuant to the Fair Trading Act and the now repealed Consumer Protection Act 1969 (New South Wales). The regulations made under the Consumer Protection Act continue in operation until repealed or varied by a regulation or order made under the Fair Trading Act. The regulations prescribe product safety standards for a variety of goods, including safety footwear, dust masks, portable fire extinguishers, kerosine heaters, sunglasses

1 Trade Practices Act, Section 65E(2).
2 Fair Trading Act 1987 (New South Wales), Section 26(2).

and fashion spectacles, folding tables, pedal bicycles, child restraints, beanbags, and some types of children's toys.

Part 4 of the Fair Trading Act permits the making of regulations prescribing product information standards. A product information standard for goods consists of requirements for the disclosure of such information as is reasonably necessary to give persons using the goods information as to their origin, quantity, quality, nature, durability, or value.[1] Such information includes:

(1) Price, performance, composition, contents, method of manufacture or processing, design, construction, finishing, or packaging of the goods;
(2) Place of manufacture or production of the goods;
(3) Identity of the manufacturer, producer, or supplier of the goods;
(4) Date of the manufacture or production and the durable life of the goods; and
(5) Care and storage of the goods.

The Fair Trading (Product Information Standards) Regulation 1992 prescribes product information standards for the following goods: leather goods, bedding and upholstered furniture, millet brooms, textile products, toys, footwear, and care labelling of certain goods.

3.2.3 Victoria

Under the Consumer Affairs Act 1972 (Victoria), regulations may be made with respect to any prescribed class or description of goods for the purpose of preventing or reducing risk of death or personal injury. The regulations may specify requirements as to the composition of contents, design, construction, finishing, or packaging and as to the making of any prescribed warning or instructions on goods of a prescribed class or description or any component part of the goods. Regulations also may be made which require identification on the goods of the name of the manufacturer and place of manufacture.

Regulations have been prescribed for certain goods, including children's nightclothes, spirit stoves, portable fire extinguishers, children's toys, airpots, pedal bicycles, marking of footwear and trade

---

1 Fair Trading Act 1987 (New South Wales), Section 38(2).

descriptions in relation to textile products, leather goods, bedding, upholstered furniture, and artificial imitation leather.

3.2.4 Other Legislation

In addition to the Trade Practices Act 1974 and the various state Fair Trading Acts, there is other Commonwealth and state legislation which prescribe standards in relation to certain products, such as legislation on standards for foods and therapeutic substances. These are discussed below.

Of particular importance are the standards in relation to weights and measures. The Commonwealth legislation sets uniform standards of measurements,[1] while the state laws ensure that physical quantities stated in these standard measurements are accurate.[2]

The state laws prescribe the verification and inspection of measuring instruments and the regulation of retail sales by weight and measure. The state laws also may require labelling to state the weight, and the name of the manufacturer of the goods. They also provide for standardization of package quantities and size range of goods.

3.3 Standing

3.3.1 Trade Practices Act 1974 (Cth) and Fair Trading Act 1987 (New South Wales)

Under the Trade Practices Act 1974 (Cth) and the Fair Trading Act 1987 (New South Wales), the provisions concerning standing are similar and are considered here together. The provisions of the Fair Trading Act 1985 (Victoria) also are similar; however, product standards in Victoria are largely governed by the Consumer Affairs Act 1972 (Victoria), rather than the Fair Trading Act 1985 (Victoria). Standing under the Consumer Affairs Act is, therefore, considered separately.

It is an offense to supply goods that are intended to be used by a consumer or are likely to be used by a consumer if the goods are the subject of a prescribed consumer product safety standard or a prescribed

---

1 *See*, e.g., the Weights and Measures (National Standards) Act 1960.

2 *See*, e.g., the Weights and Measures Act 1915 (New South Wales) and the Weights and Measures Act 1958 (Victoria).

consumer information standard and if the goods do not comply with that standard.[1] It also is an offense under the Trade Practices Act 1974 to export goods which fail to comply with product safety standards unless the Minister has, by notice in writing, given the corporation approval to export those goods. However, product information standards do not apply to goods that are intended to be used outside Australia.

Any person who suffers loss or damage by another's contravention of consumer protection laws may recover the amount of loss or damage by an action against that other person, or against any person involved in the contravention.[2]

Section 80 of the Trade Practices Act 1974 provides that, on the application of the Minister, the Trade Practices Commission or any other person, a court may grant an injunction if it is satisfied that a person has engaged, or is proposing to engage, in conduct that constitutes or would constitute a contravention of Part V of the Trade Practices Act. Similar provisions are contained in Section 65 of the Fair Trading Act.

In addition, any person may seek the other civil remedies listed in Section 87 of the Trade Practices Act 1974 and Section 72 of the Fair Trading Act in relation to breaches of the consumer protection provisions of those Acts.

In addition to these remedies, the Trade Practices Act 1974 gives the Minister powers to ban and recall unsafe goods. The Minister or the Trade Practices Commission also can apply to the court for a corrective advertising order.[3] A consumer has no standing to seek the recall of goods, a banning order, or a corrective advertising order.

Criminal prosecutions under the Trade Practices Act 1974 can only be brought by the Trade Practices Commission, a person authorized by the Trade Practices Commission, the Secretary to the Department, or a person who has the consent of the Minister.[4] Proceedings for an offense against the Fair Trading Act 1987 (New South Wales) may be prosecuted only by the Commissioner or a person acting with the authority of the Commissioner.[5]

---

1 Trade Practices Act 1974 (Cth), Sections 65C(1) and 65D(1); Fair Trading Act 1987 (New South Wales), Sections 27 and 39.

2 Trade Practices Act 1974 (Cth), Section 82; Fair Trading Act 1987 (New South Wales), Section 68.

3 Trade Practices Act 1974 (Cth), Section 80A; Fair Trading Act 1987 (New South Wales), Section 67.

4 Trade Practices Act 1974 (Cth), Section 163.

5 Fair Trading Act 1987 (New South Wales).

A person who has suffered loss as a result of a defect in goods has standing to seek compensation from the manufacturer for the amount of the loss under Part VA of the Trade Practices Act 1974. Part VA is considered in more detail below.

3.3.2 Consumer Affairs Act 1972 (Victoria)

It is an offense under the Consumer Affairs Act 1972 (Victoria) not to comply with a prohibition order,[1] not to comply with safety requirements,[2] or to impede an inspector appointed pursuant to the Consumer Affairs Act.[3] Proceedings for any offense committed under the Consumer Affairs Act may be instituted by an inspector, a person authorized by the Minister, or a person whose rights are impaired or who is specially aggrieved by the commission of such an offense.[4]

Where a person is obliged under Section 60 of the Consumer Affairs Act not to supply goods which do not comply with a prescribed requirement, the person owes a duty to any other person who may be affected by the contravention of or non-compliance with that requirement in question.[5] Any person who has suffered loss or damage as a result of such non-compliance will have standing to pursue an action for breach of statutory duty (*see* description of action for negligence and breach of statutory duty below).

3.4 Negligence - Breach of Common Law Duty

Statutory duty and the Common Law duty of care, although requiring the same act, are distinct duties in law, and the causes of action arising from injury to persons or property caused by a breach of either of the duties are separate and distinct.

A right of action for injury caused by negligence exists at Common Law in all states in Australia. The general principles of liability for negligence

---

1 Consumer Affairs Act 1972 (Victoria), Section 57F.
2 Consumer Affairs Act 1972 (Victoria), Section 60.
3 Consumer Affairs Act 1972 (Victoria), Section 65.
4 Consumer Affairs Act 1972 (Victoria), Section 66.
5 Consumer Affairs Act 1972 (Victoria), Section 61.

apply to a broad range of conduct. Liability for defective products or other negligent conduct of a business is but one application of these general principles.

Any person may have standing to bring an action for negligence. They will only succeed if they can establish there was a duty of care owed to them, a breach of that duty, and loss or damage as a result of the breach. In regard to physical injury to person or property, the law in Australia requires a person or company to take reasonable care to avoid causing injury or loss to persons who might reasonably be foreseen to be affected by his or her conduct. This principle stems from the 1932 decision of the House of Lords in *Donoghue* vs. *Stevenson*.[1]

Once a duty of care has been shown to exist, to establish negligence, it is necessary to demonstrate that the conduct complained of falls below the standard that the community would expect. Australian courts require a person or company to perform to the standard of a reasonable person or company in the relevant field of expertise. At times, the courts have found that, although an enterprise may have performed to a standard generally acceptable to the industry at the time, the standard itself was deficient. In these circumstances, the courts will impose their own higher standards, in effect finding that the industry had adopted a potentially negligent practice.[2]

Legislative standards can be of importance in determining the standard of care. In some cases, compliance with legislative standards provides evidence that due care has been exercised, but it is not conclusive.[3] Some legislation does not fully describe the manufacturers' or distributors' obligations or may be said to no longer prescribe an acceptable current standard of industry practice. If the legislation were deficient in this way, and the manufacturer or distributor were aware of this, it would not be open to it to say that it had taken reasonable care to avoid injury by adhering to the legislative standards. It has been said that sometimes obedience to a regulation can be the worst course to take.[4]

---

1 [1932] AC 562.

2 *Mercer* vs. *Commissioner for Road Transport* (1936) 56 CLR 580, at p. 589; *Wise Brothers* vs. *Commissioner for Railways* (1947) 75 CLR 59, at p. 72.

3 *Henwood* vs. *Municipal Tramways Trust* (1938) 60 CLR 438; *Sibley* vs. *Cais* (1967) 118 CLR 424.

4 *Tucker* vs. *McCann* [1948] VLR 222, at pp. 225-226, per Herring CJ.

Therefore, a manufacturer or distributor should be aware of standards imposed by legislation and comply with them. It may, however, need to go further.

The courts in Australia have recognized that liability for negligence will cover damage to persons or property and any economic loss suffered as a result.[1]

3.5 Breach of a Statutory Duty

In some situations, the appropriate standard of conduct is prescribed by the legislature instead of being left to be determined by the courts. Statutory standards tend to be widely promulgated and are primarily aimed at preventing accidents. The standards usually prescribe a minor criminal sanction, usually a fine, for any disobedience, whether or not it causes injury to anyone. However, the absence of any express intention to provide for a civil remedy has not prevented the courts from treating non-compliance with the statutory rule as having a bearing on civil recovery.

Non-compliance with a statute which lays down a standard of conduct for the purpose of preventing injury or loss is at least admissible as evidence of negligence (breach of the Common Law duty to take care).[2] In some circumstances, a breach of a safety statute is sometimes treated as negligence *per se*, that is negligence as a matter of law.

According to the accepted position in Australia, the negligence per se rule rests on the supposed or "presumed" intention of the legislature to provide a civil remedy, so long as this can be "inferred" as a matter of construction, having regard to the scope, purview, and structure of the provision.[3]

Conduct breaching a statutory standard, although not giving rise to a right of action under the statute to a person injured as a consequence, may amount to negligence or a breach of statutory duty. In New South Wales, the plaintiff may prefer to rely on the cause of action for breach of statutory duty because the Statutory Duties (Contributory Negligence) Act 1945 (New South Wales) precludes apportionment of damages for contributory negligence in cases of breach of statutory duty.

---

1 *Caltex* vs. *The Dredge "Willemstad"* (1976) 136 CLR 529.

2 *Henwood* vs. *Municipal Tramways Trust* (1938) 60 CLR 438; *Sibley* vs. *Cais* (1967) 118 CLR 428.

3 *O'Connor* vs. *SP Bray Ltd.* (1937) 56 CLR 464.

3.6 Procedures

The general procedures for implementing consumer rights are discussed below. An action for negligence or an action for the breach of state legislation will generally be brought in state courts and an action for the breach of Commonwealth legislation in the Federal Court. However, this is subject to the system of mutual cross vesting of jurisdiction between federal, state, and territory courts discussed below.

Certain deeming provisions or procedures may apply in respect of actions for non-compliance with some standards imposed by individual statutes. These provisions are discussed below in the context of the relevant statute.

3.7 Sanctions

The Trade Practices Act 1974 and the Fair Trading Act 1987 (New South Wales) provide for various remedies for breaches of the consumer protection provisions.

The sanctions provided for in the Trade Practices Act 1974 and the Fair Trading Act 1987 (New South Wales) are similar and are discussed here together. The Fair Trading Act 1985 (Victoria) contains provisions similar to parts of the Trade Practices Act 1974; however, product standards in Victoria are largely regulated by the Consumer Affairs Act 1972 (Victoria). The sanctions provided for in the Consumer Affairs Act 1972 (Victoria) are considered separately.

3.7.1 Injunctions

Section 80 of the Trade Practices Act 1974 (Cth) permits the Minister, the Commission, or any other person to apply for an injunction which the court may grant if it is satisfied that a person has engaged or is proposing to engage in conduct which constitutes or would constitute a contravention of a provision of Parts IV, IVA, or V.

Similar provisions are contained in Section 65 of the Fair Trading Act 1987 (New South Wales).

3.7.2 *Damages*

A person who suffers loss or damage through conduct of another that was in contravention of the consumer protection provisions of the Trade Practices Act 1974 may recover the amount of loss or damage by action against the other person or against any person involved in the contravention.[1] A similar provision is contained in Section 68 of the Fair Trading Act 1987 (New South Wales).

There are deeming provisions which facilitate the bringing of damages actions in Section 65C(8) of the Trade Practices Act 1974 and Section 27(2) of the Fair Trading Act 1987 (New South Wales). Where consumers have suffered loss and damage as a result of buying goods and where the manufacturer of the goods has not complied with the relevant consumer product safety standard, the loss or damage is deemed to have resulted from the supply of the goods. There is a similar provision regarding defective goods in Section 65H of the Trade Practices Act 1974, and similar deeming provisions apply for product information standards.[2]

Under the Fair Trading Act 1987 (New South Wales), where goods are supplied to a person in contravention of a product safety standard or the supply of goods is an offense because it is supplied in contravention to an order prohibiting or restricting the supply of goods, the person may recover from the supplier as a debt due any money paid for the goods.[3]

A court may direct that a judgment debt be satisfied by repair or modification of the goods.[4] If the goods, as repaired or modified, are accepted by the plaintiff on or before a day specified in the judgment, the judgment debt is deemed to be satisfied.[5]

3.7.3 *Other Civil Remedies*

Section 87 of the Trade Practices Act 1974 provides the court with wide powers to make remedial orders in appropriate cases relating to conduct covered by Parts IV and V. Similar provisions are contained in Section 72 of the Fair Trading Act 1987 (New South Wales).

---

1 Trade Practices Act 1974 (Cth), Section 82.

2 Trade Practices Act 1974 (Cth), Section 65D(7); Fair Trading Act 1987 (New South Wales), Section 39(2).

3 Fair Trading Act 1987 (New South Wales), Section 33(1).

4 Fair Trading Act 1987 (New South Wales), Section 33(2)(a).

5 Fair Trading Act 1987 (New South Wales), Section 33(2)(b).

3.7.4 *Fines*

Section 79 of the Trade Practices Act 1974 provides that a person who contravenes a provision of Part V (other than certain specified Sections) is guilty of an offense punishable on conviction by a fine not exceeding Aus. $20,000 in the case of an individual, or not exceeding Aus. $100,000 in the case of a company.

Similar provisions are contained in Section 62 of the Fair Trading Act 1987 (New South Wales).

3.7.5 *Imprisonment*

The Trade Practices Act 1974 contains no specific provisions providing for imprisonment of offenders, other than for the non-payment of fines.[1]

3.7.6 *Product Recall*

Section 65F of the Trade Practices Act 1974 permits the Minister to take certain actions, including the making of an order for the mandatory recall of goods, in certain circumstances. The Minister may make such an order where goods are supplied by a corporation to be used by a consumer, and:

(1) It appears to the Minister that the goods may cause injury;
(2) The goods do not comply with a prescribed consumer product safety standard; or
(3) An unsafe goods order or banning order applies in relation to the goods.

The Minister can only order compulsory recall if it appears that the supplier has not voluntarily taken satisfactory action to prevent the goods causing injury.

The Minister may require the actual recall of the goods, require disclosure by the supplier of the problem with the goods or the procedures for disposing of the goods, or require the supplier to repair or

1 Trade Practices Act 1974 (Cth), Section 79A.

replace the goods or refund the price.[1] The Minister also can give directions as to the manner in which the recall order is to be carried out.[2]

Where goods subject to a recall order have been supplied to overseas buyers, the supplier is obliged to give notice to the overseas buyers and to provide a copy of the notice to the Minister within ten days.[3]

Except in cases of goods which are likely to cause imminent risk of serious injury, the Minister is required before issuing a compulsory recall order to prepare a draft recall notice and a summary of the reasons for it. Suppliers of goods covered by the draft notice must be afforded an opportunity of a conference before a member of the Trade Practices Commission. The Minister must have regard to the Commission's recommendations before finally proceeding with the recall order.[4]

A corporation is prohibited from supplying goods of a kind to which the recall order relates.[5] Any person who suffers loss or damage as a result of a supplier failing to comply with the recall order may bring proceedings to recover damages.

Similar provisions for the recall of defective goods, and requirements for conferences are contained in Sections 34 and 35 of the Fair Trading Act 1987 (New South Wales).

3.7.7 Voluntary Recalls

Section 65R of the Trade Practices Act 1974 provides that, if a corporation voluntarily takes action to recall goods because the goods will or may cause injury to any person, the corporation is required, within two days of taking that action, to give notice in writing to the Minister stating that the goods are subject to recall and setting out the nature of the defect or dangerous characteristic of the goods.[6]

A similar provision is contained in Section 34(10) of the Fair Trading Act 1987 (New South Wales). Compliance with Section 65R of the Trade Practices Act is sufficient to comply with Section 34(10) of the Fair Trading Act 1987 (New South Wales).[7]

---

1 Trade Practices Act 1974 (Cth), Section 65F(1).
2 Trade Practices Act 1974 (Cth), Section 65F(3)).
3 Trade Practices Act 1974 (Cth), Section 65F(7) and (8).
4 Trade Practices Act 1974 (Cth), Sections 65J, 65L, and 65P.
5 Trade Practices Act 1974 (Cth), Section 65G.
6 Trade Practices Act 1974 (Cth), Section 65R.
7 Fair Trading Act 1987 (New South Wales), Section 34(11).

3.7.8 Banning Orders

The Trade Practices Act empowers the Minister to declare goods to be unsafe and to publish banning orders.[1] Except in cases where it appears to the Minister that goods constitute an imminent risk of serious injury, the Minister is obliged before publishing an order declaring goods to be unsafe to prepare a draft determination and to give interested persons the opportunity to have a conference in relation to a matter before a member of the Trade Practices Commission.[2]

A notice that goods are unsafe has a life of eighteen months after which it lapses unless previously revoked.[3] If, after eighteen months, there is no consumer protection safety standard prescribed in relation to the goods declared unsafe, the Minister may, subject to the conference procedure referred to above, publish a permanent ban in relation to the goods.[4] It is an offense to supply goods that are intended to be used by a consumer or are likely to be used by a consumer if the goods are subject to either an unsafe goods order or a banning order.[5]

Similar provisions are contained in Section 27 of the Fair Trading Act (New South Wales).

3.7.9 Actions against Manufacturer Pursuant to Part VA, Trade Practices Act

Part VA was inserted in the Trade Practices Act with effect from 9 July 1992. It is based on the European Union's 1985 Directive on Product Liability. This Part provides a series of statutory rights of action against the "manufacturer" in favor of persons suffering injury, loss, or damage caused by dangerous goods. The basis of liability is that the goods in question have a "defect" due to which injury, loss, or damage occurred.

"Manufacturer" is defined broadly to include the "importer" if goods are manufactured off-shore, and is given an extended meaning to capture persons who promote the goods as their own.[6] The term "defect" is defined broadly. Section 75AC of the Trade Practices Act 1974 defines

1 Trade Practices Act 1974 (Cth), Section 65C(5) and (7).
2 Trade Practices Act 1974 (Cth), Sections 65J and 65L.
3 Trade Practices Act 1974 (Cth), Section 65C(6).
4 Trade Practices Act 1974 (Cth), Section 65C(7).
5 Trade Practices Act 1974 (Cth), Section 65C(1).
6 Trade Practices Act 1974 (Cth), Sections 75AB and 74A(3)-(8).

goods as having a defect if their safety is not such as persons generally are entitled to expect. Section 75AC(2) sets out a series of matters to which regard is to be had in determining the extent of the safety of the goods. These are:

(1) The manner in which, and the purpose for which, they have been marketed;
(2) Their packaging;
(3) The use of any mark in relation to them;
(4) Any instructions for or warning with respect to doing or refraining from doing anything with or in relation to them;
(5) What might reasonably be expected to be done with or in relation to them; and
(6) The time when they were supplied by the manufacturer.

If a corporation, in trade or commerce, supplies defective goods manufactured by it and, because of the defect, an individual suffers injury, the corporation is liable to compensate the individual for the amount of the individual's resulting loss. An individual has standing to recover that amount by an action against the corporation. If the individual dies because of the injuries, the law of a state or territory concerning liability in respect of death of individuals will apply as if the action were for damages in respect of the injuries and the defect were the corporation's wrongful act, neglect, or default.[1]

Liability also is imposed on the manufacturer of defective goods if any individual suffers loss arising out of the death or injury of another as a result of that defect. However, there is no liability where such loss arises from a business relationship (including a relationship with employer and employee) between the injured person and the person suffering the loss.[2]

Section 75AF of the Trade Practices Act 1974 imposes liability on the manufacturer of defective goods if other goods are destroyed because of the defect and the person who used or intended to use the goods suffers loss or damage as a result. Section 74AF only applies in relation to destroyed or damaged goods of a kind ordinarily acquired for personal, domestic or household use.

Section 75AG imposes liability on the manufacturer of defective goods if land, buildings, or fixtures are destroyed or damaged because

1 Trade Practices Act 1974 (Cth), Section 75AD.
2 Trade Practices Act 1974 (Cth), Section 75AE.

of that defect, and the person who used or intended to use them suffers loss or damage as a result. This Section only applies in relation to destroyed or damaged land, buildings, or fixtures ordinarily acquired for private use.

Section 75AG provides that a notice may be served on each known supplier of the defective goods in question requiring information which identifies the manufacturer. If such information is not forthcoming within thirty days, then the suppliers who failed to respond to the request are taken to be the manufacturers of the goods.

Various defenses are available. These include:

(1) That the defect did not exist when the goods were supplied;
(2) That the defect occurred because of compliance with a mandatory standard;
(3) That the defect could not have been discovered given the state of scientific or technical knowledge when the manufacturer supplied the goods; and
(4) If the defect is in finished goods, that the defect is attributable to the design of the finished goods, the markings on them, or instructions given with them.

If the respondent claims the defect resulted from compliance with a mandatory standard, the Commonwealth becomes the defendant to the action under Section 75AL. If the defense is proven, the Commonwealth is required to meet the verdict.

3.8 Consumer Affairs Act 1972 (Victoria)

Under the Consumer Affairs Act 1972 (Victoria), it is an offense to sell goods or component parts of a prescribed class or description unless all requirements and regulations relating to the goods or component parts have been complied with.[1] It also is an offense to impede an inspector appointed under the Consumer Affairs Act or to supply goods in contravention of an order prohibiting the supply of dangerous goods.

Where a person is obliged under Section 60 of the Consumer Affairs Act 1972 not to sell any goods or component parts which do not comply with prescribed requirements, the person owes a duty to any person who may be affected by the contravention of or non-compliance with the

1 Consumer Affairs Act 1972 (Victoria), Section 60.

requirement in question.[1] A breach of that duty is actionable, although such action is subject to the defenses and other incidences applying to actions for breach of statutory duty.

A person prosecuted for an offense under Section 61 has a sufficient defense if it can be proved that he or she had reasonable cause to believe that all the requirements imposed were satisfied.

Persons guilty of offenses against the Act also are liable to fines.[2]

3.9 Special Regimes

3.9.1 Food

3.9.1.1 Legislative Scheme

There has been an attempt to develop uniform laws in relation to food throughout Australia. The Commonwealth, states, and territories have drawn up a model food legislation. The model food legislation regulates food safety, packaging, labelling and hygiene through regulations created pursuant to the legislation. The legislation has been adopted in all states and territories, although not all the new Food Acts conform to the model.[3]

The Food Act 1989 (New South Wales) and the Food Act 1984 (Victoria) are considered in this section, as examples of the various Food Acts. The Food Acts define "food" in wide terms.

The Acts provide for the making of regulations for a wide variety of matters concerning food, its packaging or labelling, and other matters.[4]

The Food Standards Code of 1987 has been adopted under the state Acts. The Foods Standards Code contains detailed provisions on a variety of matters concerning food, such as labelling and advertising, food additives, preservatives, colorings, flavorings, antioxidants, artificial sweetening substances, vitamins and minerals, modifying agents, and metals and contaminants in food. The regulations also prescribe detailed standards for a variety of specific food items.

The National Food Authority Act 1991 (Cth) gives power to the National Food Authority to develop, vary, or review existing standards.

---

1 Consumer Affairs Act 1972 (Victoria), Section 61.

2 Consumer Affairs Act 1972 (Victoria), Section 65A.

3 Food Act 1989 (New South Wales), Food Act 1984 (Victoria), Food Act 1981 (Qld), Food Act 1986 (NT), Food Act 1992 (ACT), Public Health Act 1962 (Tas), Food Act 1985 (Section A), and Health Act 1911 (WA).

4 Food Act 1989 (New South Wales), Section 90; Food Act 1984 (Victoria), Section 63.

The National Food Authority, in developing standards and variations of standards, must have regard to the following objectives in descending order of priority:

(1) The protection of public health and safety;
(2) The provision of adequate information relating to food to enable consumers to make informed choices and to prevent fraud and deception;
(3) The promotion of fair trading in food;
(4) The promotion of trade and commerce in the food industry; and
(5) The promotion of consistency between domestic and international food standards where they are at variance, providing it does not lower the Australian standard.

The standards recommended by the National Food Authority are considered by the National Food Standards Council.

In July 1991, the Commonwealth and states and territories entered into an agreement aimed at obliging each state and Territory to adopt the food standards prepared and recommended by the National Food Authority. There is provision for limited exceptions to national uniformity to allow for regional variation in food standards, where exceptional conditions in a state or territory or part thereof require some variation on the uniform standard to be allowed.

The Food Acts provide for various offenses concerning the processing for sale and sale of unwholesome food. The Food Act 1989 (New South Wales) makes it an offense to prepare for sale or to sell food which does not comply with a relevant prescribed standard. It also is an offense to supply food which is adulterated or falsely described. The Food Act 1989 (New South Wales) broadly defines food that is "adulterated or falsely described".

It is an offense to sell any food which is not of the nature, substance, or quality of the food demanded by the purchaser. If a person demands any food by a name prescribed for a food for which there is a standard prescribed, the person is to be taken to have demanded food which complies with the standard. It also is an offense for a person to tender or dispatch food which is adulterated or falsely described, to sell food which is wrongly packed, to display for sale or to sell food which is not labelled in accordance with the regulations, and to engage in false or misleading advertising. Similar offenses are specified under the Food Act 1984 (Victoria).

The Food Acts provide for a system of surveillance and inspection. For example, the Food Act 1989 (New South Wales) gives inspectors powers of entry and inspection. An inspector also is given powers to seize and detain, or take possession of, any food, appliance, package, or labelling or advertising material, or any other thing which the inspector reasonably believes is evidence that an offense against the Food Act or the regulations is being or has been committed.

The Food Act 1989 (New South Wales) and the Food Act 1984 (Victoria) contain provisions for the obtaining of samples of food for analysis and the procedures to be followed in analyzing the samples.

3.9.1.2 Procedures

The Food Act 1989 (New South Wales) provides that proceedings for an offense against the Food Act or the regulations may be dealt with in a summary manner by a local court constituted by a magistrate sitting alone.[1] Where a sample of food has been obtained for the purposes of analysis, no prosecution for an offense against the Food Act 1989 (New South Wales) or the regulations in respect of the food samples may be commenced after ninety days from the date on which the sample was obtained (other than prosecution for false warranties). Similar provisions are contained in the Food Act 1984 (Victoria).

3.9.1.3 Sanctions

The penalties for various offenses to the Food Act 1989 (New South Wales) are small monetary penalties or imprisonment. Provision also is made for the publication of the names of offenders, for clean-up notices and for orders for closure of unhygienic food stores, food vehicles, or appliances.

3.9.2 Drugs

The Commonwealth government has enacted the Therapeutic Goods Act 1989 (Cth), which provides a national system of controls relating to the quality, safety, and efficacy of therapeutic goods used in Australia, whether produced in Australia or elsewhere, or exported from Australia. Section 6(3) of this Act provides that the Act is intended to apply to the exclusion of any law of a state or territory, other than laws identified in the regulations (which were to take effect on 15 February 1994). The

---

1 Food Act 1989 (New South Wales), Section 57.

laws identified by the regulations for the purpose of Section 6(3) include various state and Territory Acts relating to therapeutic goods, drugs, and poisons.

However, the Health and Community Services Legislation Amendment Act (Number 2) 1993 (Cth) contains provisions which repeal Section 6(3) and amend the objects of the Therapeutic Goods Act to express the intention that the Therapeutic Goods Act is not intended to apply to the exclusion of a state or territory law which is capable of operating concurrently with the Therapeutic Goods Act 1989 (Cth). These provisions are to commence on a day fixed by Proclamation, but no such date has yet been fixed. Thus, it would appear that state and federal legislation will continue to operate concurrently.

The Therapeutic Goods Act 1989 (Cth) provides for the determination of quality and safety standards, the establishment of an Australian Register of Therapeutic Goods, and licensing requirements for manufacturers of therapeutic goods in Australia.

In general, a therapeutic good is any thing which can be used for the prevention, diagnosis, or treatment of diseases and other bodily conditions, or which can be taken for such through advertising or other means. Therapeutic goods are divided broadly into two classes, drugs and devices. In general, therapeutic devices are defined in the Act as therapeutic goods which do not achieve their principal intended action by pharmacological, chemical, immunological, or metabolic means.

Before therapeutic goods can be imported, exported, or supplied in Australia, most must be entered in the Australian Register of Therapeutic Goods. In general, the goods which are declared to be exempt from registration are simple pharmaceutical formulations for external application or therapeutic devices presenting no greater risk than other readily available consumer products. The Register is divided into two parts, one for "registered" goods and the other for "listed" goods. In general, goods which are registerable are those which are judged to require thorough evaluation with regards to their quality, safety, and efficacy.[1] Those which are listed tend to be less hazardous and more akin to other products readily available to consumers.[2]

Manufacturers of most therapeutic goods in Australia must be licensed and must comply with the Australian Code of Good Manufacturing Practice for Medicinal Products.

---

1 Schedule 3 of the Regulations.
2 Schedule 4 of the Regulations.

Under Section 10 of the Therapeutic Goods Act 1989 (Cth), the Minister may determine standards in relation to therapeutic goods or a class of therapeutic goods. An order establishing a standard for therapeutic goods may:

(1) Be specified by reference to the quality of the goods, the quantity of the goods when contained in specified containers, procedures to be carried out in the manufacture of the goods, a monograph of the British Pharmacopoeia or the British Pharmacopoeia (Veterinary), a monograph in another publication approved by the Minister or such a monograph as modified in a manner specified in the order establishing a standard, a standard published by the Standards Association of Australia, or such other matters as the Minister thinks fit;
(2) Require that a matter relating to the standard be determined in accordance with a particular test; or
(3) Require that the therapeutic goods or class of therapeutic goods identified in the order be labelled or packaged in a manner, or kept in containers that comply with requirements, specified in the order.

Standards also may concern the packaging and labeling of therapeutic goods.

Except with consent in writing of the Secretary, a person may not import therapeutic goods into Australia or supply therapeutic goods for use in Australia if the goods do not conform with the standard applicable to the goods.[1] Similar penalties apply in respect of the export of therapeutic goods which do not conform with the standard.

The states have re-enacted controls on the manufacture, distribution, labelling, and advertising of therapeutic goods and cosmetics.[2]

In addition, the states and territories operate separate systems of poisons scheduling under local Poison Acts or their equivalents.[3] The poisons schedules classify substances according to potency, addictive qualities, and suitability for ingestion by humans or animals. The Poisons Acts and regulations to those Acts contain provisions relating to the substances listed in these schedules, including provisions on the packaging and labelling of those poisons and the supply and storage of the drugs.

---

1 Therapeutic Goods Act 1989 (Cth), Section 14.

2 Therapeutic Goods and Cosmetics Act 1972 (New South Wales).

3 Poisons Act 1966 (New South Wales) and the Drugs, Poisons, and Controlled Substances Act 1981 (Victoria).

3.9.3 Motor Vehicles

There is an extensive national scheme for the prescription of standards for motor vehicles and vehicle components. The Commonwealth Motor Vehicle Standards Act 1989 aims to establish uniform standards which apply to road vehicles when they begin to be used in transport in Australia. The Act also prohibits the supply and importation of non-standard vehicles.

The Act states that compliance plates (indicating that a vehicle complies with the National Standards and has been granted approval) are to be attached to road vehicles.

The Act creates offenses with respect to the manufacture, supply, importation, and use of non-standard road vehicles, as well as modifications to make standard road vehicles non-standard. It also provides for court proceedings and injunctions that may be granted on the application of the Minister or any other person. Applications for review of the decision of a Minister, or a decision of another authority relating to compliance plates, may be made to the Administrative Appeals Tribunal.

The Minister has the power to determine procedures to be observed by manufacturers and importers relating to the testing and inspection of road vehicles, and all steps involved in their manufacture.

The national standards prescribed by this Act have the effect of a prescribed consumer product safety standard under Section 65C of the Trade Practices Act. Therefore, the enforcement procedures provided under that Act also are available.

State regulations, while they do not adopt the National Scheme, achieve a similar effect by the adoption of Australian Design rules and Australian Standards for motor vehicles.[1]

The existing state regulations deal with such subjects as lamps and reflectors, mud guards, rear markings, brakes, seatbelts, child restraint anchorages, and tires.

In addition to safety standards prescribed under Motor Vehicle Regulations, some standards are required under general consumer protection legislation. For example, under Section 65C(2) of the Trade Practices Act 1974, there is a Product Safety Standard specifically set for motor vehicle child restraints. Similarly, there is a banning order

---

1 Motor Traffic Regulations 1935, made under the Traffic Act 1909 (New South Wales), and Road Safety (Traffic) Regulations 1988, made under the Roads Safety Act 1986 (Victoria).

under Section 65C(5) of the Trade Practices Act 1974 for motor vehicle headlight covers allowing less than eighty-five per cent optical transmission. There are similar standard requirements under state legislation.[1]

3.9.4 Electrical Appliances

Control over the sale of electrical appliances and equipment is dealt with by the states, rather than by the Commonwealth. There is no uniform law, but the various state schemes for approval of electrical goods are based on similar principles. In addition, cooperation between the relevant state authorities has achieved a significant degree of uniformity in practice. This practical uniformity is recognized in the reciprocal nature of the various schemes, an electrical article approved or certified for a particular purpose in one state being considered safe for that purpose throughout Australia.

The New South Wales scheme, which may be considered as a typical example, is set out in the Electricity Act 1945 and the accompanying Approval of Electrical Articles Regulations. The scheme divides electrical goods into declared articles and non-declared articles. There are more than sixty categories of declared articles. These include such items as electrical household appliances, electrical tools, electric lights, accessories, such as plugs, wires, cords, switches, and components. It is an offense to sell (defined broadly) a declared electrical article if the article:

(1) Is not approved by the relevant authority;
(2) Is not marked in accordance with the regulations; or
(3) Does not comply with the relevant specifications or other prescribed requirements for that article.

Approval can be given by the relevant state authority.[2] A previous approval in another state or territory is sufficient, without further formalities. Alternatively, the electrical article can be certified under the Standards Australia Type Test or Standards Mark Scheme. Both are a certification trademark granted on behalf of the Standards Association of Australia. A Standards Mark is awarded to electrical appliances and

---

1 Product Safety Regulation 1988 (New South Wales).

2 For example, the Office of Energy in New South Wales and the State Electricity Commission in Victoria.

equipment manufactured under a quality assurance program endorsed by the Standards Association. The Electrical Safety Type Test Program provides a nationally recognized mark, indicating that an article has been type-tested against an Australian Standard for electrical safety.

Approval is contingent on the article in question conforming to the applicable specification. The specifications most often used for approvals are the Australian Standard Approval and Test Specifications. For approval to be granted, the applicant must have obtained satisfactory examination and test results from an approved, independent testing facility. All pre-sale modifications to the design, materials, or construction of an approved article require new approval by the relevant authority. Certificates of approval must be renewed after five years. A declared article must be sold marked with an "approved marking" indicating the state of original approval and the certificate of approval number.

It is an offense to sell an electrical article in contravention of the above provisions. It is also an offense to make a false and misleading application for approval. In addition, it is misleading to represent that the authority approves the overall performance and energy efficiency of the electrical article as approval in New South Wales relates only to the electrical safety of the article when constructed in accordance with the approved design. Such a misleading representation could give rise to liability under the Trade Practices Act or the Fair Trading Acts of New South Wales and Victoria.

3.9.5 Tools

There is no uniform regime regulating manufacture and design standards for tools. Where tools are electrical they will be covered by the regimes for product and safety standards for electrical articles. There are a number of Australian Standards relating to the manufacture and design of particular tools but, unless they are prescribed by state or Commonwealth legislation they are non-mandatory.

Examples can be found of mandatory standards in relation to specific classes of tools, such as explosive powered tools. Part 9A, Construction Safety Regulations 1950 (New South Wales), made under the Construction Safety Act 1912 (New South Wales), prescribe that the Australian Standard "Explosive Powered Hand-Held Fastening Tools, Fasteners and Explosive Charges" (AS1873-1978) is a mandatory standard in New South Wales.

The regulations establish a scheme whereby an explosive powered tool must be granted approval before it is sold or offered for sale, hired out, lent, or used. The approval regime is similar to that for the approval of electrical articles. In addition, the regulations require certain warning notices to be placed on the tools themselves and in areas where the tools are used. There are also provisions for the inspection and repair of explosive powered tools, their care and storage, their use, and the provision of protective devices for the operator.

3.9.6 Textiles

3.9.6.1 Product Safety

There is no uniform or comprehensive scheme in place for the mandatory prescription of standards for the manufacture, design, and testing of textiles. The exception to this is the control of certain flammable fabrics. The Standards Association of Australia has developed detailed standards with respect to the manufacture of some garments from flammable fabrics, such as the Australian Standard for "Children's Night Clothes Having Reduced Fire Hazard" (AS1249-1983, as variously updated). Various pieces of legislation have made compliance with the Australian Standard for children's nightclothes mandatory.[1]

In addition to specific standards in relation to children's flammable clothing, there is a general Australian Standard specification of "Methods of Test for Combustion Characteristics of Textile Materials" (AS1176-1976). This has been prescribed as a mandatory standard in various circumstances, for example, for children's tents and playhouses under Part 16 of the Product Safety Regulation 1988 (New South Wales).

3.9.6.2 Product Information

The regime for requiring the labelling of textiles is more fully developed. As for product safety, there are significant standards published by the Standards Association. The required labelling includes the following:

(1) The country of origin of the textile product if it was made outside Australia;[2]

---

1 Trade Practices Act 1974 (Cth), Section 65E(1); Consumer Affairs (Children's Night Clothes) Regulations 1987 (Victoria); Product Safety Regulation 1988 (New South Wales), Part 17.

2 Schedule 4, Fair Trading (Product Information Standards) Regulation 1992 (New South Wales).

(2) The fiber composition of the textile product; there are also detailed prescriptions for labelling that may be affixed to a textile product when a certain fiber forms only a percentage of the product;[1]
(3) Care instruction labelling; the Australian Standard "Care Labelling of Clothing, Household Textiles, Furnishings, Piece Goods and Yarns" (AS1957-1987) has been adopted as a mandatory product information stanard under Section 65D of the Trade Practices Act, and also in certain states;[2] and
(4) Safety warnings, which are required particularly if the textile product is flammable; the relevant Australian Standard divides products into those of the low fire-hazard type, those designed to reduce fire hazard, and those which have specifications for reduced but high fire danger, a different level of labelling warning being prescribed for each.[3]

For all of the above information standards, there are requirements for the affixing of the information to the product. Such requirements relate to the language, the type of label, the visibility, the permanence of the affixing, and the method of affixing to the textile goods or packaging.

3.9.7 Toys

There is no uniform national regime that covers toys. However, there is a significant quantity of ad hoc legislation concerning the design, manufacture, and labelling of certain classes of toys, and certain individual products. The existence of Australian Standards contributes significantly to uniformity in practice.

3.9.7.1 Standards Applicable to All Toys

It is rare for there to be standards prescribed for all toys. An exception to this is the regulation of any toys manufactured, designed, labelled, or marketed for the use by children under the age of three years. The Australian Standard "Children's Toys (Safety Requirements), Part 2 -

---

1 For example, in New South Wales, there needs to be ninety-five per cent wool by weight in a textile product before it can be labelled "pure wool" or "all wool".

2 For example, Schedule 7, Fair Trading (Products Information Standards) Regulation 1992 (New South Wales).

3 For example, the Consumer Affairs Children's Night Clothes Regulations 1983 (Victoria).

Constructional Requirements" (AS1647, Part 2-1981), is prescribed as a mandatory product standard in several legislative schemes. This deals with prohibits the construction of hazardous toys, including ingestion and inhalation hazards.[1]

There are also general provisions concerning toxicological requirements.[2]

Additionally, there are product information standards. For example, in certain states, there is a requirement that toys made outside Australia be marked with a statement indicating the country of origin.[3] Similarly, there may be a requirement that the age range of toys wholly or partially intended for children under the age of three years be marked on the toys.[4]

3.9.7.2 Standards Applicable to Particular Classes of Toys

There are certain generic types of toys for which standards are prescribed. These include such items as children's flotation toys, swimming aids, and underwater toys and games. The requirements are for permanent and conspicuous labelling, attached to both the toy and its packaging, advising of the dangers and limitations of the products.[5]

There are also banning orders in place under the various Acts for such products as liquid-filled toys and novelties, toy rockets and guns with spring-loaded firing mechanisms, stuffed venomous snakes, and toys incorporating poisonous seeds.

3.9.7.3 Standards Applicable to Particular Named Products

It is common in the various jurisdictions for specific brands and items to be banned. Examples include so-called "victim toys" (toys showing

---

1 *See*, for example, mandatory product safety standards under Section 65C of the Trade Practices Act 1974 (Cth); Part 14, Product Safety Regulation 1988 (New South Wales); Consumer Affairs (Product Safety) (Children's Toys Regulation) 1987 (Victoria).

2 For example, the prohibition in Section 245A of the Health Act 1958 (Victoria) on the manufacture or sale of toys composed wholly of, or containing more than a prescribed quantity, of lead. *See also* Australian Standards "Children's Toys (Safety Requirements Part 3 - Toxicological Requirements)" (AS1647, Part 3 - 1982).

3 Schedule 5, Fair Trading (Product Information Standards) Regulation 1992 (New South Wales).

4 Consumer Affairs (Product Safety) (Children's Toys) Regulations 1987 (Victoria).

5 *See* mandatory standards under Section 65C of the Trade Practices Act 1974 (Cth); Part 15, Product Safety Regulation 1988 (New South Wales); order made under Section 39E(1), Consumer Protection Act 1969 (New South Wales).

children in various states of injury and disfigurement), water toys capable of increasing their volume by 200 per cent or more when immersed in liquid, and certain, named projectile toys. Such toys are frequently banned by more than one state.

3.9.8 Insurance

Despite the very extensive law relating to insurance, there is only minimal regulation of the form and content of insurance policies. Freedom of contract prevails, despite the inequality of bargaining power between insurer and insured which inevitably results in the insurer being able to impose its standard terms and conditions on the insured without significant negotiation.

There is, however, some legislation that deals with insurance contracts. The area is largely regulated by the Commonwealth under the Insurance Act 1973, the Insurance Contracts Act 1984, and the accompanying Insurance Contract Regulations. Other relevant legislation includes the Life Insurance Act 1945, the Insurance Agents and Brokers 1984, and the Insurance and Superannuation Commissioner Act 1987. Although a significant number of insurance contracts are thereby regulated by Commonwealth legislation, the Insurance Contracts Act does not apply to the following:

(1) Contracts of insurance entered into, renewed, extended, varied, or reinstated before 1 January 1986;
(2) Contracts of re-insurance, health insurance (where the insurer is a registered fund), marine insurance, compulsory workers' compensation insurance, and compulsory third-party motor vehicle insurance;
(3) Contracts of insurance entered into by a Friendly Society and the Australian Trade Commission;
(4) Contracts in respect of aircraft engaged in commercial operations; and
(5) Contracts entered into in the course of state insurance (where the insurer is a Government Insurance Office).

These contracts are regulated by the states and territories.[1]

---

1 For example, the Insurance Act 1902 (New South Wales) and the Contracts Review Act 1980 (New South Wales).

3.9.8.1 General Requirements for Formation of Insurance Contracts

There are certain requirements prescribed under the Insurance Contracts Act 1984 which generally cannot be contracted out of:

(1) In every insurance, contract there is an implied provision requiring each party to act with the utmost good faith toward the other;[1]

(2) The insurer is required to inform the insured in writing before a contract is entered into of the general nature and effect of the duty of disclosure.[2] The insured's duty of disclosure is limited only to those facts reasonably known to be relevant to the insurer's assessment of the risk.[3] An untrue statement does not constitute a misrepresentation where the person making it reasonably believes it to be true.[4] Innocent non-disclosure or misrepresentation does not entitle the insurer to avoid a contract; instead, the insurer's liability is reduced by an amount which represents the loss suffered by the insurer by reason of the non-disclosure or misrepresentation.[5] Non-disclosure or misrepresentation only entitles an insurer to avoid a contract of general insurance if it is fraudulent, although the court will be able to disregard such avoidance if it would be harsh or unfair not to do so, and the insurer has not been prejudiced by the non-disclosure or misrepresentation, or any prejudice is minimal.[6]

(3) Where a loss occurs as a result of a latent defect in property or a latent sickness or disability of the insured, the insurer will not be able to rely on any provision in the contract excluding liability if the insured was not reasonably aware of the latent defect, sickness or disability.[7] Regulations have been made excluding certain classes of insurance from thc opcration of the pre-existing defect section.

(4) An insurer may cancel a contract of general insurance only if there has been a breach of the duty of utmost good faith, a breach of the duty of disclosure, a misrepresentation, a breach of the terms of

---

1 Insurance Contracts Act 1984, Section 13.
2 Insurance Contracts Act 1984, Section 22 and Regulation 3.
3 Insurance Contracts Act 1984, Section 21.
4 Insurance Contracts Act 1984, Section 26.
5 Insurance Contracts Act 1984, Sections 28 and 29.
6 Insurance Contracts Act 1984, Sections 28(2), 29(2), and 31.
7 Insurance Contracts Act 1984, Sections 27 and 46.

the contract, a fraudulent claim by the insured under the contract or under any other contract of insurance which overlaps in time, or a failure to notify the insurer of a specified act or omission as required by the contract.[1]

(5) There are provisions in the Insurance Contracts Act which deal with interim cover, installment contracts (where a premium is paid in installments over a year), maximum cover, claims, subrogation, contribution, arbitration, and the effect of co-existing insurance cover for an insured event.

3.9.8.2 Standard Policies

The Insurance Contracts Act allows for the prescription of standard covers. The Insurance Contracts Regulations have prescribed standard covers for:

(1) Motor vehicle insurance;
(2) Home buildings insurance;
(3) Sickness and accident insurance;
(4) Consumer credit insurance; and
(5) Travel insurance.

Each standard cover states the prescribed contracts to which the regulations apply, and the prescribed risks insured against. The standard cover lists exclusions from standard cover. These are those which would usually be found in contracts of insurance, such as the sickness and accidents insurance standard cover which excludes death or disablement resulting from deliberately self-inflicted injuries, war, nuclear materials, the insured person being under the influence of, or addicted to, drugs or alcohol, the insured taking part in a riot, the insured acting maliciously, or the insured engaging in professional sporting activities. Lastly, the standard cover provides for minimum amounts payable under the prescribed classes of insurance.

The standard covers, however, are not mandatory. Insurers are free to offer policies which contain more or less than the standard cover, provided that in the latter case the insured's attention is drawn to the limitations on the cover. This can be done by providing the insured with a document containing the provisions, or clearly informing the insured

---

1 Insurance Contracts Act 1984, Section 60.

in writing of the variations.[1] The same applies for unusual terms in insurance contracts for which standard cover has not been prescribed.[2]

Under Section 11(10) of the Insurance Contracts Act 1984, where the insurer has given such information once, it is not required to repeat it on any renewal of the contract, despite the fact that it is scarcely reasonable to expect an insured to remember a warning about non-standard exclusions from cover years after they have been drawn to his or her attention.

3.9.8.3 Illegibility and Incomprehensibility

One of the most significant problems with insurance contracts concerns their illegibility and lack of plain English. Insurance contracts have long been notorious for their "fine print" and general incomprehensibility. This is a problem both with the policies themselves, and with any notifications of derogations from standard covers. The various bodies that review insurance law (e.g., the Trade Practices Commission, the Australian Law Reform Commission, the Insurance and Superannuation Commission, and the Australian Consumer's Association) have all identified unintelligibility as a major problem. It is also a factor behind a significant percentage of consumer complaints to these bodies.

Neither the Insurance Contracts Act nor state legislation require general insurance policies to be written in simple and easily intelligible language. Section 73 of the Insurance Contracts Act allows for the prescription of legibility standards, but it has not yet been used. Only for consumer credit insurance is there any sign of legislative change. In July 1993, the Commonwealth government's working party on consumer credit insurance made recommendations for plain English pre-sale, point of sale, and post-sale documentation, in addition to disclosure in plain English of derogations from standard cover. In September 1993, the Commonwealth Treasurer and Minister for Consumer Affairs announced a far-reaching program of reform to the Consumer Credit Insurance system, implementing these and other recommendations in the report.

In New South Wales, the Contracts Review Act 1980 provides that the physical form of a contract and the intelligibility of its language are factors to be taken into account in determining whether a contractual provision is unjust at the time of making the contract.[3] This Act, however, only applies to contracts not regulated by the Commonwealth Insurance Contracts Act.

---

1 Insurance Contracts Act 1984, Section 35.

2 Insurance Contracts Act 1984, Section 37.

3 Contracts Review Act 1980 (New South Wales), Section 9(2).

Otherwise, reform of the situation is in the hands of individual insurers. Several large insurance companies now voluntarily use plain English policies; but, for the majority, there has been no change.

3.9.9 Travel

There are many abuses that can arise in connection with the marketing and provision of travel services. The approach of the legislatures in Australia has been to regulate the industry of travel agents, rather than to prescribe standards for the services they provide. The legislation in each state provides for the licensing of travel agents, the conduct of a travel agent's business, and compensation for clients who suffer pecuniary losses arising out of a travel agent's failure to account.[1] The travel agents' licensing scheme has been adopted with only minor variations in all states and territories. This legislation comes more properly under the heading of occupational licensing.

In addition to remedies under the licensing regime, the consumer also has recourse to both contract law principles and consumer protection legislation. The Trade Practices Commission in 1976 published its "Travel Advertising Guidelines", dealing with the application of the Trade Practices Act to the travel industry.

The Commission highlighted two broad areas of conduct giving rise to concern, and for which the Trade Practices Act can provide a remedy:

(1) Representations in promotional literature that create misleading impressions of a price at which services are offered, the quality or range of services offered, or the time at which the services are to be provided and their duration; and
(2) Failure to inform consumers of variations to price, quality, itineraries, or the like on which claims in promotional literature material to a consumer's decision to travel are based.

The Commission also provided detailed guidelines on liability arising from representations as to:

(1) Price and variations in price;
(2) Quality or extent of services;

---

1 For example, the Travel Agents Act 1986 (New South Wales) and Travel Agents Act 1986 (Victoria).

(3) Duration of a tour, holiday, or the time of travel;
(4) Availability and nature of finance;
(5) Extent of travel insurance; and
(6) Duty-free prices.

In addition to any action taken by the Commission, Section 82 of the Trade Practices Act 1974 gives an individual the right to bring proceedings for the recovery of damage suffered as a result of contravention of the Act. The Commission noted that, in addition to compensation for monetary loss, damages may cover mental distress, inconvenience, or disappointment caused as a result of misleading or deceptive statements in literature promoting travel.

3.9.10 Correspondence Courses

There is no specific regime for controlling correspondence courses as such. Correspondence courses are not differentiated from any other educational or training courses. Therefore, they must meet the same national and state accreditation requirements.

Accreditation is the procedure by which an authority provides certification that the standards of an educational or training course are appropriate to the award to which it leads and that the course and the methods adopted in delivering it are likely to achieve the purpose for which the course was or will be introduced.

Accreditation powers have been granted to two types of authorities:

(1) Higher education institutions, empowered by their various Acts of establishment to accredit or approve their own courses; these bodies are regulated by various Higher Education Acts;[1] and
(2) Statutory bodies which accredit tertiary award courses offered through institutions of technical and further education (TAFE), those few higher education institutions not self-accrediting, and private education and training providers.

In New South Wales, the major authority is the Vocational Education and Training Accreditation Board (VETAB), established under the

1 For example, the Higher Education Act 1988 (New South Wales) and the Tertiary Education Act 1993 (Victoria).

Vocational Education and Training Accreditation Act 1990 (New South Wales). There are equivalent bodies in other states.[1]

One of the functions of statutory accreditation authorities is to establish guidelines for the accreditation of vocational courses. VETAB in New South Wales has issued guidelines relating to standards for course documentation and premises. These include guidelines relating to the following issues:

(1) An underpinning educational philosophy for the commercial education or training establishment;
(2) Adequate and safe premises;
(3) Availability of and access to adequate resources and facilities;
(4) Misleading advertising, and misleading names of commercial education establishments which do not accurately convey the types and levels of courses or programs being offered;
(5) Availability of information about the course and the commercial education establishment;
(6) Safeguards to protect fee-paying students from financial exploitation;
(7) Permissible entry requirements, including English language proficiency requirements;
(8) Legal acquisition and use of computer software, and compliance with applicable regulations and standards concerning intellectual property;
(9) Recognition of prior learning;
(10) Structure and sequence of a course or training program, and appropriate modes of delivery;
(11) Numbers of appropriately qualified and experienced staff;
(12) Arrangements for the maintenance of students' records for a period of at least thirty years, particularly where the organization ceases business; and
(13) Review procedures for monitoring curriculum development, course implementation, and the continued relevance of the course to industry and learners.

In addition to the VETAB guidelines, there are guidelines for course nomenclature and course classification laid down in the Register of Australian Tertiary Education, established by the Australian Education Council.

---

1 For example, the Vocational Education and Training Act 1990 (Victoria).

The accreditation scheme is voluntary. It is, however, open to a particular industry to recognize only training provided through an accredited training program. It is an offense to falsely advertise or otherwise falsely represent that a particular vocational course has been accredited, endorsed or otherwise approved by a state authority.

Australia has a National Framework for the Recognition of Training, operating to ensure consistency in the accreditation and recognition of training. The Framework agreement is designed to produce:

(1) National consistency in the accreditation of courses and recognition of training programs;
(2) National consistency in the registration of providers of training;
(3) National recognition and portability of individual competencies;
(4) National recognition of training in the public and private sectors; and
(5) Nationally recognized standards of training.

The Australian National Training Authority, established under the Australian National Training Authority Act 1992 (Cth), oversees the development of a national vocational educational and training system in consultation with state authorities, and administers funding to state bodies.

3.9.11 Mail Order

There is no specific legislative regime for the regulation of mail-order selling. There are, however, general controls that are exercisable in respect of the advertisements which invite the consumer to purchase a product and which provide the only information by which a consumer can decide as to the merits of the offer.

The advertisements are covered by the general prohibition of misleading and deceptive conduct in the Trade Practices Act, and the equivalent state Fair Trading legislation. In addition to this general consumer protection legislation, mail-order selling may be caught by Section 58 of the Trade Practices Act and the equivalent state provisions.[1] This provides a remedy for both non-delivery and the supply of defective goods.

1 For example, Section 53 of the Fair Trading Act 1987 (New South Wales) and Section 20 of the Fair Trading Act 1985 (Victoria).

The provisions state that a person shall not accept payment or other consideration for goods or services where, at the time of the acceptance, the person intends:

(1) Not to supply the goods or services;
(2) To supply goods and services materially different from the goods or services in respect of which the payment or other consideration is accepted; or
(3) There are reasonable grounds, of which the person is aware, or ought reasonably to be aware, for believing that the person will not be able to supply the goods or services within the period specified, or within a reasonable time.

Section 58 is not an infallible remedy for non-delivery of mail-ordered goods, as the offense relies on an objective test of the intention of the purported supplier. Mere non-supply will not suffice to prove intention without some circumstances from which the intention may be proved or inferred.

The problem of the supply of defective goods can be remedied by the prohibition on supplying goods materially different as described in item (2), above. It also could constitute a breach of implied terms as to merchantability and fitness for purpose.

A problem to which mail-order selling is susceptible is that the description in the advertisement may be vague enough to permit the supply of more than one kind of good or service. Section 58 provides no guarantee that the consumer will receive the goods or services they believe have been ordered.

Goods supplied by mail-order are still required to comply with general sale-of-goods legislation and any special regulation applying to the product or service supplied. For example, the supply of alcohol by mail-order may not contravene any laws prohibiting the sale of liquor to minors.

In addition to consumer protection legislation, there are certain non-mandatory but influential Codes of Practice that regulate aspects of mail-order selling. The advertising industry is a self-regulating profession and has evolved detailed Codes and complaint procedures. The Media Council of Australia has published a Mail Order Advertising Code. It applies to all mail-order advertisements published in a newspaper or magazine, and the publication of such an advertisement by the electronic media. It deals with the following issues:

(1) Publication of the name and physical address of the advertiser;
(2) The circumstances in which goods or samples can be described as "free";
(3) The use of contests or lotteries as marketing incentives;
(4) Fictitious or misleading testimonials;
(5) Prohibitions on certain products, such as goods purporting to impart a good-luck advantage to the possessor, and medical products which do not conform to relevant health laws;
(6) Adequate facilities and samples at the address for enquiries;
(7) Refunds;
(8) Prompt filling of orders; and
(9) The correspondence between the goods dispatched and the description given.

In addition to remedies under consumer affairs legislation, a consumer can make a complaint to the Advertising Standards Council for a breach of this or any other relevant code (e.g., the Media Council of Australia Advertising Code of Ethics, or the Australian Association of National Advertisers Code of Advertising Standards).

3.10 Testing

There are numerous Commonwealth and state requirements for testing and for the distribution of test results. Many of these requirements are imposed by or in conjunction with product standards in relation to specific goods. For example, the various state laws on food and drugs contain provisions relating to the ongoing surveillance and inspection of food and drugs, which enable inspectors to obtain samples and to set in chain a process of analysis.

The various pieces of legislation which permit standards to be made in relation to certain products also may permit standards to be made relating to testing. For example, the Trade Practices Act 1974 provides that a standard in respect of goods of a particular kind may contain requirements as to the testing of goods during, or after the completion of manufacture or processing.[1] The requirements as to testing in relation to a number of specific goods, in particular food, drugs, motor vehicles, electrical appliances, and textiles, are discussed above.

---

1 Trade Practices Act 1974 (Cth), Section 65C.

In addition to the testing requirements in relation to specific products, there are some general requirements as to testing. One of these is found in occupational health and safety legislation. These legislative schemes impose a duty on employers to provide a safe working environment for their employees. The Occupational Health & Safety Act 1983 (New South Wales) also provides that manufacturers and suppliers of plant and substances for use at work must ensure that the plant or substance is safe and without risk when properly used. Such a manufacturer also is required to carry out such research, testing and examination as may be necessary for the purpose of discovery and the elimination or minimization of any risks to health which a product may cause and to take such steps as are necessary to make available in connection with the use of its product at work adequate information about the results of any relevant tests which have been carried out on the product and about any conditions necessary to ensure that it will be safe without risk to health when properly used. Similar requirements are contained in the Occupational Health and Safety Act 1985 (Victoria).

Another important example is found in legislation relating to standards of measurement. The legislation in each state is part of a scheme for uniform trade measurement legislation throughout Australia. For example, the Trade Measurement Act 1989 (New South Wales) contains provisions relating to the verification and certification of measuring instruments. Where an inspector reasonably believes that an article is for sale by reference to the measurement of the article or it is a pre-packed article, an inspector has certain powers, including the power to examine the article.

If an inspector reasonably believes that an offense against the Act has been committed involving an article, the inspector has certain powers which include the power to seize and retain the article and to measure it. The inspector also has the power to examine and test any measuring instrument he or she reasonably believes is used for trade. Similar provisions are contained in the Weights and Measures Act 1958 (Victoria).

The Mutual Recognition legislation discussed above may apply to requirements for inspection. Part 2 of the Mutual Recognition legislation provides that goods produced or imported into one state, that may lawfully be sold in that state, may be sold in a second state without the need to comply with requirements that the goods be inspected, passed or similarly dealt with for the purposes of the second state. As discussed above, certain goods are not affected by the operation of Part 2, and certain laws still must be complied with, including laws which regulate the manner of sale of goods laws directed at matters affecting the health and safety of persons within the second state or at environmental pollution matters.

Section 4

Advertising Claims

4.1 Introduction

Advertising in Australia is primarily regulated by the Trade Practices Act 1974 and by fair trading legislation enacted by the states and territories.[1] The fair trading legislation broadly parallels the relevant provisions in the Trade Practices Act 1974. Despite this, the fair trading legislation serves a useful purpose since it covers activities undertaken by persons generally, while, as is discussed below, the operation of the Trade Practices Act 1974 is more limited. Since the fair trading legislation broadly reproduces the relevant provisions of the Trade Practices Act, this discussion will not analyze the fair trading legislation but will focus on the Trade Practices Act.

There are also numerous other Acts which control advertising concerning particular products. For instance, some Acts prohibit false or misleading advertising relating to credit and false and misleading advertising of therapeutic goods. However, this legislation tends to be of less significance than the Trade Practices Act because very few actions have been brought under it.

The television and radio media are subject to a special legislative regime which controls advertising on commercial television and radio stations, among other things. This legislative regime is discussed below.

In addition to the legislative regulation, various media bodies have published non-binding standards concerning advertising. These standards are discussed below.

Finally, the Common Law provides some controls on advertising, such as giving traders a cause of action in the tort of passing off and thus regulating advertising indirectly. There is considerable overlap between the relevant provisions of the Trade Practices Act and the passing off action.

---

1 For example, the Fair Trading Act 1987 (New South Wales) and the Fair Trading Act 1985 (Victoria).

4.2 Trade Practices Act: Part V, Division 1

The consumer protection provisions of the Trade Practices Act 1974 that apply to advertising are found in Part V, Division 1, of the Act. Although these provisions are stated to apply to conduct by a corporation in trade or commerce, the Act also covers individuals and entities other than corporations if they engage in conduct which involves the use of postal, telegraphic, or telephonic services, or which takes place in a radio or television broadcast.[1] Therefore, most forms of advertising are subject to the Act, no matter which sort of entity is responsible for the advertising. However, advertising by unincorporated firms and business persons in newspapers and magazines falls outside the operation of the Act but will usually be caught by the fair trading legislation.

The scheme of Part V, Division 1, of the Act is broadly as follows. Section 52 of the Trade Practices Act, which is the first provision in Part V, Division 1, prohibits in very general terms misleading or deceptive conduct or conduct that is likely to mislead or deceive. The remaining relevant provisions of Division 1, Sections 53, 53A, 53B, 55, 55A, and 56, prohibit false representations relating to specific matters in connection with the supply or promotion of goods or services and practices such as bait advertising. The specific conduct in these sections also may amount to "misleading or deceptive conduct" under Section 52 of the Act.

Contravention of Section 52 exposes an advertiser to private civil actions in which persons injured by the misleading or deceptive conduct can recover damages from the offender.[2] In addition, an injunction may be issued,[3] and, on the application of the Minister responsible for the Act, or the Trade Practices Commission, a public information disclosure order or corrective advertising order may be made.[4] The court also may make remedial orders, such as orders declaring contracts void, orders refusing to enforce contracts, or orders that money be refunded.[5]

Contraventions of the remaining provisions expose an advertiser to private civil actions and also carry criminal penalties consisting of fines of up to Aus. $400,000 for a corporation and Aus. $40,000 for an individual.[6] The Trade Practices Commission has general responsibility

---

1 Trade Practices Act 1974 (Cth), Section 6(3).
2 Trade Practices Act 1974 (Cth), Section 82.
3 Trade Practices Act 1974 (Cth), Section 80.
4 Trade Practices Act 1974 (Cth), Section 80A.
5 Trade Practices Act 1974 (Cth), Section 87.
6 Trade Practices Act 1974 (Cth), Section 79.

for instituting prosecutions for offenses against the consumer protection provisions of the Act.[1] A person has a defense to prosecutions for contraventions of Part V of the Act if he or she establishes that the contravention was due to:

(1) Reasonable mistake;
(2) Reasonable reliance on information supplied by another person; or
(3) An act or default of another person or an accident or cause beyond the defendant's control and where the defendant took reasonable precautions and exercised due diligence to avoid the contravention.[2] Similarly, a publisher will have a defense to both civil and criminal contraventions of provisions in Part V arising out of the publication of an advertisement if the publisher establishes that it is his or her business to publish advertisements and that he or she received the advertisement for publication in the ordinary course of business and did not know and had no reason to suspect that its publication would amount to a contravention of a provision of that Part.[3]

4.2.1 Misleading or Deceptive Conduct

Section 52 of the Trade Practices Act 1974 is of great importance to businesses, not only because of possible action against them for breach of the section, but also because businesses can use the section to protect themselves from competitors whose unfair business practices could or do injure them. Section 52 provides that:

> "A corporation shall not, in trade or commerce, engage in conduct that is misleading or deceptive or is likely to mislead or deceive."

Some general points should be noted about the operation of the section.

(1) The term "trade or commerce" is broad, covering not only ordinary commercial or business dealings and communications, but also dealings and communications that do not occur in the market

---

1 Trade Practices Act 1974 (Cth), Section 79.
2 Trade Practices Act 1974 (Cth), Section 85(1).
3 Trade Practices Act 1974 (Cth), Section 85(3).

place. In *Larmer* vs. *Power Machinery Pty. Ltd.*,[1] the defendant company displayed brochures in the foyer of its premises. This was held to be a representation in trade or commerce.

(2) "Conduct" is defined to include the doing or refusing to do any act, including the making of or giving effect to a provision of a contract or arrangement, and arriving at or giving effect to an understanding.[2]

(3) To be misleading or deceptive, conduct must convey a misrepresentation.[3]

(4) Whether a particular advertisement is misleading or deceptive is a question of fact to be answered in the context of the evidence concerning the alleged conduct and the relevant surrounding facts and circumstances. One relevant factor is the understanding or impression conveyed by the advertisement to the persons affected by it, who usually include its target audience. The relevance of the target audience is discussed below.

(5) Australian courts recognize that a "robust approach" is needed in determining whether advertisements, as opposed to other conduct, are misleading or deceptive, since the public is accustomed to advertisers making somewhat exaggerated claims for their products and services.[4]

(6) In determining whether advertisements breach Section 52, Australian courts assume that the ordinary customer is of average intelligence, that he or she reads between the lines of advertisements in light of ordinary experience, and that he or she does not draw strained or utterly unreasonable interpretations of advertisements.[5]

(7) Section 52 does not require that the advertiser intends to mislead or deceive consumers. An advertiser will breach Section 52 if its advertisement is misleading or deceptive or is likely to mislead or deceive, irrespective of the state of mind of the advertiser.[6]

---

1 (1977) 14 ALR 243.

2 Trade Practices Act 1974 (Cth), Section 4(2).

3 *Taco Co. of Australia* vs. *Taco Bell Pty. Ltd.* (1982) 42 ALR 177.

4 *Stuart Alexander and Co. (Interstate) Pty. Ltd.* vs. *Blenders Pty. Ltd.* (1981) 53 FLR 307.

5 *Typing Centre of New South Wales Pty. Ltd.* vs. *Northern Business College Ltd.* (1989) ATPR 50-279; *FAI Insurance Co. Ltd.* vs. *RAIA Insurance Brokers Ltd.* (1992) ATPR 41-176.

6 *Hornsby Building Information Centre Pty. Ltd.* vs. *Sydney Building Information Center* (1978) 140 CLR 216.

(8) It is not necessary to prove that damage is caused or that people are actually misled; merely that the advertisement is capable of misleading is sufficient.
(9) Statements in advertisements which are literally true will offend Section 52 if they are likely to mislead a consumer.
(10) What is left unsaid in an advertisement may be important since failure to disclose relevant information can constitute misleading or deceptive conduct.[1]
(11) Ambiguous statements which are capable of having one true meaning and one false meaning are also likely to lead a person into error and to be in breach of Section 52.
(12) Since it is the overall impression created by a particular advertisement which is important in assessing whether it is likely to mislead or deceive, fine-print qualifications may not be sufficiently prominent to correct an overall impression which is likely to mislead consumers.

4.2.2 Further Provisions

The remaining provisions of Division 1 of Part V of the Act contain specific prohibitions, of which the ones relevant to advertising are as follows:

(1) Sections 53(a) and 53(aa) of the Act prohibit false representations that goods or services are of a particular standard, quality, value, or grade, or that goods are of a particular composition, style, or model or have a particular history or particular previous use.
(2) Section 53(b) of the Act prohibits false representations that goods are new.
(3) Sections 53(c) and 53(d) of the Act prohibit representations that corporations, goods, or services have sponsorship, approval, or affiliation they do not have or that goods or services have performance characteristics, accessories, uses, or benefits they do not have.
(4) Section 53(e) of the Act prohibits false or misleading representations with respect to the price of goods or services.
(5) Section 53(ea) of the Act prohibits false or misleading representations concerning the availability of facilities for the repair of goods or of spare parts for the goods.

---

1 *Demagogue Pty. Ltd.* vs. *Ramensky* (1992) 110 ALR 608; *General Newspapers Pty. Limited* vs. *Telstra Corp Ltd.* (1993) ATPR 41-274.

(6) Section 53(eb) of the Act prohibits false or misleading representations concerning the place of origin of goods.
(7) Section 53(f) of the Act prohibits false or misleading representations concerning the need for any goods or services.
(8) Section 53(g) of the Act prohibits false or misleading representations concerning the existence, exclusion, or effect of any condition, warranty, guarantee, or remedy.
(9) Section 53A of the Act prohibits false representations and other misleading conduct in relation to land. This is to prevent promotions involving the sale of land where the buyer buys sight unseen.
(10) Section 53B of the Act prohibits conduct that is liable to mislead persons seeking employment as to its availability, nature, terms or conditions. This section was introduced to prohibit the publication of false or misleading advertisements for employment (for example, by an employment agency advertising positions which do not exist with a view to expanding their pool of available employees).
(11) Sections 55 and 55A of the Act prohibit conduct liable to mislead the public as to the nature, characteristics, suitability for purpose, or the quantity of any goods or services or the manufacturing process of any goods.
(12) Section 56 of the Act prohibits bait advertising, which is advertising goods at specified prices without intending or being able to supply them as advertised for a reasonable period.

4.3 Comparisons

Comparative advertising involves advertising the qualities of a product by reference to the qualities of competing products.[1]

If a comparison is false or likely to mislead or deceive, the advertiser risks civil action and possibly criminal penalties for contravening provisions of Part V Division 1 of the Act. The advertiser also may be disciplined under the self-regulatory activities of media bodies. This latter point is discussed below.

If, on the other hand, the comparison is accurate and is not in any way misleading, it is legally legitimate. Indeed, the Trade Practices Commission

---

1 *Stuart Alexander & Co. (Interstate) Pty. Ltd.* vs. *Blenders Pty. Ltd.* (1981) 53 FLR 307; *State Government Insurance Commission* vs. *JM Insurance Pty. Ltd.* (1984), ATPR 40-465.

holds the view that accurate comparisons perform a valuable information function. Note, however, that the courts impose a heavy responsibility on advertisers to ensure that advertisements showing their competitors' goods in an unfavorable light are correct, since a consumer will be less likely than otherwise to suspect that the advertisement contains exaggerated claims.[1]

Some administrative bodies do not favor comparative advertising. The Therapeutic Goods Administration, a Commonwealth statutory body set up under the Therapeutic Goods Act 1989 (Cth), is opposed to comparative advertising of therapeutic goods.

While the law creates no obstacle to accurate comparative advertising, the media does through the Media Council of Australia's Advertising Code of Ethics and the activities of an industry body, the Joint Committee for Disparaging Copy.

Clause 11 of the Advertising Code of Ethics states that "[a]dvertisements shall not disparage identifiable products, services or competitors in an unfair or misleading way". The Joint Committee for Disparaging Copy (JCDC) investigates and settles complaints within the advertising industry relating to Clause 11. On receiving a complaint, it will rule that an advertisement breaches Clause 11 if it contains a specific identifiable misleading or unfair disparagement of a particular product or service provided by a competitor. If an advertisement breaches Clause 11, the JCDC can veto it.

4.4 Media Channels

In addition to the Trade Practices Act, which can apply to all forms of advertising, the television and radio media and advertising through them are subject to a special legislative regime. Under the Broadcasting Services Act 1992 (Cth), commercial television and radio stations, among others, cannot be operated except by persons holding a license. The licenses are issued on certain standard conditions, one of which directly concerns advertisements and two others of which concern advertisements indirectly. A licensee which does not comply with a condition of a license is guilty of an offense carrying a penalty of Aus. $2,000,000.

1 *Stuart Alexander & Co (Interstate) Pty. Ltd.* vs. *Blenders Pty. Ltd.* (1981) 53 FLR 307; *State Government Insurance Commission* vs. *JM Insurance Pty. Ltd.* (1984) ATPR 40-465.

The first standard condition is the condition that the licensee not advertise cigarettes, cigarette tobacco, or any other tobacco products. The second standard condition is that the licensee comply with program standards set by the body administering the Broadcasting Services Act, the Australian Broadcasting Authority (ABA). Relevant ABA program standards for television include standards concerning children and advertising,[1] Australian content in advertising,[2] advertisements for cinema films,[3] and advertisements related to betting and gambling.[4]

The third standard condition is that the licensee must comply with any conditions imposed on it by the ABA. The ABA can require that a licensee comply with a code promulgated by an industry group, such as the Federation of Australian Television Station (FACTS) or the Federation of Australian Radio Broadcasters Limited (FARB), once the code has been registered with the ABA.

FACTS has promulgated a Code of Practice which has been endorsed by all Australian commercial television stations. The Code of Practice provides, among other things, for the classification and placement of commercials with a view to ensuring that television commercials are classified and broadcast appropriately, that commercials for products and services such as alcoholic drinks, betting, and gambling are subject to additional restrictions, and that public health and safety messages are not unreasonably restricted.

FARB has promulgated Commercial Radio Codes of Practice and Guidelines, which require that advertisements broadcast by a licensee not be presented as news programs or other programs and not, among other things, present as desirable the use of tobacco or the misuse of drugs, narcotics, or alcoholic liquor.

As mentioned above, another facet of the regulation of advertising in Australia is the advertising standards published by media industry bodies. The principal industry scheme for regulation of advertising in Australia is administered by the Media Council of Australia (MCA). The MCA is an unincorporated voluntary association of commercial media including newspapers, magazines, radio, television, cinema, and outdoor display contractors. Its regulation of advertising coincides with an accreditation system for advertising agents which it administers through an MCA committee, the Australian Media Accreditation Authority.

---

1 Television Advertising Standard 5.
2 Television Program Standard 23.
3 Television Advertising Standard 6(c)(i)-(ii).
4 Television Advertising Standard 9.

The accreditation rules provide that accredited advertising agencies must observe the MCA's advertising codes. The codes also must be observed by MCA members and any persons who lodge advertisements with an MCA member.

The MCA currently has five codes: the Advertising Code of Ethics and four separate codes for advertisements concerning therapeutic goods, cigarettes, alcohol, and slimming preparations. The purpose of the Advertising Code of Ethics is to promote honesty, fairness, and responsibility in advertising. The Code requires that advertisements be clearly recognizable as such, that they be truthful, and that they not be misleading or deceptive. The Code also requires that advertisements not encourage dangerous behavior, not engage in unlawful discrimination, and not contain material which is likely to cause serious offense to a significant section of the community.

Each of the four product codes imposes more detailed requirements for advertisements concerning those products. For instance, the Cigarette Advertising Code provides that the advertising of cigarettes should not have a strong or evident appeal to children or adolescents, should not encourage people to start smoking or, if already smoking, to increase their consumption, but should only effect or deter a change of brand, should not depict or represent persons, and should not depict sexual, social, or business success or distinction as being attributable to the act of smoking. The Cigarette Advertising Code also sets out detailed requirements for the size of health warnings to be printed on taxi panels, shopping center posters, van posters, bus panels, and outdoor posters.

Each of the product codes requires advertisers or agencies to get a pre-clearance for their advertisement before submitting it for publication or broadcast by an MCA member.

Each branch of the media (radio, television, print, cinema, and outdoor) maintains a clearance office for this purpose. They are the Federation of Australian Commercial Television Stations (FACTS), the Federation of Australian Radio Broadcasters Limited (FARB), the Australian Publishers' Bureau (APB), the Outdoor Advertising Association of Australia Incorporated (OAAA), and the Australian Cinema Advertising Council (ACAC).

An accredited advertising agency should not submit, and an MCA member should not accept, an advertisement that is governed by one of the four product codes unless the advertisement has been pre-cleared by the appropriate body.

An advertiser or agent whose advertisement is refused pre-clearance approval can appeal from the decision to the Advertising Standards Council. The Advertising Standards Council consists of representatives of advertisers, advertising agencies, the public, and the media. Complaints about advertising can be made to the Advertising Standards Council by anyone, including members of the public, advertisers, advertising agencies, or government instrumentalities. If the Advertising Standards Council finds that an advertisement has breached a Code, MCA members will stop broadcasting and publishing it. If an accredited advertising agent breaches the Codes, the Australian Media Accreditation Authority may remove the agent's accreditation.

4.5 Target Audiences

As mentioned in the discussion of Section 52 of the Trade Practices Act above, in considering whether a particular advertisement is misleading or deceptive or has a capacity to mislead or deceive, Australian courts consider the class of persons likely to be affected by the advertisement, whether the class may be defined in terms such as geography, age, or the persons exposed to the particular medium in which the advertisement appears, such as television viewers.

This class of persons may be wider than the target audience that the advertiser hoped to reach. The court then determines the impact of the advertisement on members of that class. In one case, for example, a corporation had copied designs from album covers of records produced by the band INXS and reproduced the designs on tee-shirts. The tee-shirts and the market stall from which the tee-shirts were sold bore the words "Bootleg Company". However, the court held that this phrase was insufficient to remedy the misrepresentation that the tee-shirts were merchandise authorized by INXS. This is because the section of the public likely to be affected by the sale of the tee-shirts were INXS followers, a major proportion of which were teenagers and persons in their twenties. Not all of these would understand the significance of the term "Bootleg Company".[1]

One particular target audience - children - has been afforded special protection with regard to television commercials. Television Advertising Standards have been promulgated concerning advertising directed at children. As discussed above, licensees must comply with these standards as a condition of their license, and breach of the license could attract penalties of Aus. $2,000,000. The Television Advertising Standards require that:

1 *Hutchence* vs. *South Seas Bubble Co Pty. Ltd.* (1986) 6 IPR 473.

(1) Special care and judgment be exercised in respect of advertisements directed at children;

(2) A licensee may not broadcast advertisements during times set aside for broadcasting to preschool children; and

(3) Advertisements directed to children comply with specified Children's Television Standards, which broadly provide that advertisements broadcast during times set for broadcasts for primary school children may not, among other things:
   (a) Present images or events which depict unsafe uses of a product or unsafe situations which may encourage children to engage in activities dangerous to them;
   (b) Mislead or deceive children;
   (c) Put undue pressure on children to ask their parents or other people to purchase an advertised product or service; or
   (d) State or imply that a product or service makes children who own or enjoy it superior to their peers or that a person who buys an advertised product or service for a child is more generous than a person who does not.

Media industry bodies also consider the target audience of an advertisement when determining whether the advertisement conforms with MCA codes.

Section 5

Standard Terms (Adhesive Contracts)

5.1 Introduction

Standard term contracts are common in Australia. They have the potential to be unjust and unconscionable because they are often prepared by traders for transactions with consumers and contain terms very favorable to the traders which are not negotiable. The consumer must either take the contract as is, or leave it. However, since other traders usually also have standard term contracts, consumers often cannot improve their position by doing business elsewhere.

Australian legislatures have recognized this situation and have enacted legislation to address it. Consequently, the regulatory system concerning consumer contracts now comprises three levels. First, contracts for the sale of goods are generally covered by the sale-of-goods legislation of each state.[1] These Acts are largely uniform and codify Common Law principles, such as those relating to title, payment and delivery terms, and risk in the sale of goods.

The sale of goods legislation also implies certain conditions and warranties, such as conditions of conformity, fitness for purpose, and merchantability into contracts for the sale of goods. However, in some cases, these implied conditions and warranties can be excluded, or the seller's liability for breach of those conditions and warranties can be limited, by express terms in the contracts, by the course of dealing between the parties, or by usage, if the usage is such as to bind both parties to the contract.

Additional layers of regulation are imposed on the codification of the Common Law governing sale of goods to provide consumer protection. One additional layer is provided by legislation which implies non-excludable conditions and warranties into contracts for consumer transactions. The Sale of Goods Act 1923 (New South Wales) provides in Part VIII that none of the conditions and warranties that the Act implies into contracts can be excluded or restricted in a consumer sale except those relating to title.

1 For example, the Sale of Goods Act 1923 (New South Wales); Goods Act 1958 (Victoria).

The Trade Practices Act, Part V, Division 2, implies similar non-excludable conditions and warranties into contracts for the supply of goods or services by corporations to consumers. Provisions with a similar effect are contained in the Goods Act 1958 (Victoria).

The other additional layer of regulation is created by laws relating to unfair or unconscionable contracts. The Contracts Review Act 1980 (New South Wales), Section 51AB of the Trade Practices Act, and provisions in various other state Acts[1] all regulate unjust and unconscionable contracts in consumer transactions.

Finally, the Trade Practices Act in Part V, Division 2A, imposes liability on manufacturers direct to consumers for:

(1) Goods not fit for purpose;
(2) Goods which do not correspond with description;
(3) Goods of unmerchantable quality;
(4) Goods not conforming to sample; and
(5) Failure to comply with express warranties.[2]

5.2 Sale of Goods Act

The Sale of Goods Act 1923 (New South Wales) is typical of the sale of goods legislation in other states, and it will be the focus of the following discussion. The Sale of Goods Act 1923 generally applies only to contracts for the sale of goods: that is, contracts whereby the seller transfers or agrees to transfer the property in goods to the buyer for a money consideration called the price.[3] It does not apply to contracts concerning things other than goods, such as land, shares, debts, or intellectual property.

5.2.1 Delivery and Payment Terms

The obligations of the parties to a contract for the sale of goods with regard to payments and delivery and the times at which these obligations arise are matters which depend on the terms of the contract. However,

1 Fair Trading Act 1987 (New South Wales), Section 43, and Fair Trading Act 1985 (Victoria), Section 11A.
2 Trade Practices Act 1974 (Cth), Sections 74A-74E.
3 Sale of Goods Act 1923 (New South Wales), Section 6.

if there is no other agreement, delivery of goods and payment of the price are concurrent conditions. That is, the seller must be ready and willing to give possession of the goods to the buyer in exchange for the price, and the buyer must be ready and willing to pay the price in exchange for possession of the goods.

Again, if there is no other agreement, the place of delivery is the seller's place of business or, if the seller does not have a place of business, the seller's residence.[1]

5.2.2 Risk

The Sale of Goods Act 1923 provides that, unless otherwise agreed, the goods remain at the seller's risk until the property in the goods is transferred to the buyer. When the property in the goods is transferred to the buyer, the goods are at the buyer's risk whether delivery has been made or not.[2] The term "delivery" means the voluntary transfer of possession from the seller to the buyer.[3]

The general rule that risk passes with property is subject to the proviso that where the delivery has been delayed through the fault of either the buyer or the seller, the goods are at the risk of the party at fault as regards any loss which might not have occurred but for the fault.

5.2.3 Title

The Sale of Goods Act 1923 codifies the Common Law rule that no one can transfer a better title to goods than he or she possesses.[4] The effect of this rule is that an owner who has an immediate right to possess goods is entitled to recover them from someone who has not acquired a good title to them, unless the owner of the goods is by his or her conduct precluded from denying the seller's authority to sell. The true owner of goods may be estopped from denying the seller's authority to sell if the owner represented by words or conduct, or allowed another person to represent, that another person is the owner of the goods.

---

1 Sale of Goods Act 1923 (New South Wales), Section 31.
2 Sale of Goods Act 1923 (New South Wales), Section 25.
3 Sale of Goods Act 1923 (New South Wales), Section 5.
4 Sale of Goods Act 1923 (New South Wales), Section 26.

The Sale of Goods Act 1923 also provides that, where a seller of goods has a voidable title but the title has not been avoided at the time of the sale, the buyer acquires a good title to the goods provided that he or she buys in good faith and without notice of the defect in the seller's title.[1] A seller's title might be voidable if it was obtained by fraud, misrepresentation, non-disclosure, duress, or undue influence.

The Sale of Goods Act 1923 implies conditions and warranties concerning title, quiet possession, and freedom from encumbrances into contracts for the sale of goods unless the circumstances of the contract show a different intention.[2]

A condition is a vital term of a contract, the slightest breach of which will give the other party a right to treat the contract as at an end and to claim damages for any losses incurred as a result. A warranty is an agreement which is collateral to the main purpose of a contract, the breach of which gives rise to a claim for damages but not a right to reject the goods and treat the contract as repudiated.[3]

The implied conditions and warranties are as follows:

(1) An implied condition that the seller has a right to sell the goods or, in the case of an agreement to sell, that the seller will have a right to sell the goods at the time when the property is to pass - The condition will be breached where, at the time of the sale, the seller has a defective title or no title at all. If the seller does not pass title, the buyer is entitled to terminate the contract and claim damages even if he or she still possesses the goods, and even if the seller subsequently acquires title. However, if the defect in title is cured before the buyer terminates the contract, the title will be "fed" along the chain of transactions, and the buyer will receive good title.

(2) An implied warranty that the buyer will have and enjoy quiet possession of the goods - This warranty gives the buyer some redress against the seller if the seller passes a defective title and there is an interference with the buyer's possession of the goods. If the buyer's possession of the goods is disturbed, the buyer has a right to sue the seller for breach of this warranty. This warranty also contains the promise that the seller will not wrongfully repossess the goods from the buyer where, for instance, they have not been fully paid for.

---

1 Sale of Goods Act 1923 (New South Wales), Section 27.
2 Sale of Goods Act 1923 (New South Wales), Section 17.
3 Sale of Goods Act 1923 (New South Wales), Section 5.

(3) An implied warranty that the goods will be free from any charge or encumbrance in favor of any third party not declared or known to the buyer before or at the time when the contract is made - This warranty gives the buyer a right of action against the seller if it turns out that charges or encumbrances exist on the goods which were not disclosed to the buyer before or at the time the contract was made.

5.3 Trade Practices Act

The Trade Practices Act 1974 implies similar conditions and warranties into every contract for the supply of goods by a corporation to a consumer.[1] These conditions and warranties cannot be excluded.

For the purposes of the Trade Practices Act 1974, a person is taken to have acquired goods as a consumer if and only if:

(1) The price of the goods did not exceed Aus. $40,000; or
(2) Where the price exceeded Aus. $40,000, the goods were of a kind ordinarily acquired for personal domestic or household use or consumption, or the goods consisted of a commercial road vehicle, and the person did not acquire the goods, or hold himself out as acquiring the goods for the purpose of re-supply.

"Goods" are defined broadly, to include ships, aircraft, animals, fish, gas, electricity and minerals, and trees and crops, whether on, under, or attached to land or not.[2]

5.4 Conformity

The Sale of Goods Act 1923 implies into contracts for the sale of goods by description an implied condition that the goods will correspond with their description. Moreover, if the sale is by sample as well as by description, the bulk of the goods must correspond with both the sample and with the description.[3]

---

1 Trade Practices Act 1974 (Cth), Section 69.
2 Trade Practices Act 1974 (Cth), Section 4.
3 Sale of Goods Act 1923 (New South Wales), Section 18.

Sales by description occur when descriptive statements are used regarding the goods either in the contract or during negotiations, and the goods are sold by reference to those descriptions. The description must identify the goods and not merely describe the quality of the goods. Parties can describe the goods by conduct, for example, by displaying illustrations of the goods on the container in which they are packaged.

There also can be a sale by description if goods are displayed on a counter: a thing can be sold by description although it is a specific item, as long as it is not sold merely as a specified thing, but rather as a thing corresponding to a description.

Part VIII of the Sale of Goods Act 1923 provides that a provision in or applying to a contract for a consumer sale and purporting to exclude or restrict the operation of Section 18 is void.[1] For the purposes of Part VIII of the Sale of Goods Act 1923, "consumer sale" means a sale of goods (other than a sale by auction) by a seller in the course of a business where the goods:

(1) Are of a kind commonly bought for private use or consumption; and
(2) Are sold to a person who does not buy or hold himself out as buying them in the course of a business.[2]

The Trade Practices Act 1974 implies similar conditions into contracts for the supply of goods (other than by way of sale by auction) by a corporation in the course of a business to consumers.[3]

Section 70(2) of the Trade Practices Act 1974 provides that a sale is not prevented from being a sale by description because the goods are exposed for sale or hire and are selected by the consumer. This is intended to protect a consumer who chooses goods from a range of displayed goods.

Unlike state legislation, which requires that the seller be a person who deals in goods of that description in order for this condition to be implied into a contract, the Trade Practices Act 1974 only requires that the goods be sold to a consumer in the course of a business.

---

1 Sale of Goods Act 1923 (New South Wales), Section 64(1).
2 Sale of Goods Act 1923 (New South Wales), Section 62.
3 Trade Practices Act 1974 (Cth), Section 70(1).

5.4.1 Fitness for Purpose

The Sale of Goods Act 1923 provides in Section 19 that a condition of fitness for a particular purpose will be implied into a contract for the sale of goods under certain circumstances. Specifically, where the buyer expressly or by implication makes known to the seller the particular purpose for which the goods are required so as to show that the buyer relies on the seller's skill or judgment, and the goods are of a description which it is in the course of the seller's business to supply (whether the seller is the manufacturer or not), there is an implied condition that the goods must be reasonably fit for the purpose. However, in the case of a contract for the sale of a specified article under its patent or other trade name, there is no implied condition as to its fitness for any particular purpose.

A buyer can inform the seller of a particular purpose for which he or she requires the goods by implication or by express words. The purpose must be stated with sufficient particularity to enable the seller to exercise his or her skill and judgment in making or selecting appropriate goods. Where goods normally are used for only one purpose, it will often be implied that the consumer made it known that the goods were being acquired for that purpose.

As with implied conditions as to conformity with description, the implied condition as to fitness for purpose cannot be excluded or limited in a consumer contract in New South Wales.[1]

The Trade Practices Act 1974 implies a similar condition into contracts for the supply of goods (other than by way of sale by auction) by a corporation to a consumer in the course of a business.[2]

Section 71(2) of the Trade Practices Act provides that, where a corporation supplies goods to a consumer in the course of a business and the consumer, whether expressly or by implication, makes known to the corporation or the person by whom any antecedent negotiations are conducted that are imputable to the corporation any particular purpose for which the goods are being acquired, there is an implied condition that the goods supplied under the contract be reasonably fit for that purpose, whether or not that is a purpose for which the goods are commonly supplied.

---

1 Sale of Goods Act 1923 (New South Wales), Section 64.
2 Trade Practices Act 1974 (Cth), Section 71(2).

There are two exceptions to this provision. First, the implied condition of fitness for purpose is not implied into sales by auction. Second, the term is not implied into contracts made in circumstances which show that the consumer did not rely, or that it was unreasonable for him or her to rely, on the skill or judgment of the corporation or the person who conducted the antecedent negotiations.

5.4.2 Merchantable Quality

The Sale of Goods Act 1923 provides that, in a contract for the sale of goods, there will be an implied condition that the goods be of merchantable quality if the goods are bought by description from a seller who deals in goods of that description (whether the seller is the manufacturer or not) and the buyer has not examined the goods or, if he or she has, the defects are such as would not be discoverable on an examination.[1]

For the purposes of consumer sales, the phrase "merchantable quality" is defined in the Sale of Goods Act 1923. The definition of merchantable quality provides that goods of any kind which are the subject of a consumer sale are not of merchantable quality if they are not as fit for the purpose or purposes for which goods of that kind are commonly bought as is reasonable to expect having regard to their price, to any description applied to them by the seller, and to all other circumstances.[2]

This definition means that, where goods are suitable for a number of common uses, they must be fit for each and every one of those common uses before they will be of merchantable quality. However, if the seller describes the goods in a manner that indicates that they are suitable for only some of the normal purposes for which the goods are commonly used, the seller may be able to limit his or her liability.

Part VIII of the Sale of Goods Act 1923 further provides that in any legal proceedings for breach of the condition of merchantable quality in a consumer sale related to second-hand goods, the liability of the seller is, subject to any contrary agreement, limited to the amount of the cash price of the goods in question.[3]

---

1 Sale of Goods Act 1923 (New South Wales), Section 19(2).
2 Sale of Goods Act 1923 (New South Wales), Section 64(3).
3 Sale of Goods Act 1923 (New South Wales), Section 64(9).

Under the provisions of Section 64(4) of the Sale of Goods Act 1923, in a consumer contract, there is no implied condition of merchantable quality regarding defects in the goods that are brought to the buyer's notice before the contract is entered.

Section 71(1) of the Trade Practices Act 1974 provides that where a corporation provides goods to a consumer in the course of a business, there is an implied condition that the goods supplied are of merchantable quality. The condition is not implied into sales by auction. The condition does not apply to defects which are specifically drawn to the consumer's attention before the contract was made. If the consumer examines the goods before the contract is made, the condition is not implied as regards defects which that examination ought to have revealed.

Section 66(2) of the Trade Practices Act 1974 defines merchantable quality as follows:

> "Goods of any kind are of merchantable quality within the meaning of this Division if they are as fit for the purpose or purposes for which goods of that kind are commonly bought as it is reasonable to expect having regard to any description applied to them, the price (if relevant) and all other relevant circumstances."

Under this definition, goods must be reasonably fit for all purposes for which they are commonly bought. Consequently, if the goods are not fit for one purpose for which goods of that description are commonly bought they will not be of merchantable quality.

5.4.3 Supply of Services

The Trade Practices Act 1974 implies terms into contracts for the supply of services to consumers by corporations. These are implied warranties that the services will be rendered with due care and skill and that any material supplied in connection with those services will be reasonably fit for the purpose for which they are supplied.[1]

If the consumer either expressly or by implication makes known the purpose for which the services are acquired or the result that he or she desires the services to achieve, there is an implied warranty that the services supplied and any materials supplied in connection with those

1 Trade Practices Act 1974 (Cth), Section 74.

services will be reasonably fit for that purpose or are of such a nature and quality that they may reasonably be expected to achieve that result.[1]

This warranty is not implied into the contract if the circumstances show that the customer does not rely, or that it is unreasonable for the customer to rely, on the corporation's skill and judgment.

The references to "services" above do not include a reference to services that are provided under a contract for or in relation to the transportation or storage of goods for the purposes of a business carried on by the person for whom the goods are transported or stored or for a contract of insurance. Nor does the term include the supply of goods or the performance of work under an employment contract.[2]

However, "services" does include any right, benefit, privilege, or facility that is to be provided in trade or commerce, including those to be provided under:

(1) A contract for or in relation to the performance of work, the provision of, or the use or enjoyment of, facilities for amusement, entertainment, recreation, or instruction, or the conferring of rights, benefits, or privileges for which remuneration is payable in the form of a royalty, tribute, levy, or similar exaction;
(2) A contract of insurance;
(3) A contract between a banker and a customer of the banker entered into in the course of the banker's business of banking; or
(4) Any contract for or in relation to the lending of money.

5.5 Rejection and Refund

Where there is a breach of condition implied in the contract between a seller and a consumer, the consumer is entitled to return the goods to the seller and obtain a refund and, where appropriate, compensation for any consequential damage caused by the breach. Alternatively, the buyer can choose to retain the goods and seek damages instead. In cases where there is a breach of an implied warranty, there is a right to damages but no right to return the goods. In either case, a notice at the point of sale such as "we exchange goods or give credit, but do not refund money", has no effect because it cannot restrict or modify a consumer's legal rights.

---

1 Trade Practices Act 1974 (Cth), Section 74(2).
2 Trade Practices Act 1974 (Cth), Section 4.

Moreover, the display of such a notice puts sellers at the risk of contravening the Trade Practices Act 1974, which prohibits conduct which misleads consumers about their legal rights or remedies.

5.6 Replacement, Warranty, and Service

As discussed above, Parts V and VA of the Trade Practices Act 1974 imposes on manufacturers and importers a direct liability to consumers for defective products. Division 2A does not apply where there is a contract between the manufacturer and a consumer. It applies where the manufacturer supplies goods to another person, usually a distributor or retailer, who re-supplies the goods, ultimately to the consumer.

Division 2A imposes obligations on the manufacturers and importers to ensure that:

(1) Goods are reasonably fit for any purpose for which they are acquired by the consumer which is directly or indirectly made known to the manufacturer;
(2) Where a manufacturer applies or allows a description to be applied to the goods, that the goods correspond with the description;
(3) The goods are of merchantable quality; and
(4) Where the goods are supplied by sample, that they correspond with the sample.

These obligations render the manufacturer or importer concurrently liable with the actual seller of goods to compensate the consumer for his or her loss or damage.

Division 2A also imposes obligations on manufacturers and importers to provide either repair facilities and spare parts for goods sold to distributors or retailers for ultimate re-supply to a consumer or to ensure that consumers get notice that repairs and spare parts are unavailable or of limited availability before or at the time the consumer buys the goods.[1] If a consumer suffers loss as a result of a manufacturer's unreasonable failure to ensure that repair facilities and spare parts are available to the consumer, the manufacturer is liable to compensate the consumer for that loss.

If a manufacturer makes an express warranty in relation to goods and fails to comply with the warranty, the manufacturer will be liable to

1 Trade Practices Act 1974 (Cth), Section 74F.

compensate the consumer for any loss or damage arising from the breach of warranty.[1] For purposes of this provision, an "express warranty" in relation to goods is defined as an undertaking, assertion, or statement in relation to the quality, performance, or characteristics of the goods, given or made in connection with the supply of the goods or in connection with the promotion by any means of the supply or use of the goods, the natural tendency of which is to induce people to acquire the goods.[2]

5.7 Unjust or Unconscionable Contracts

The Contracts Review Act 1980 (New South Wales) empowers courts to grant various kinds of relief against consumer contracts, or terms in them, which are found to be "unjust" within the meaning of the Contracts Review Act 1980. A court may refuse to enforce the contract in whole or in part, may declare the whole or part of the contract void, may vary the contract, or may order the execution of an instrument varying or terminating the operation of a land-sale instrument.[3] A court also may grant ancillary relief, including orders for payment of compensation, the supply or repair of goods, the supply of services, and orders in respect of property.[4]

The Contracts Review Act 1980 does not provide relief from contracts for the Crown, public or local authorities, corporations, or persons who entered into the contract in the course of or for the purposes of a trade, business, or profession carried on or proposed to be carried on by them, other than a farming undertaking.[5]

The term "unjust" is defined in Section 4(1) of the Contracts Review Act 1980 to include harsh, oppressive, or unconscionable.

Section 9(1) of the Contracts Review Act 1980 lists some factors that are relevant in determining whether a contract is unjust in the circumstances relating to the contract at the time it was made. These factors include material inequality of bargaining power, opportunity for negotiation, difficulty of complying with provisions, the ability of a party to protect its own interests, the language of the contract, the form and

---

1 Trade Practices Act 1974 (Cth), Section 74A.

2 Trade Practices Act 1974 (Cth), Section 74A(1).

3 Contracts Review Act 1980 (New South Wales), Section 7.

4 Contracts Review Act 1980 (New South Wales), Section 8 and Schedule 1.

5 Contracts Review Act 1980 (New South Wales), Section 6.

intelligibility of a written contract, the use of unfair tactics, similar dealings, and the commercial setting of the contract. A provision in a contract that purports to exclude the operation of the Contracts Review Act 1980 is void.[1]

Section 51AB of the Trade Practices Act prohibits a corporation from engaging in conduct that is, in all the circumstances, unconscionable in connection with the supply or possible supply of goods or services to a consumer.

The following factors are examples of those to which a court may have regard in determining whether a corporation has acted unconscionably:

(1) Unequal strength of bargaining position;
(2) Forcing the consumer to comply with unnecessary conditions;
(3) The consumer's understanding of the documents;
(4) Undue influence or undue pressure exerted on or unfair tactics used against the consumer; and
(5) The amount for which and the circumstances under which the consumer could have acquired identical or equivalent goods or services from a person other than the corporation.[2]

In determining whether a corporation has contravened the provision, a court is able to have regard to conduct before the section was enacted, but is unable to examine circumstances that were not reasonably foreseeable at the time of the alleged contravention.[3]

Identical provisions governing the conduct of natural persons have been incorporated in the Fair Trading Acts of New South Wales and Victoria.

---

1 Contracts Review Act 1980 (New South Wales), Section 71(1).
2 Trade Practices Act 1974 (Cth), Section 51AB(2).
3 Trade Practices Act 1974 (Cth), Section 51AB(4).

Section 6

Reasonable Pricing and Price Controls

6.1 Price Information

Mechanisms exist at both federal and state levels to provide consumers with accurate information as to the price of goods and services. Regardless of these governmental schemes, the primary sources of price information remain manufacturers, merchants, and the non-government consumer organizations.

Most significant of the governmental bodies involved in the collation and dissemination of price information is the Prices Surveillance Authority. This Authority was established by the federal government in 1983 under the Prices Surveillance Act 1983.

The Prices Surveillance Act 1983 makes provision for the selective surveillance of, and the holding of inquiries into, prices charged or proposed to be charged for the supply of goods and services within Australia.

Consistent with the underlying philosophy of the Act, the Prices Surveillance Authority perceives its role as being "to promote price restraint and accountability consistent with competitive market outcomes".[1] To this end, the Authority has identified three major goals:

(1) To identify excessive prices or price increases;
(2) To deter businesses from charging excessive prices; and
(3) To operate as an expert, independent pricing body fully accountable to the Australian public.

The application of the Act is expressly limited (primarily for constitutional reasons) to the supply of goods or services within Australia for which a price is charged:

(1) By a Commonwealth authority;
(2) By a foreign corporation;
(3) By a trading corporation in the course of, or for the purposes of, its trading operations;

---

1 Prices Surveillance Authority, Annual Report 1991-1992.

(4) By a financial corporation in the course of, or for the purposes of, its business operations;
(5) By a body corporate incorporated in a territory (other than the Northern Territory or Norfolk Island);
(6) In an internal territory (other than the Northern Territory); or
(7) In the course of, or in connection with, trade or commerce among the states and territories.

Thus, the Act has no application to the supply of goods or services by a state, the Northern Territory, Norfolk Island, or a public authority established by or under a law of any of them.

The statutory functions of the Prices Surveillance Authority are:

(1) To consider notices given under the Act to the Authority by declared persons of proposed price increases or new prices of notified goods or services, and to take in relation to such notices such action in accordance with the Act as it considers appropriate; and
(2) To hold public inquiries in accordance with the Act into matters relating to the supply of goods or services, and to report to the responsible government minister the results of each such inquiry.[1]

Over the past decade, some fifty inquiries have been held, investigating the pricing policies of goods and services ranging from fruit juices and cigarettes to coastal shipping freight prices, funeral services, and compact disks.

The availability of price information under state law is much narrower. In New South Wales, the Fair Trading Act 1987 prescribes "price" as one of the elements of product information which are standard for all goods and must be disclosed.[2]

There is little application of this Act to the price of services. Victoria's legislation applies to both goods and services. It is an offense under the Victoria Fair Trading Act 1985 to make a false and misleading representation with respect to the price of goods or services.

In Victoria, the Office of Fair Trading, which is a division of the Department of Justice, contributes to deterrence of excessive prices through:

---

1 Prices Surveillance Act 1983 (Cth), Section 17(1).
2 Fair Trading Act 1987 (New South Wales), Section 38(2)(a).

(1) Consumer awareness activities;
(2) Submissions to Commonwealth government inquiries into price-related issues;
(3) Participation in national policy development; and
(4) Provision of research support to the Prices Commissioner.

The Office of Fair Trading is thus intimately involved with the collation of price information.

Victoria also has a Prices Commissioner, who is appointed under the Fuel Prices Regulation Act 1981 and is attached to the Office of Fair Trading. Price information is within the responsibility of the Commissioner.

6.2 Residual Controls against Extortionate Prices and Usury

The archaic laws relating to the charging of interest for monies lent and usury have been repealed in both New South Wales and Victoria. They have been replaced by a modern regime of consumer credit legislation.

There exist residual remedies against extortionate prices in both Common Law and equity through the doctrines of consideration and unconscionability respectively. However, it is difficult to see these private rights as amounting to price control.

Price control in Australia has tended to be applied in an industry-specific environment. Traditionally, staples and basic requirements (such as bread and pharmaceuticals) have been more susceptible to price regulation. The federal government, for example, exercises effective price control over the sale of many pharmaceutical products through the operation of a pharmaceutical benefits scheme, as provided for in the National Health Act 1953 and administered by the Commonwealth Department of Health.

Pharmaceutical price control is not wholly intended for the benefit of the consumer, as the federal government foots a large part of the bill as part of Medicare, the compulsory national medical insurance scheme.

The prices of telecommunications services are also determined by ministerial regulations under the Telecommunications Act 1991. This legislation applies to the dominant telecommunications provider in any given market sector and may soon apply to prices set by non-governmental bodies if the current rate of telecommunications deregulation continues space (for example, if Optus were to become the dominate carrier of mobile digital communication). The government carrier (Telecom) is also subject to price capping for particular services. The mechanism is based on a basket of various services (not including pay phones) and effectively requires price reduction as the price is based on the Consumer Price Index (CPI) less a percentage, currently at five per cent.

There is some price control exercised in Victoria by the Price Commissioner. The Commissioner does not "fix" prices per se, but rather is empowered by the Fuel Prices Regulation Act 1981 to declare the maximum price at which declared fuels may be sold. In addition, the Commissioner may from time to time review certain professional fees at the request of the relevant minister. For example, the Commissioner acts as the Attorney-General's nominee on the Supreme Court Solicitors' Remuneration Order Committee.

The Victoria Dairy Industry Authority, established under the Dairy Industry Act 1992, is responsible for the regulation of prices for the sale of milk. New South Wales has a similar scheme under the New South Wales Dairy Industry Act 1979 and regulations made pursuant to it (most recently, the Dairy Industry (Pricing) Regulations 1984). With the exception of milk, all previously existing statutory controls on the prices of agricultural products have now been removed.

Prices set by non-agricultural statutory authorities in Victoria include taxi fares, private hire car charges and private route bus fares, estate agent and auctioneer commissions, conveyancing charges, and finance broker commissions.

In New South Wales, the Prices Regulation Act 1948 provides a statutory framework to facilitate comprehensive direct price control, but this is not currently used. Nevertheless, a Prices Commission exists under the Act with a power to fix maximum prices for goods and services which the Minister has determined should be subject to price control. The stated objectives of the Act, which originated as a means of winding down wartime price controls, include the prevention of undue price increases and the regulation so far as is necessary of prices of essential goods and services. Although there are no present indications that the Prices Commission will again become active in price control, this remains a possibility depending on the inclination of the government of the day.

In 1992, the Pricing Tribunal was established, under the Government Pricing Tribunal (New South Wales) Act 1992, with powers to conduct periodic reviews of pricing policies and determine maximum prices for government monopoly services supplied by specified government agencies. The Act is primarily, but not exclusively, concerned with the supply of water or electricity, and the provision of public transport.

New South Wales, like Victoria, also has regulations controlling solicitors' fees and the price of conveyancing services.

6.3 Competition Law

Legislation exists, primarily at the Federal level, to promote competition within the marketplace. Such legislation indirectly has an effect on price control, and price minimization (much like the federal antitrust laws of the United States).

The Trade Practices Act 1974 prohibits all manner of anti-competitive practices which in turn have a significant influence on price. For example, acquisitions and covenants which tend to lessen competition are expressly prohibited.[1] The Act also provides sanctions against the misuse of market power.[2]

Several sections of the Trade Practices Act 1974 deal directly with the issue of price and are designed to ensure fair consumer prices. The prohibitions are quite comprehensive and are thus an effective mechanism of consumer price protection. For example, the prohibition against price fixing[3] provides a sanction against any "fixing, controlling or maintaining, or providing for the fixing, controlling or maintaining of, the price for, or a discount, allowance, rebate or credit in relation to goods or services".

The Trade Practices Act 1974 also prohibits:

(1) Predatory pricing;[4]
(2) Resale price maintenance,[5] such as entering into an agreement for the supply of goods containing a provision that the purchaser will not sell below the supplier's specified price;
(3) Price discrimination,[6] where a vendor discriminates between buyers of goods in relation to the price charged, discounts allowed, credit and rebates given, and services provided with the goods; and
(4) False and misleading statements as to price,[7]

Failure to comply with Part IV of the Act may result in penalties up to Aus. $10-million for a corporation or Aus. $500,000 for an individual.[8]

---

1 Trade Practices Act 1974 (Cth), Sections 50 and 45B.
2 Trade Practices Act 1974 (Cth), Section 46.
3 Trade Practices Act 1974 (Cth), Section 45A.
4 Trade Practices Act 1974 (Cth), Section 46.
5 Trade Practices Act 1974 (Cth), Section 48.
6 Trade Practices Act 1974 (Cth), Section 49.
7 Trade Practices Act 1974 (Cth), Section 53(e).
8 Trade Practices Act 1974 (Cth), Section 76.

Section 7

Consumer Credit

7.1 Introduction

In 1984, substantially uniform consumer credit legislation was introduced into most states in Australia. The relevant Acts are as follows:

(1) Credit Act 1984 (New South Wales);
(2) Credit Act 1984 (Victoria);
(3) Credit Act 1984 (WA);
(4) Credit Ordinance 1985 (ACT); and
(5) Credit Act 1987 (Qld).

The aim of the legislation is to regulate the provision of credit transactions worth no more than Aus. $20,000. The limit in Queensland is Aus. $40,000. The legislation regulates the following types of transactions:

(1) Credit sale contracts - A credit sale contract is deemed to include contracts for hire or lease where there are indications or expectations that the goods will not be returned to the supplier at the conclusion of the hire.
(2) Loan contracts where interest is charged at a rate exceeding fourteen per cent - A loan contract is a contract under which a credit provider gives credit to a person, other than a body corporate. Continuing credit contracts are excluded from the definition of loan contract.
(3) Continuing credit contracts - A continuing credit contract is a contract where the credit provider agrees to provide credit to a borrower in the form of a payment to a third party in fulfillment of the obligations of the borrower to the third party, e.g., the usual credit card or retail store charge card is within the definition of continuing credit contract.

These transactions are known as regulated credit contracts.

The Standing Committee of Consumer Affairs Ministers (SCOCAM), which is comprised of the Minister for Consumer Affairs of each state and territory and of New Zealand, have reached agreement to introduce uniform credit laws. A Draft Consumer Credit Code has been published, and it is planned to introduce the Code into the Parliaments of the states and territories during 1994. The new Codes will significantly expand the scope of consumer credit regulation in Australia.

The existing Credit Acts are complex, and what follows can only be a brief outline of their operation. This will be followed by a list of the key changes which will be implemented by the Credit Code if it is introduced in its current form.

References will be to the Credit Act 1984 (New South Wales) and the Credit Act 1984 (Victoria), unless otherwise specified. There are very few differences between the Victoria and New South Wales legislation, and most of the Section numbers correspond. The Acts attempt to regulate consumer credit through:

(1) A scheme of licensing of credit providers;
(2) Compulsory disclosure requirements;
(3) Imposing obligations on linked credit providers for the liabilities of the supplier of goods;
(4) The review of unfair contracts; and
(5) Restrictions on the manner in which credit contracts can be terminated and enforced by credit providers.

A "credit provider" is defined in Section 5 of the Acts to be a person providing credit under contract in the course of a business carried on by him or her. Persons providing credit occasionally are excluded. However, a person who provides credit as part of or incidental to another business is a credit provider.[1]

Legislation governing the licensing of credit providers has been in force in Australia for many years.[2] Licensing schemes have always been viewed as a significant source of regulation of consumer credit.

In New South Wales, the Commissioner for Consumer Affairs has special functions in relation to the Credit Act. The Commissioner may appear before the New South Wales Tribunal:

(1) On the Commissioner's own accord;
(2) On behalf of consumers; and
(3) Intervening in any proceedings in the public interest.

---

1 Credit Act 1984 (New South Wales) and Credit Act 1984 (Victoria), Section 16.

2 Pawnbrokers Act 1902 (New South Wales); Moneylending Act 1941 (New South Wales); Dealers and Pawn Brokers Act 1989 (Victoria).

In addition, in New South Wales, the Commercial Tribunal hears disputes arising under the Credit Act.

The Victoria Director of Consumer Affairs has similar functions to the Commissioner in New South Wales.

7.2 Rates

There is no maximum credit charge set by the Acts. The Acts aim to protect consumers through extensive disclosure requirements. The philosophy is that the consumer should know the true amount of the credit charge. There also is some provision for review of unfair contracts.

Credit sales contracts and loans contracts must contain a statement of the total of the credit charge. It is important that this statement be completely accurate, as even a trivial error will prevent a contract from complying with the legislation.[1] The contract also must state the annual percentage rate.[2] The annual percentage rate is the interest rate applicable to the contract. The Acts provide a method for calculating the rate so that there will be uniformity and consistency for comparison between the different rates charged by credit providers.

A debtor must have notice of the annual percentage rate with respect to a continuing credit contract prior to first incurring a debt.[3] Section 60(1) of the Acts gives the credit provider the power to unilaterally vary a continuing credit contract. If the variation increases the credit charge or shortens the time in which the debtor must pay, the credit provider must give the debtor at least two billing-cycles' notice. For any other variation in the terms of the contract, the debtor must be given seven days notice.

Under Section 147 of the Acts, the Tribunal has extensive powers to vary the terms of a regulated credit contract. One of the factors that can make a contract unjust is if the annual percentage rate is excessive, having regard to the risk, the value of any security, the amount of consideration, the time for repayment, the amount financed, and any other relevant circumstances.[4]

---

1 Credit Act 1984 (New South Wales) and Credit Act 1984 (Victoria), Sections 35 and 36.

2 Credit Act 1984 (New South Wales) and Credit Act 1984 (Victoria), Section 38.

3 Credit Act 1984 (New South Wales) and Credit Act 1984 (Victoria), Section 59.

4 Credit Act 1984 (New South Wales) and Credit Act 1984 (Victoria), Section 145(b).

The Commercial Tribunal has the power to adjust the amount payable under a regulated credit contract. However, as going to the Tribunal is an expensive and risky exercise, this provision does not offer the debtor as much protection as would a compulsory ceiling on interest rates.

7.3 Disclosure Requirements

Different disclosure regimes apply for credit sale contracts and continuing credit contracts.

7.3.1 Credit Sale Contracts and Loan Contracts

Under Section 31(1) of the Acts, a credit provider is not to enter into a credit sale contract or loan contract that is not in writing signed by the debtor. The documents must be readily legible.[1] It is an offense for a credit provider to give or issue a document under the Acts that is not legible.[2]

A credit sale contract which relates to goods or services must include a description of the goods or services.[3]

The Acts require the contract to set out the amounts payable under the contract in such way as to allow the debtor to clearly identify what amounts are principal and what amounts are charges made for the credit. For a credit sale contract, for example, the contract must show the amount to be paid as a deposit, the cash price of the goods or services, and the balance of the cash price after deduction of the deposit.[4] The loan contract and credit contract also must have a statement of the total of all the amounts payable under the contract. It is important that the borrower know the full amount paid for the provision of credit.

There must be a separate statement of stamp duty and legal fees payable.[5] Under Section 47 of the Acts, the debtor can apply to the Tribunal if he or she believes the amount charged for legal fees is unreasonable.

---

1 Credit Act 1984 (New South Wales) and Credit Act 1984 (Victoria), Section 151(1).

2 Credit Act 1984 (New South Wales) and Credit Act 1984 (Victoria), Section 154.

3 Credit Act 1984 (New South Wales) and Credit Act 1984 (Victoria), Section 35(1)(b).

4 Credit Act 1984 (New South Wales) and Credit Act 1984 (Victoria), Section 35, Schedule 2.

5 Credit Act 1984 (New South Wales) and Credit Act 1984 (Victoria), Schedules 2 and 4.

The New South Wales Commercial Tribunal and the Supreme Court of Victoria have taken different approaches to the issue of what type of fees and charges must be disclosed. The Supreme Court of Victoria, in *Custom Credit Corporation Limited* vs. *Gray*,[1] held that a loan contract need only disclose stamp duty payable to the creditor under the contract. If stamp duty were payable as a result of the transaction, but not payable to the credit provider under the contract, it need not be disclosed. In *Australian Guarantee Corporation Limited* vs. *Faint and Another*,[2] however, the Commercial Tribunal of New South Wales held that the disclosure of any mortgage registration and search fees payable in respect of the contract must be disclosed.

Under Sections 35(1)(g) and 36(1)(f) of the Acts, a contract must include a statement of exactly where payments are to be made. In *Custom Credit Corporation Limited* vs. *Gray*, it was held that a statement that payments are to be made at any branch of a bank is sufficient to comply with the legislation.

7.3.2 Continuing Credit Contracts

As stated above, the credit provider must notify the debtor of the annual percentage rate prior to any debt being incurred under a continuing credit contract. Under Section 59, notice also must be given to a debtor of:

(1) The credit limit;
(2) The method by which the credit charge will be determined for each billing cycle;
(3) The time within which, at the expiration of a billing cycle, the amount owed is payable;
(4) Particulars of stamp duty payable in relation to the contract; and
(5) The method by which the contract can be varied.

Under Section 61(1), a credit provider must give the debtor a statement for each billing cycle. There is an exemption from the requirement to provide a statement of account for each billing cycle if there was no amount owing at the end of a billing cycle and there was no amount entered in the account at any time during the billing cycle.[3]

---

1 [1992] 1 VR 540.
2 (1992) ASC 56-153.
3 Credit Act 1984 (New South Wales) and Credit Act 1984 (Victoria), Section 65.

The contents of the statement for each billing cycle must be in accordance with Schedule 7 to the Act. That Schedule prescribes a number of things which must appear on the statement, including:

(1) The last day of the cycle;
(2) The opening and closing balance;
(3) The date of purchase and price of the goods purchased under the continuing credit contract; and
(4) The particulars of any cash supplied.

Under Section 62, a debtor may query an amount included in a statement of account by giving the creditor written notification of the query prior to the due date for payment.

Where a query is made, the obligations of the debtor will be suspended for two complete billing cycles to give time for the query to be determined. During the period of suspension, the debtor may apply to the Commercial Tribunal for a determination, in which case the credit provider's rights are suspended until the Commercial Tribunal has made a determination.

7.4 Cancellation

The debtor, under a regulated credit contract, has a right to end the contract at any time by paying to the credit provider the net balance due. The parties cannot contract out of this right,[1] and any attempt to do so is void.[2]

Under Section 107, it is a condition precedent to a credit provider taking any steps for enforcement that:

(1) The debtor is in default under the regulated credit contract;
(2) A notice has been served on the debtor; and
(3) The notice has not been complied with.

In some circumstances, a Section 107 notice will not be required.[3] Those circumstances include if:

(1) The credit provider has reasonable reason to believe that it was induced to enter into the contract by fraudulent misrepresentation;

---

1 Credit Act 1984 (New South Wales) and Credit Act 1984 (Victoria), Section 105.
2 Credit Act 1984 (New South Wales) and Credit Act 1984 (Victoria), Section 157.
3 Credit Act 1984 (New South Wales) and Credit Act 1984 (Victoria), Section 107(6).

(2) The debtor cannot be located; or
(3) On reasonable grounds, the creditor believes the goods may be removed, concealed, damaged, or disposed of by the debtor.

The Section 107 notice must include the following information:

(1) The default relied on must be specified so that the debtor knows what he or she must do to remedy the default;
(2) The notice must specify that the creditor intends to exercise certain remedies unless the default is rectified within one month; and
(3) A statement of how the amount payable will increase if the debt remains unpaid; this includes not only interest which will become due but also any default charges which might become payable.

If the credit provider fails to comply with Section 107, a penalty of Aus. $2,000 may be imposed. Compensation can be awarded to the debtor for any loss suffered as a result of the credit provider's non-compliance with Section 107.[1] A broad meaning has been given to the word "compensation".[2]

Section 164 of the Acts covers service of notices. A notice must be served on the debtor personally or sent to the debtor's last known address. If the notice is properly addressed, pre-paid and posted, there is a presumption that it has been served at the time when it normally would have been delivered in the ordinary course of the post.[3] If a letter is returned with an indication that the debtor is not at that address, this will rebut the presumption.

To invoke the presumption, the credit provider must be in a position to put forward evidence from an officer of the credit provider with personal knowledge of the issues required to be proved. That is, it is not enough for the officer to give evidence of usual practice.

Under Section 107(4), a notice is complied with if the amount due along with enforcement expenses are paid within one month.

7.5 Loans Secured by Mortgage over Goods

There is a particular risk of unfairness to a mortgagor when a mortgagee terminates a loan and takes possession of mortgaged property.

---

1 Credit Act 1984 (New South Wales) and Credit Act 1984 (Victoria), Section 107(8).
2 *Wilson* vs. *Australian Guarantee Corporation Limited* (1987) ASC 55-598.
3 Credit Act 1984 (New South Wales) and Credit Act 1984 (Victoria), Section 165.

Where the outstanding balance of the amount financed is less than a quarter of the total amount financed, the credit provider is not entitled to take possession of the security, except in accordance with the consent of the Tribunal.[1]

A mortgagee is not entitled to enter property to repossess goods other than with the mortgagor's consent or an order of the court.[2] The mortgagor's consent must be real consent. The mortgagee bears the onus of proving the mortgagor's consent. If the premises are not owned or leased by the mortgagor then the consent of the owner of the premises also must be obtained. If an application is made to the Commercial Tribunal for entry onto the premises, the owner of the premises must be joined as a party to the proceedings.[3]

A mortgagee in possession of goods cannot sell the goods until twenty-one days after serving a notice on the mortgagor[4] unless the mortgagor consents in writing to the sale. A mortgagee is not entitled to sell where there are proceedings being taken by the mortgagor in relation to the taking of possession of the goods, for variation or for postponement.

A mortgagee must exercise the power of sale as soon as becoming entitled to do so, and it must be exercised so as to receive the best price reasonably obtainable.[5]

If repair work is required, will not cost much and is likely to result in an increased sale price, it should be done by the mortgagee. The costs of repair, in many circumstances, will be able to be charged to the mortgagor as an enforcement expense.

Consumer credit arrangements often contain provisions making the debtor liable for expenses incurred by the creditor in enforcing the contract after default by the debtor. Section 76 provides that any term which does not limit this amount to sums reasonably incurred by the credit provider will be void.

The costs of bringing an action for enforcement in the Commercial Tribunal may, in some circumstances, be enforcement expenses.[6]

---

1 Credit Act 1984 (New South Wales) and Credit Act 1984 (Victoria), Section 110.

2 Credit Act 1984 (New South Wales) and Credit Act 1984 (Victoria), Section 95.

3 *Australian Guarantee Corporation Ltd.* vs. *Gretton* (1991) ASC 56-102.

4 Credit Act 1984 (New South Wales) and Credit Act 1984 (Victoria), Section 112(1)(a).

5 Credit Act 1984 (New South Wales) and Credit Act 1984 (Victoria), Section 114; *see Universal Guarantee Pty. Ltd.* vs. *Carlile* [1957] VR 68 and *Harrison & Another* vs. *Mercantile Credits Limited* (1987) ASC 55-537.

6 *General Motors Acceptance Corporation Australia* vs. *Smith* (1991) ASC 56-106.

The mortgagee is liable to account to the mortgagor for the actual proceeds of sale less:

(1) The net balance due at the time the mortgagee received the proceeds of sale;
(2) The reasonable selling expenses of the mortgagee; and
(3) Amounts payable in respect of certain other mortgages and debts secured over the goods; a mortgagee must pay prior mortgagees and subsequent mortgagees of which he or she had notice, before accounting to the debtor.

If the amount recovered does not cover the amount due, the mortgagee may sue the mortgagor on the personal covenant.

A mortgagor, a prior mortgagee, or subsequent mortgagee of which the vendor mortgagee has notice may seek compensation for any improper use by a mortgagee of the power of sale.[1]

7.6 Imposition of Liability on Linked Credit Providers

A consumer who has suffered loss or damages as the result of the supply of goods may have a right of action against a linked credit provider. The imposition of this liability is designed to prevent the situation where defective goods have been acquired, but a consumer still has a liability under a credit contract. Before the Acts, situations would arise where a debtor had useless goods and a major debt burden, even though there existed a close relationship between the supplier and the creditor.

The liability only applies to a "linked credit provider". A linked credit provider is a credit provider:

(1) Who has a trade or tie agreement with the supplier of the goods;
(2) To whom the supplier, by arrangement with the credit provider, regularly refers debtors;
(3) Whose credit application forms are made available by the supplier; or
(4) Who has a formal or informal agreement with the supplier, under which applications or contracts for credit may be signed at the premises of the supplier.

---

1 Credit Act 1984 (New South Wales) and Credit Act 1984 (Victoria), Section 114(7).

The liability of the linked credit provider is established under the Credit Acts and under Sections 73, 73A, and 73B of the Trade Practices Act 1974.

If a consumer brings proceedings against the credit provider, he or she also must sue the supplier. The only exceptions are where the supplier has been wound up or judgment against the supplier is unlikely to be satisfied.[1] Under Section 73(7), the liability of the linked credit provider is limited to the amount financed, and any interest and costs. The judgment must be enforced against the supplier first.[2] The clear purpose of the provisions is to relieve the debtor from the liability to the credit provider rather than to give an alternate avenue for redress.

It is a defense against liability for a linked credit provider if it can be established that the credit was given as a result of an approach by the consumer which was independent of the supplier.[3]

7.7 Review of Unfair Contracts

The New South Wales credit legislation applies the principles underlying the Contracts Review Act 1980 to credit contracts. The Tribunal has the power to re-open a transaction which gave rise to a contract if it finds the transaction to be unjust in the circumstances. A contract is "unjust" if it is unconscionable harsh or oppressive or if the annual percentage rate is excessive. In determining whether a contract is unjust, the Tribunal is to take account of the factors outlined in Section 147(2) of the Acts.

It is clear, however, that these factors are only relevant if they lead the Tribunal to determine in all the circumstances that the contract is "unjust". The fact that the circumstances fall within the wording of one or more of the criteria does not mean that the contract will be found to be unjust.[4]

The factors set out in Section 147(2) of the Acts include the following:

(1) Any material inequality of bargaining power of the parties;
(2) Whether the terms of the contract were the subject of negotiation; it should be noted, however, that the mere fact that a standard form

---

1 Trade Practices Act 1974 (Cth), Section 73(5) and (6).

2 Credit Act 1984 (New South Wales) and Credit Act 1984 (Victoria), Section 73(8).

3 Credit Act 1984 (New South Wales) and Credit Act 1984 (Victoria), Section 24(2)(a).

4 *Esanda Finance Corporation Ltd.* vs. *Murphy* (1989) ASC 55-703; *Morlend Finance Corporation (Victoria) Pty. Ltd.* vs. *Westendorp* (1993) ASC 56-200.

of contract was used will not be enough to make a contract unjust, standard form contracts being used frequently in consumer finance transactions;

(3) Whether any of the conditions were unreasonably difficult to comply with or not reasonably necessary to protect the interest of one or both of the parties;

(4) Whether the debtor was reasonably able to protect his or her interests because of age or physical or mental capacity; the existence of a special weakness or disability is a crucial factor under the Contracts Review Act;[1]

(5) The form of the contract and language in which it is expressed;

(6) The existence of independent legal or other expert advice; the mere fact that a borrower has not obtained legal advice, if none of the provision are otherwise unfair, will not be enough to re-open a contract;[2]

(7) The extent to which provisions of the contract were understood by and explained to the applicant; the importance of explaining the legal and practical effects of a provision will depend on the seriousness of its potential effects;[3] and

(8) Whether undue influence, unfair pressure, or unfair tactics were exerted on the applicant; this includes unfair conduct by a person who is not a party to the contract if it is to the knowledge of a party to the contract.

The Commercial Tribunal has wide powers under Section 146(2) which arise on a finding that a contract is unjust. The Tribunal can even relieve the debtor of the obligation to repay the principal sum. It would, however, be only in very rare circumstances where the debtor would not be required to pay the principal.[4] The Tribunal's powers include:

(1) Relieving the debtor, mortgagor or guarantor from payment of any amount in excess of such amount as the Tribunal might consider reasonable;

---

1 *Baltic Shipping* vs. *Dillon* (1991) 22 *New South Wales Law Review* 1; *St Clair* vs. *Petricevic* (1988) ASC 55,688.

2 *Custom Credit Corporation Limited* vs. *Lynch* (1993) ASC 56-201. However, it has been held that, where there is a guarantor who receives no financial benefit from a transaction, there may be a requirement for the credit provider to take steps to advise the guarantor to attain independent advice; *see Jones* vs. *Santor Pty. Ltd.* (1992) ASC 56-161.

3 *Wade* vs. *Avco Financial Services Ltd.* (1991) ASC 56-081.

4 *Esanda Finance Corporation Ltd.* vs. *Murphy* (1989) ASC 55-703.

(2) Setting aside a contract in whole or in part; and
(3) Giving judgment for an amount which the Tribunal thinks just or making an order for delivery of the goods.

For a contract to be re-opened, there must be actual injustice, not just a failure to comply with the requirements of the Credit Act.[1] There are, of course, civil consequences prescribed by the Credit Act for breaches of its provisions.

There is conflict among the authorities as to whether a credit provider's knowledge that a debtor has no capacity to repay a loan or a disregard by a credit provider of whether the debtor has capacity is sufficient to make a contract unjust. In *Murphy* vs. *Esanda Finance Corporation*[2] and *Bryant* vs. *Melbourne Money Pty. Ltd.*,[3] it was said that this could result in a contract being unjust. The decision in *Custom Credit Corporation Limited* vs. *Lynch*,[4] however, was to the effect that it is the debtor's responsibility to consider the risk and that this was in its own interest.

If the Tribunal finds that the annual percentage rate is excessive, it can relieve the debtor from the obligation to pay anything more than what the Tribunal determines to be a reasonable rate.[5] It does not necessarily follow from a finding that a contract is unjust that the contract will be re-opened.[6]

7.8 Bona Fide Purchase for Value

In all Australian states except South Australia,[7] there is no protection for the consumer who makes a purchase without notice of a security interest. If the purchaser, acquires goods from a mortgagor in breach of the security interest of the creditor, the creditor remains entitled to enforce its interest. There is, however, in all states systems of registration of interests in vehicles. The relevant Acts in New South Wales and Victoria are:

---

1 *Custom Credit Corporation Limited* vs. *Gray* (1991) ASC 56-906.
2 (1988) ASC 55-650.
3 (1992) ASC 56-185.
4 (1993) ASC 56-201.
5 Credit Act 1984 (New South Wales) and Credit Act 1984 (Victoria), Section 146(2).
6 *Peters* vs. *Commonwealth Bank of Australia* (1992) ASC 56-135.
7 *See* Consumer Credit Act 1974 (SA), Section 36.

(1) Registration of Interest in Goods Act 1986 (New South Wales);
(2) Collateral Securities Act 1987 (Victoria); and
(3) Motor Car Traders Act 1986 (Victoria).

Under that legislation, a public register of security interests in motor vehicles has been established. If a person buys a vehicle from a dealer and the vehicle is subject to a security interest which could have been registered, the purchaser will take free of the interest. If an interest has been registered, the dealer must compensate the holder of the interest. If a person does not buy from a dealer, the purchaser will take free of the interest if he or she has obtained a search certificate that the vehicle is free from encumbrances from the authority which conducts the register. The goods must have been purchased *bona fide* and for value.

7.9 Credit Reporting

In Australia, there are a number of credit reference bureaus which, for a fee, provide information to various credit providers regarding the past behavior of applicants for credit.

A bad reference will usually result in the refusal of credit. There has been publicity concerning the misuse of confidential reports by credit reporting agencies. In 1991, Commonwealth legislation was introduced to regulate credit-reporting agencies.[1] Under this legislation, the Privacy Commissioner issued a Code of Conduct. Credit providers may not pass on information about an applicant for credit to a credit-reporting agency unless the person has been informed that the information may be disclosed to a credit reporting agency. The agency must take steps to ensure that its information is accurate and up-to-date.

If an application for credit is refused because of information derived from a credit report, the credit provider must give the individual notice in writing, specifying the credit-reporting agency from which the information was obtained. The applicant for credit also must be notified of his or her right to obtain access to the information. An individual must be able to obtain access to his or her file in order to have inaccurate information corrected.

---

1 Privacy Act 1988 (Cth), Part IIIA.

7.10 New Uniform Consumer Credit Code

It is envisaged that the new Uniform Consumer Code will be of greater scope than the existing legislation. The following is a summary of the major changes:

(1) The legislation will apply to all credit provided in the course of a credit provider's business where the borrower is an individual or a strata corporation, provided that the credit is wholly or predominantly for private purposes;
(2) There is no maximum amount;
(3) The Code will regulate the activities of all financial institutions and other providers of personal credit;
(4) The Code will regulate housing finance; and
(5) All credit will be presumed to be regulated, and the onus will be on the credit provider to establish that the credit is not regulated.

Section 8

Occupational Licensing

8.1 Introduction

In Australia, licensing of occupational groups is a primary method of regulation. In recent years, the emphasis has been placed on ensuring that licensing schemes are truly aimed at achieving consumer protection rather than entrenching unfair competition within an industry.

Many occupational groups are regulated by licensing controls in all states of Australia (e.g., pharmacists, medical practitioners, solicitors, barristers, dentists, veterinary surgeons, architects, optometrists, hairdressers, and real estate agents).

The Prime Minister and each of the State Premiers entered into an agreement on 11 May 1992 to establish a scheme of mutual recognition of occupational registration and certain standards applying to goods. Under Section 17 of the Mutual Recognition (New South Wales) Act 1992, any person registered in another state, so as to be entitled to carry a certain occupation in that state, is entitled to be registered in New South Wales to carry on the equivalent occupation. There is equivalent legislation in Victoria.

8.2 Scope and Application

In New South Wales, the Commercial Tribunal exercises jurisdiction to deal with the licensing of various occupational groups.

The Business Licenses Act 1990 (New South Wales) establishes a Director of Business Licenses.[1] The purpose of the Act is to centralize the system of granting business licenses in order to avoid duplication. The individual licensing authorities maintain the responsibility for determining whether a license should be granted to a particular applicant. The Director performs the administrative tasks involved and maintains centralized data.

The licenses covered by the Act are set out in Schedule 1. They include:

---

1 Business Licenses Act 1990 (New South Wales), Section 40.

(1) Motor vehicle dealers and repairers;
(2) Travel agents;
(3) Hairdressers;
(4) Bakers;
(5) Tobacco retailers;
(6) Licenses under the Dangerous Goods Act 1975; and
(7) Pest control operators.

The legislation generally operates to prohibit a person who does not hold a license from undertaking a certain activity. It usually is a criminal offense for an unlicensed person to operate in an occupation which requires a license. Most occupational licensing schemes are enacted in an attempt to protect the public from dealing with fraudulent or incompetent people in an industry. One important feature of such schemes is that they aim to prevent consumers from suffering loss rather than to compensate for losses already incurred. This is a useful goal as consumers often face practical difficulties getting redress even when they have a legal right. Further, an offender risks not just an occasional lawsuit but being prevented from continuing in business.

It is important that a licensing system not be used to protect the economic interests of the occupational group by preventing new competitors entering the market. This would restrict competition and disadvantage consumers. There is a greater risk of a scheme being used as a means of conferring monopoly rights where the administration of the scheme is entrusted to the occupational members rather than to outside interests.

There is a risk of injustice to operators under a licensing scheme. This danger can be minimized where the legislation establishes objective standards on which an operator's conduct must be judged. The granting and revoking of licenses attracts the rules of procedural fairness.[1] The power to revoke licenses attracts higher standards than the power to grant licenses. There is, however, at least a duty to act fairly in making the decision whether to grant a license.[2]

8.3 Credit Providers

A "credit provider" for licensing purposes is a person who is in the business of providing credit or who provides credit as a part of or

1 *Kioa* vs. *Minister for Immigration and Ethnic Affairs* (1985) 62 ALR 321.
2 *Trivett* vs. *Nivison* [1976] 1 *New South Wales Law Review* 312.

incidental to the carrying on of another business. Licensing is only required when financial accommodation is given with respect to a "regulated credit contract". The following are regulated credit contracts:

(1) Credit sale contracts -These are contracts for sale by credit, and they include contracts for hire or lease where there are indications or expectations that the goods will not be returned to the supplier at the conclusion of the hire;
(2) Loan contracts - These are contracts providing for the loan of money where the interest rates exceeds fourteen per cent and where the credit is given to a person other than a body corporate; and
(3) Continuing credit contracts - The definition of continuing credit contract covers the usual credit card arrangements.

Certain entities, such as banks and insurance companies, are exempted from the requirement to be licensed. Exempted entities are licensed under other specific legislation.

An application for a license is made to the Commercial Tribunal in New South Wales. In Victoria, the application is made to the Licensing Registrar of the Credit Licensing Authority. Licenses can be granted to natural persons and to body corporates.

There is a penalty of Aus. $5,000 for knowingly or recklessly making a false or misleading statement in relation to an application for a credit provider's license. It is a defense if the person believed on reasonable grounds that the false information was in fact correct.[1]

The financial position of an applicant is relevant to an application for a credit provider's license. A credit provider must be in a position to meet potential claims if there is a breach of the legislation.

In New South Wales, where an application for a credit provider's license has been made, the Commercial Tribunal will send a copy of the application to the Commissioner for Consumer Affairs, who will make enquiries with respect to the applicant. The Commissioner is to make enquiries as specified in the request and may make such other enquiries as he or she considers necessary which relate in some way to the fitness of the applicant to hold a credit provider's license. In Victoria, the enquiries are made by the Director of Consumer Affairs. The Director's power to

---

1 Credit (Administration) Act (New South Wales), Section 9; the Credit (Administration) Act (Victoria), Section 39(2).

make enquiries is completely discretionary. It can be inferred, however, that the power is limited by the aims of the legislation.

In New South Wales, the Registrar of the Commercial Tribunal must publish a notice giving particulars of an application in a newspaper circulating in New South Wales. In Victoria, the Licensing Registrar may cause notice of the application to be published. In both states, any person can object to the granting of a license within fourteen days of the publication of the notice. The reasons for the objection must be stated by notice in writing and served on the applicant within fourteen days. In New South Wales, the objection, to be valid, must be based on a reason which requires the Tribunal to refuse a license application.

8.4 Motor Dealers and Repairers

A license is required to carry on business as a motor vehicle dealer, auto-dismantler, wholesaler, motor vehicle parts reconstructor, car market operator or motor vehicle consultant. It is an offense to carry on the business of a dealer or to advertise that one is carrying on the business of a dealer without a license.[1]

The Victoria legislation was modelled on the New South Wales legislation. The provisions in those two states, therefore, are very similar. In New South Wales, applications for a license can be made:

(1) By a natural person over eighteen years of age; or
(2) By a body corporate if all persons involved in the management of the body corporate are over eighteen years of age.

The Commissioner of Corporate Affairs can make such enquiries as the Commissioner considers necessary in relation to the application for a license.[2]

An application must be refused in certain circumstances. For an individual, those circumstances include that the applicant:
(1) Has not attained eighteen years of age;
(2) Is disqualified from holding a license;
(3) Is an undischarged bankrupt;
(4) Does not have sufficient financial resources to carry on the business;
(5) Is not likely to carry on the business honestly and fairly;

---

1 Motor Vehicle Dealers Act 1974 (New South Wales), Section 9; Motor Car Traders Act (1986) (Victoria), Section 7.

2 Motor Vehicle Dealers Act 1974 (New South Wales), Section 11.

(6) Does not have sufficient qualifications or expertise to carry on the business; or
(7) Is not a fit and proper person to be holder of a license.[1]

Equivalent factors are set out in Section 12(4) of the Motor Vehicle Dealers Act 1974 in relation to applications by a body corporate.

Section 12(3) of the Act contains factors which the Commissioner may have regard to when determining whether an applicant is a fit and proper person to hold a license.

Section 21 stipulates that the holder of a license must keep a register recording the details of every secondhand motor vehicle acquired in the course of the business and the details of the disposal of each vehicle. Section 21(9) states that the entry in the register must be made within one trading day of the transaction taking place.

Section 23 provides that the register must be available for inspection at all times when the licenseholder is open for business.

A statutory warranty is imposed by the legislation with respect to motor vehicles sold by dealers.

Under Section 27, the dealer must repair or make good a defect in a vehicle, whether or not that defect existed at the time of sale, so as to place the vehicle in a reasonable condition having regard to its age for the following periods:

(1) For a new vehicle, until it has driven 20,000 kilometers or until twelve months after sale, whichever occurs first; and
(2) For a secondhand vehicle, until it has driven 5,000 kilometers after sale or a period of three months has expired, whichever occurs first.

Under Section 31(1), if a dispute arises in relation to the dealer's obligation to repair, the purchaser or owner may apply to the Commissioner to investigate and determine the disagreement.

Section 32 states that the Commissioner must use best endeavors to settle the dispute but, if the dispute cannot be settled, the Commissioner must determine the dispute.[2]

Section 39 of the Motor Vehicle Dealers Act establishes a Motor Vehicle Dealers Compensation Fund. The Fund is financed out of dealers' and car market operators' license fees. The claimant may be paid out of the fund, if the Commissioner is satisfied that:

1 Motor Vehicle Dealers Act 1974 (New South Wales), Section 12(2).
2 Motor Vehicle Dealers Act 1974 (New South Wales), Section 35(1).

(1) A claimant's loss was incurred because a dealer or car market operator had failed to comply with the requirements of the Act or regulations;
(2) A dealer has not passed unencumbered title to a claimant and the claimant suffered loss; or
(3) A dealer failed to repay an amount paid by way of deposit or trade in.

Section 8 of the New South Wales Motor Vehicle Repairs Act 1980 provides for the establishment of the Motor Vehicle Repair Council. The Council's function is to review the standard of motor vehicle repair work and promote improvement in the quality of motor vehicle repair work. The Council makes reports to the Minister with respect to the motor vehicle repair industry.

A licensed dealer is prohibited from engaging in certain conduct by the Motor Vehicle Dealers Regulation 1986. This regulation includes the following:

(1) A dealer may not publish an advertisement stating or implying a price for a secondhand or demonstrator motor vehicle unless the cash price also is disclosed; for a new vehicle, the advertisement must specify the manufacturer's recommended retail price;
(2) All advertisements relating to the sale of motor vehicles must include the licenseholder's name, license number, and business telephone number;
(3) All advertisements which refer to a specified motor vehicle must state the registration number of that vehicle;
(4) A dealer may not represent that a vehicle is for sale knowing that it is not;
(5) A dealer may not advertise a given odometer reading if the dealer knows or has reasonable cause to know that the reading is false; and
(6) It is an offense to misrepresent the year of manufacture of a motor vehicle, the year in which it was first registered, or the model designation.[1]

Part 3 of the Motor Vehicle Dealers Act contains provisions dealing with the licensing of motor vehicle repairers. Applications for the grant of licenses are made to the Director of Business Licenses in accordance with the Business Licenses Act. A license will only be granted if the applicant:

---

1 Motor Dealers Regulation 1986 (New South Wales), Section 47(1).

(1) Is above the age of eighteen;
(2) Is a fit and proper person to hold a license; and
(3) Has sufficient material, manpower, and financial resources to carry on the work permitted by the license.

Equivalent provisions relate to corporations.

8.5 Travel Agents

8.5.1 Legislative Scheme

There is legislation in every state in Australia making provision for the licensing of travel agents. The legislation was enacted following concern about the dishonest and incompetent practices of some travel agents. There are variations in the legislation from state to state, but the provisions are largely uniform. Reference will be to the New South Wales Travel Agents Act 1986. The other relevant Acts are:

(1) Travel Agents Act 1986 (Victoria);
(2) Travel Agents Act 1988 (Qld);
(3) Travel Agents Act 1986 (SA);
(4) Travel Agents Act 1987 (Tas);
(5) Travel Agents Act 1985 (WA); and
(6) Travel Agents Act 1986 (ACT).

The licensing provisions in New South Wales and Victoria are substantially uniform and also have been adopted in Tasmania.

A license is required to carry on business as a travel agent.[1] In New South Wales, the Commissioner for Consumer Affairs is responsible for issuing licenses. In Victoria, the Travel Agents Licensing Authority issues licenses.

Under Section 10(2) of the New South Wales and Victoria Acts, an applicant is not able to obtain a license if the applicant is:

(1) Under eighteen years of age;
(2) Disqualified from holding a license under the legislation of that state or of the corresponding law of another state or territory;

1 Travel Agents Act 1986 (New South Wales) and Travel Agents Act 1986 (Victoria), Section 6.

(3) Not likely to carry on the business honestly or fairly; or
(4) Not a fit and proper person to hold a license.

For each place of business of the licenseholder, there must be a manager who is suitably qualified.[1]

For a corporation, the requirement is that each person concerned in its management meet equivalent criteria to those specified for individuals.[2]

A licensee must pay an annual fee[3] and must lodge an annual statement.[4]

It is a condition of the grant of a license that the licensee be prepared to become a participant in the co-operative compensation scheme.[5] The grant of any license is subject to the participant remaining a member of the scheme.

The Cooperative Compensation Scheme was established in 1986 by the Ministers for Consumer Affairs of New South Wales, Victoria, South Australia, and Western Australia. The other states and the ACT have since joined the scheme. Under the scheme, a trust fund has been established, with the licensees being the contributors to the fund. The trustees can pay compensation out of the fund to persons who suffer loss arising from the failure of a participant to the scheme to account for money or other valuable consideration. The other conditions before the claimant will receive compensation out of the fund are that:

(1) The person suffering loss is a client of a participant;
(2) The person suffering loss is not insured; and
(3) The failure to account resulted from an act or omission of the participant in the scheme or an employee of a participant in the scheme.

All printed advertisements must contain the licensee's license number and the name or names under which the licensee is authorized to trade.[6]

---

1 Travel Agents Act 1986 (New South Wales), Section 33, and Travel Agents Act 1986 (Victoria), Section 36.

2 Travel Agents Act 1986 (New South Wales) and Travel Agents Act 1986 (Victoria), Section 10.

3 Travel Agents Act 1986 (New South Wales) and Travel Agents Act 1986 (Victoria), Section 16.

4 Travel Agents Act 1986 (New South Wales) and Travel Agents Act 1986 (Victoria), Section 17.

5 Travel Agents Act 1986 (New South Wales) and Travel Agents Act 1986 (Victoria), Section 10.

6 Travel Agents Act 1986 (New South Wales), Section 34, and Travel Agents Act 1986 (Victoria), Section 31.

The license number also must appear on all commercial documents used by a licensee in the course of business.[1] A licensee must keep accounting records which enable a true and fair balance sheet and profit and loss account to be prepared.[2]

8.5.2 Licensing Policy

The general policy behind occupational licensing can be seen from the above consideration of licensing schemes.

The licensing provisions attempt to ensure that licenseholders and the operators of corporate licenseholders are of good character. It is hoped that consumers will be protected by preventing people who are not "fit and proper" from operating.

The schemes also seek to ensure that licenseholders are financially sound. This is an attempt to prevent a situation arising where a consumer has a valid claim against an operator but cannot obtain satisfaction because the operator has no money. Closely linked to this objective are the establishment of funds, such as the Travel Agent's Cooperative Compensation Scheme, to provide compensation to consumers who have suffered loss as the result of the conduct of a licensed operator.

Another important objective of licensing schemes is to ensure that licenseholders are suitably qualified. A related aim is to ensure that operators work together to improve the service provided to consumers by their industry generally.

8.6 Sanctions

8.6.1 Credit Providers

Under the Credit Acts, there is a fine of Aus. $10,000 for carrying on the business of providing credit without a license. Holding oneself out as a person carrying on the business attracts a penalty of Aus. $5,000. A credit provider also is liable to lose the amount financed and the credit charge if providing credit unlicensed.

---

1 Travel Agents Act 1986 (New South Wales), Section 35, and Travel Agents Act 1986 (Victoria), Section 32.

2 Travel Agents Act 1986 (New South Wales), Section 41, and Travel Agents Act 1986 (Victoria), Section 39.

The liability of a debtor under a continuing credit contract is removed in respect of the billing cycle during which the credit provider was unlicensed.[1] A license may be cancelled if the annual fee is not paid.

In New South Wales, the Tribunal may hold an enquiry to see whether a licensee should be reprimanded, ordered to comply, or fined, or whether the license should be suspended or cancelled. In New South Wales and Victoria, the grounds for holding an inquiry include the following:

(1) That the licensee has failed to comply with the credit legislation;
(2) That a licensee cannot meet the licensee's liabilities;
(3) That the licensee has charged an excessive interest rate or has taken excessive security; and
(4) That the business is not carried on honestly and fairly.

If a Tribunal suspends or cancels a license, it must be returned to the registrar, in New South Wales, within the time specified by the Tribunal[2] and, in Victoria, as soon as the licensee knows of the cancellation.[3] A license may be suspended for a period not exceeding twelve months.

8.6.2 Motor Vehicle Dealers and Repairers

It is an offense to carry on the business of a dealer or to advertise that one is carrying on the business of a dealer without a license.[4]

Under Section 20D of the New South Wales Motor Vehicle Dealers Act, the Commissioner for Corporate Affairs can, in certain circumstances, serve notice on the holder of a license to show cause, in less than fourteen days, why the holder of the license should not be dealt with under the disciplinary measures set out in Division 3 of the Act. Those circumstances include the Commissioner forming the opinion that there are reasonable grounds for believing that:

(1) The license may have been improperly obtained;
(2) The holder of the license has been convicted of an offense under the Act;

---

1 *Re Crowell International Pty. Ltd.* (1991) ASC 56-069.
2 Credit (Administration) Act (New South Wales), Section 21.
3 Credit (Administration) Act (Victoria), Sections 56, 58, and 59.
4 Motor Vehicle Dealers Act 1974 (New South Wales), Section 9; Motor Car Traders Act 1986 (Victoria), Section 7.

(3) The holder of the license has failed to comply with a condition of the license;
(4) The business of the licenseholder has been carried on in an unfair or dishonest manner; or
(5) The holder of the license is not a fit and proper person to continue to hold a license.

The Commissioner may conduct an inquiry or make such investigations in relation to the matter as the Commissioner thinks fit.[1] The Commissioner has a number of powers if a matter referred to in Section 20D of the Act is established. The Commissioner can:

(1) Reprimand the holder of the license;
(2) Require the holder of the license to comply with a requirement specified by the Commissioner;
(3) Suspend the license for a period not exceeding twelve months;
(4) Disqualify the holder of the license from being concerned in any business for the carrying on of which a license is required;
(5) Impose a condition or restriction on the license; or
(6) Cancel the license.

Under Section 15 of the Motor Vehicle Repairs Act 1980, it is an offense if a person:

(1) Advertises that he or she will carry on the business of repairing motor vehicles; or
(2) Carries on the business of a motor vehicle repairer, unless he or she is the holder of a license; the holder of a license can carry on business only at the place specified in the license.

8.6.3 Travel Agents

Section 28 of the New South Wales Travel Agents Act 1986 gives a definition of unjust conduct by travel agents. Conduct is unjust if it is conduct that:

(1) Is dishonest or unfair;
(2) Involves breach of contract, even if proceedings are not brought in respect of the breach;

---

1 Motor Vehicle Dealers Act 1974 (New South Wales), Section 20D(3).

(3) Contravenes the Act or regulations; or
(4) Is a failure to comply with a condition or restriction on a license.

If the Commissioner forms the view that a licenseholder has repeatedly engaged in unjust conduct, the Commissioner may:

(1) Seek an undertaking from the licenseholder that the conduct will not be continued; or
(2) Apply for an order restraining the licenseholder from continuing the unjust conduct.

It is an offense to breach an undertaking to desist from unjust conduct.[1]

1 Travel Agents Act 1986 (New South Wales), Section 30(4); Travel Agents Act 1986 (Victoria), Section 27(4).

Section 9

Merchandise Classes for Bulk Products

9.1 Sale by Sample

A sale by sample occurs where goods are sold and where it is an express or implied condition of the contract that the goods to be acquired will correspond with a sample of the goods shown to the buyer before contracting. In some cases, there is an express term in the contract that the goods will be as per the sample. In other cases, the term will be implied by the showing of a sample to the buyer before contracting.

Section 20(2) of the Sale of Goods Act 1923 (New South Wales) provides that:

"In the case of a contract for sale by sample:

"(a) there is an implied condition that the bulk shall correspond with the sample in quality;

"(b) there is an implied condition that the buyer shall have a reasonable opportunity of comparing the bulk with the sample;

"(c) there is an implied condition that the goods shall be free from any defect rendering them unmerchantable which would not be apparent on reasonable examination of the sample."

Section 20 of the Goods Act 1958 (Victoria) has the same provisions.

An examination of a sample during negotiation of a contract for sale of goods does not necessarily make a sale by sample.[1] The question is whether, on the facts of a given transaction, the seller is representing that the bulk is like the sample[2] or merely showing the goods to give some indication of the nature of the goods offered.

---

1 *JS Robertson (Aust) Pty. Ltd.* vs. *Martin* (1956) 94 CLR 30.
2 *Cameron* vs. *Slutzkin Pty. Ltd.* (1923) 32 CLR 81.

If there is a written contract which does not make reference to the sample, it will be difficult for the buyer to establish that it is a sale by sample because the buyer would have to overcome the extrinsic evidence rules.[1]

The requirement that the bulk correspond with the sample in quality will vary depending on the nature of the goods. In some cases, all that is necessary is that the goods correspond on a visual comparison. In other cases, chemical analysis might be the appropriate test to determine whether the goods actually correspond. The parties may decide to leave the determination of whether the bulk corresponds with the sample to a third party.[2]

The provision in Section 20(2)(b) of the New South Wales Act is equivalent to the provision in Section 37 of the Act. Under Section 37(1), the buyer does not have to accept goods unless he or she has an opportunity to examine the goods for the purpose of ascertaining whether they are in conformity with the contract.

As the buyer has had an opportunity to examine the sample, the buyer will have no protection if there is any defect in the goods which would have been discoverable on reasonable examination of the sample. There is, however, expressed in Section 20(2)(c), an implied condition that the goods be free from latent defects, i.e., defects that could not be discovered on examination of the sample.

9.2 Mislabeling of Bulk Merchandise

Section 53(A) of the Trade Practices Act 1974 prohibits a corporation, in connection with the supply of goods or services, from falsely representing that goods are of a particular standard, quality, value, grade, composition, style, or model.

Most states have comparable legislation prohibiting persons who are not corporations from falsely representing that goods are of a particular standard.[3]

Any system of classification of goods which the consumer is made aware of either through labelling on the product itself or by labelling on

---

1 *Service* vs. *Walker* (1877) 3 VLR 348; *Thorne & Co. Pty. Ltd.* vs. *Thomas Borthwick & Sons* (1955) SR (New South Wales) 81; *Ship Agencies Aust* vs. *Fremantle Fishermen's Co-op Society Ltd.* [1991] 8 SR (WA) 109.

2 *Briscoe* vs. *Victorian Railways Commissioners* [1907] VLR 523.

3 Fair Trading Act 1987 (New South Wales), Section 44, and Fair Trading Act 1985 (Victoria), Section 12.

a shelf or bin containing large quantities of the product will be a representation as to the standard, quality, value, grade, or composition of the goods. If there are individual products within the bulk which do not conform with the label given to the bulk, this will be a breach of Section 53(A) of the Trade Practices Act 1974 and the corresponding Sections of the Fair Trading Act 1987.

There have been several decisions in which Section 53(A) has been held to have been breached because of descriptions attached to items. In *Ducret* vs. *Chaudhary's Oriental Carpet Palace Pty. Ltd.*,[1] a rug was labelled as a "Shah Prayer Rug" when it was actually an "Afghan Runner". The company was held to have misrepresented the style of the rug.

In *Wilkinson* vs. *Katies Fashions (Aust) Pty. Ltd.*,[2] a retailer was convicted of misrepresenting the composition of skirts due to a label which was attached to the inner side of the skirts. The labels made statements about the wool content of the skirts which were incorrect.

In *Thompson* vs. *Magnamail Pty. Limited*,[3] a magazine advertisement advertised spoons as "silver plate teaspoons". The spoons actually contained no silver and the company was convicted of misrepresenting the composition of the goods.

Section 52 of the Trade Practices Act 1974 provides further protection to consumers.[4]

In a number of cases, it has been found that inaccurate labelling is a breach of Section 52 of the Trade Practices Act 1974.[5]

---

1 (1987) 16 FLR 562.

2 (1986) 11 FCR 390.

3 (1977) ATPR 40-033.

4 *See also* Section 42 of the Fair Trading Act 1974, 1987 (New South Wales) and Section 11 of the Fair Trading Act 1974, 1985 (Victoria); if products are sold to consumers after being mislabeled, these Sections will have been contravened.

5 *Siddons Pty. Ltd.* vs. *Stanley Works Pty. Ltd.* (1990) ATPR 41-044; *Netcomm (Australia) Pty. Ltd.* vs. *Dataplex Pty. Ltd.* (1988) 81 ALR 101.

Section 10

Implementing Consumer Rights

10.1 Information

Consumers may obtain information from the Executive or from statutory consumer protection authorities.[1]

In the federal arena, the Trade Practices Commission has the function of disseminating information in relation to matters affecting the interests of consumers.[2]

It is the function of the Trade Practices Commission to:

(1) Make available to persons general information for their guidance in respect of the carrying out of the functions, or the exercise of the powers, of the Commission;
(2) Make available to the public general information in relation to matters affecting the interests of the consumers; and
(3) Make known for the guidance of consumers the rights and obligations of persons under provisions of laws enforced in Australia that are designed to protect the interests of consumers.[3]

A number of publications are produced by the Trade Practices Commission. They include:

(1) A newsletter on fair trading;
(2) A leaflet on the Trade Practices Commission;
(3) The Trade Practices Commission annual report;
(4) The Guide to the Trade Practices Act 1974 and Trade Practices Commission procedures;

---

1 Commonwealth - National Consumer Affairs Advisory Council, Trade Practices Commission; New South Wales - Commissioner of Consumer Affairs within the Department of Consumer Affairs, Fair Trading Act 1974, 1987 (New South Wales), Section 9; Victoria - Consumer Affairs Committee, Consumer Affairs Act 1972 (Victoria), Section 8.

2 Trade Practices Act 1974 (Cth), Section 28.

3 Trade Practices Act 1974 (Cth), Section 28(1).

(5) Consumer information leaflets on matters such as green marketing claims, buying jewelry, spare parts and servicing, warranties, and the right to safe goods;
(6) Business information leaflets and news sheets;
(7) Information on banking and insurance (for example, studying competition, efficiency, and the welfare of customers in the market for consumer credit insurance); and
(8) Study of the professions, including the accountancy, architectural, and legal professions.

In addition to the function of disseminating information to the community, the various state and federal bodies conduct research, receive complaints, investigate complaints, and engage in consumer education.

There are federal and state Freedom of Information Acts by which the public may be granted access to government information.[1] There are relatively low application and processing fees under these Acts.

The Commonwealth Ombudsman is a public official whose job it is to investigate the complaints of citizens who are aggrieved by the exercise of Commonwealth governmental powers. He or she has jurisdiction to investigate action that relates to a matter of administration by a department or by a proscribed authority.[2] The remedy available to the Ombudsman is the making of a report.[3] Although the Ombudsman cannot directly implement his or her decision, a recommendation usually will be acted on.

In New South Wales, under the Ombudsman Act 1974, any person may complain to the Ombudsman about the conduct of a public authority.[4] If the Ombudsman finds fault with that conduct, he or she may make a report giving reasons and making further recommendations.[5] The Ombudsman may report to the complainant[6] and must prepare an annual report of the Ombudsman's work and activities.[7] The equivalent legislation in Victoria is the Ombudsman Act 1973.

---

1 Freedom of Information Act 1982 (Cth); Freedom of Information Act 1989 (New South Wales); Freedom of Information Act 1982 (Victoria).

2 Ombudsman Act 1976 (Cth), Section 5(1).

3 Ombudsman Act 1976 (Cth), Sections 15-19.

4 Ombudsman Act 1974 (New South Wales), Section 12(1).

5 Ombudsman Act 1974 (New South Wales), Section 26(1).

6 Ombudsman Act 1974 (New South Wales), Section 29.

7 Ombudsman Act 1974 (New South Wales), Section 31.

10.2 Material Incentives (Punitive Awards)

Generally, punitive or exemplary damages are unavailable as a remedy in Australia. However, exemplary damages may be awarded if the following criteria are satisfied:

(1) The conduct must amount to "conscious wrong doing in contumelious disregard of another's rights";[1]
(2) The plaintiff is a victim of the punishable behavior;[2] and
(3) The damages must otherwise serve the purposes of retribution and deterrence.

It is uncertain whether exemplary damages are available in negligence[3] and for breach of contract.[4]

In certain circumstances, businesses and their owners and directors may face criminal sanctions.

Contravention of a number of Sections of Part V of the Trade Practices Act 1974 (but not Sections 52 or 52A) are criminal offenses punishable by fines. A corporation may be fined up to Aus. $200,000 and an individual Aus. $40,000.[5]

However, there is a limitation in that if a person is convicted of two or more offenses of a similar or the same nature committed at about the same time, the maximum penalty cannot exceed the maximum penalty for a single offense.[6]

Imprisonment is not an available option under the Trade Practices Act 1974, although the Federal Court may impose a limited sentence of imprisonment for unpaid fines.[7]

Similarly, offenses may be committed under Section 62 of the Fair Trading Act 1974 (New South Wales) and Section 32 of the Fair Trading Act 1974 (Victoria). Enforcement is the responsibility of the Consumer Affairs authority in the relevant jurisdiction.

---

1 *Whitfield* vs. *DeLauret* (1920) 29 CLR 71, at p. 77, per Knox CJ.

2 *XL Petroleum (New South Wales) Pty. Ltd.* vs. *Caltex Oil (Aust) Pty. Ltd.* (1985) 155 CLR 448, at p. 469.

3 *Midalco Pty. Ltd.* vs. *Rabenalt* [1989] VR 461.

4 *Addis* vs. *Gramophone Co Ltd.* [1909] AC 488; *Butler* vs. *Fairclough* (1917) 23 CLR 78, at p. 89.

5 Trade Practices Act 1974 (Cth), Section 79.

6 Trade Practices Act 1974 (Cth), Section 79(2); as to what is meant by "at about the same time", *see Ducret* vs. *Colourshop Pty. Ltd.* (1981) 35 ALR 503.

7 Trade Practices Act 1974 (Cth), Section 79A.

Section 87 of the Trade Practices Act 1974 confers a broad power on the courts to make remedial orders in appropriate cases relating to conduct covered by Parts IV and V. Orders may be made under Section 87 where:

(1) In proceedings under one of the other provisions of the Act, it appears to the court that a party has suffered or is likely to suffer loss or damage as a result of the contravention of Part IV and V;[1]
(2) Where a party applies under Section 87 for remedial orders in circumstances where the party applying has suffered or is likely to suffer loss or damage as a result of the contravention of Part V;[2] and
(3) The Trade Practices Commission makes application for a remedial order on behalf of identified persons who have consented to the Commission applying on their behalf.[3]

Section 87(2) of the Trade Practices Act 1974 sets out the orders which the court may make. They include orders:

(1) Declaring the whole or any part of any contract or arrangement void;
(2) Varying any contract or arrangement in such manner and from such date as the court thinks fit;
(3) Refusing enforcement of any contract;
(4) That money be refunded or property returned;
(5) For payment of compensatory damages;
(6) For repair or the provision of parts for goods supplied;
(7) For supply of specified services; and
(8) An order varying or terminating the operation or effect of an instrument creating or transferring an interest in land.

Despite the wide range of discretionary orders available under Section 87, there appears to be a reluctance both on the part of applicants to seek alternatives to damages and on the part of the courts to make alternative orders.[4] However, in certain instances, the courts have been prepared to rewrite contracts.[5]

---

1 Trade Practices Act 1974 (Cth), Section 87(1).

2 Trade Practices Act 1974 (Cth), Section 87(1)(a).

3 Trade Practices Act 1974 (Cth), Section 87(1)(b).

4 *Melchas Investments Pty. Ltd.* vs. *Larkin* (1989) 96 FLR 464, at p. 477; *Futuretronics International Pty. Ltd.* vs. *Gadzhis* [1992] 2 VR 217, at p. 245.

5 *Pont Data Australia Pty. Ltd.* vs. *ASX Corporations Pty. Ltd.* (1990) 21 FCR 385.

Similar provisions exist in Section 72 of the Fair Trading Act 1974 (New South Wales) and Section 41 of the Fair Trading Act 1974 (Victoria).

By Section 80A of the Trade Practices Act 1974, on the application to the Minister or the Trade Practices Commission, a court may order, in the case of a contravention of Part V of the Act, that a person disclose information and/or publish corrective advertisements.

That advertising may be required to be at the expense of the person involved in the contravention, and there is no statutory monetary upper limit.

In addition, the court may use its injunctive power to allow a particular state of affairs to continue, but on the condition of particular advertising occurring.[1]

10.3 Class Actions

Class actions are available in the Federal Court in matters within its jurisdiction. A similar form of action is available in Victoria. In New South Wales, a limited form of representative action is available.

10.3.1 Federal Legislation

Under Section 87(1B) of the Trade Practices Act 1974, the Trade Practices Commission may apply to the court for orders on behalf of persons who have suffered loss. The Trade Practices Commission must receive written consent to the making of such an application. In essence, the provision relates to consumers who have suffered loss or damage as a result of the contravention of the consumer protection provisions of the Trade Practices Act 1974.

Similar provisions are found in Section 72 of the Fair Trading Act 1974 (New South Wales) and Section 41(3) of the Fair Trading Act 1974 (Victoria).

In addition, Section 75AQ of the Trade Practices Act 1974 permits the Trade Practices Commission to commence action on behalf of consumers under the manufacturer's liability provisions (Part VA) of the Trade Practices Act 1974.

Of greater note is the introduction in 1992 of class or representative actions procedures in the Federal Court of Australia.[2]

---

1 *Mundine* vs. *Layton-Taylor Productions Pty. Ltd.* (1981) ATPR 40-211.

2 Federal Court of Australia Act 1976 (Cth), Part IVA.

The class action procedure is available only in respect of claims by which the Federal Court has direct jurisdiction, i.e., excluding jurisdiction given solely by virtue of the Jurisdiction of Courts (Cross-vesting) Act 1987 (Cth).

The action may be brought by one or more of a group of persons having the claim on behalf of the whole of, or part of the affected group or class. An "opt-out" procedure is used, and the consent of the other members of the group is not required.

There must be at least seven persons having claims against the same person.[1] Each claim must be in respect of, or arise out of, the same, similar, or related circumstances, and the claims must give rise to a substantial common issue of law or fact.

The consent of a person to be a member of the class is not required.[2]

The court will make an order to advise potential class members of the existence of the proceedings. A person may "opt-out" of a claim if he or she gives written notice to the court prior to a date fixed by the court.[3]

The approval of the court must be required to acceptance of settlement offers.[4] Individual claims may be settled at any stage with leave of the court.[5] The court has wide remedial powers.[6]

If a class action is successful, the court has a discretion to award damages to individual members of the group for a specified amount or to award damages for a total amount without specifying the sum awarded in respect of each individual group member.[7] The court may make provision for the constitution of the fund.[8]

There are no contingency fee arrangements allowed in the Federal Court. A representative who brings proceedings will principally be liable for costs. There is doubt about the liability of members of the class for legal costs if the action is unsuccessful. If the class action is successful, the court can order that any difference in the representative's actual legal costs and those recovered from the defendant be paid to the representatives from any damages awarded to the class.[9]

---

1 Federal Court of Australia Act 1976 (Cth), Section 33C(1)(a).
2 Federal Court of Australia Act 1976 (Cth), Section 33E.
3 Federal Court of Australia Act 1976 (Cth), Section 33J.
4 Federal Court of Australia Act 1976 (Cth), Section 33V.
5 Federal Court of Australia Act 1976 (Cth), Section 33W.
6 Federal Court of Australia Act 1976 (Cth), Section 33Z.
7 Federal Court of Australia Act 1976 (Cth), Section 33Z.
8 Federal Court of Australia Act 1976 (Cth), Section 33ZA.
9 Federal Court of Australia Act 1976 (Cth), Section 33ZJ(2).

10.3.2 Victoria

The Supreme Court Act 1958 (Victoria), Sections 34 and 35, provides for a representative action where three or more persons have the right to the same or substantially the same relief.

However, problems are faced by consumers in using this legislation, particularly in respect of possible exposure to costs.[1]

10.3.3 New South Wales

A limited form of representative action is available in the New South Wales Supreme Court.[2] This rule is modelled on a similar provision in the English High Court Rules. It provides that, where numerous persons have the same interests in any proceedings, proceedings may be commenced and/or continued by or against any one or more of them representing all or all except one or more of them.

The problem with this rule is that it only applies where the plaintiffs sue with respect to the same common right. The law is not effective in an action for damages in tort where each plaintiff is relying on recovery for his or her own personal loss and not a common one.[3]

However, all jurisdictions contain procedures for joinder, which permits a number of plaintiffs to join their claim in a single proceeding. While joinder may be successfully used for procedures encompassing a narrow scope of events and a limited number of parties, it does not lend itself (usually) to the large-scale, class-action style of litigation.[4]

10.4 Streamlined Procedures

Resort to private litigation through the court system is expensive and cumbersome. While the courts are tiered so that smaller monetary disputes are dealt with in smaller courts, the delays to hearing are often long and the procedures outmoded.

---

1 *Burns Philip and Co. Ltd.* vs. *Bhogat*, unreported, Supreme Court of Victoria, Appeal Division, 31 January 1992.

2 Supreme Court Rules, Part 8, Rule 13.

3 *Prudential Assurance Co. Ltd.* vs. *Newman Industries Ltd.* [1981] Ch 229.

4 But *see Springfield Nominees Pty. Ltd.* vs. *Bridgeland Securities Ltd.* (1991) ATPR 41-078.

Originally, the Federal Court had exclusive jurisdiction to hear and determine "consumer protection" claims under Part V of the Trade Practices Act 1974. However, as a result of the Jurisdiction of Courts (Miscellaneous Amendments) Act 1987, it shared its original jurisdiction in civil matters arising under Division 1 and 1A of Part V of the Trade Practices Act 1974 with the state and territory courts. These divisions include provisions dealing with product safety and product information.

Since 1 July 1988, a system of mutual cross-vesting of jurisdiction has operated between federal, state, and territory courts. State and territory Supreme Courts are vested with much of the civil jurisdiction of the Federal Court.

To ensure that a proceeding is heard in the appropriate court, the cross-vesting legislation provides that, in certain circumstances, the court in which proceedings have been commenced must determine whether it is "more appropriate" or otherwise in the interests of justice that the matter be dealt with by another court. An application for transfer may be made by the party or by an Attorney General, or the court may transfer the proceedings on its own motion.[1]

The Trade Practices Act 1974, Section 170, allows a person who has instituted, or who proposes to institute, proceedings under the Act to apply to the Attorney General for assistance. An application may be granted if it would involve hardship to that person to refuse the application and it is reasonable that the application should be granted.

In Victoria, a director of Consumer Affairs may institute or defend proceedings on behalf of consumers where:

(1) A consumer made a complaint under the Act;
(2) The director is satisfied that the consumer has a cause of action or a good defense to action relating to a matter to which the complaint refers and that it is in the public interest to institute or defend proceedings on behalf of the consumer.[2]

The director may not institute or defend proceedings on behalf of the consumer unless:

(1) The amount involved does not exceed Aus. $10,000;
(2) The Minister has given his or her consent in writing subject to such conditions (if any) as he or she determines; and

---

1 Jurisdiction of Courts (Cross-vesting) Act 1987 (Cth), Section 5.
2 Consumer Affairs Act 1972 (Victoria), Section 9B(1).

(3) The consumer has given his or her consent in writing and has not revoked that consent.[1]

In New South Wales, a consumer who wishes to bring legal proceedings may apply to the Commissioner of Consumer Affairs for assistance in the conduct of the proceedings.[2]

The Commercial Tribunal in New South Wales is a statutory body established under the Commercial Tribunal Act 1984. Its functions are to:

(1) Determine applications by debtors and credit providers under the Credit Act 1984 and cognate Acts;
(2) License and discipline credit providers and finance brokers;
(3) Hear appeals concerning the licensing of builders, motor dealers, travel agents, and verifiers of weighing equipment; and
(4) Hear applications under mandatory codes under the Fair Trading Act 1987.

In New South Wales and Victoria, there are tribunals that deal only with small claims.[3]

The tribunal is constituted by a referee who sits alone. In Victoria, the referee must be legally qualified, unlike in New South Wales.

In New South Wales, the tribunal has jurisdiction to hear claims up to Aus. $10,000 in the case of building claims and Aus. $6,000 for other claims.[4] In Victoria, the jurisdiction is up to Aus. $5,000.[5]

The claim must arise from the supply of goods or provision of services by a trader or supplier. In New South Wales, the claim need not arise out of the contract;[6] in Victoria, it must.[7]

The Acts cover claims in relation to contracts of insurance except life insurance.

---

1 Consumer Affairs Act 1972 (Victoria), Section 9B(2).
2 Fair Trading Act 1987 (New South Wales), Section 12(1).
3 New South Wales - Consumer Claims Tribunal, Consumer Claims Tribunal Act 1987; Victoria - Consumer Claims Tribunal, Small Claims Tribunals Act 1973.
4 Consumer Claims Tribunal Act 1987 (New South Wales), Section 32.
5 Small Claims Tribunals Act 1973 (Victoria), Section 2.
6 Consumer Claims Tribunals Act 1973 (New South Wales), Section 3(1).
7 Small Claims Tribunals Act 1973 (Victoria), Section 2.

In Victoria, the claim must be against a trader. Claims may not be available against persons carrying on a profession in Victoria.[1] In New South Wales, the position is different.[2]

The referee is required to attempt to settle all claims through a process of conciliation. In New South Wales, the Tribunal may make orders which are "fair and equitable" in the circumstances. In Victoria, the Small Claims Tribunal's function is to bring the parties to a settlement. If that fails, the referee must apply the law in determining the matter, including the whole law of contract.[3] The Small Claims Tribunal is only empowered to make one of the following orders:

(1) That a party to the proceeding before it pay money to a person specified in the order;
(2) That a party to the proceeding before it perform work to rectify a defect in goods; or
(3) To dismiss the claim.[4]

The Tribunals are not bound by the strict rules of evidence.[5] In Victoria, proceedings are generally held in public,[6] while the opposite is true in New South Wales.[7] Representation by legal practitioners is prohibited, except with leave of the Tribunal and consent of all parties.[8] Corporations may be represented in Victoria by a non-lawyer with the Tribunal's approval[9] and in New South Wales by one of its officers.[10]

There is no right of appeal from orders of the Tribunal which are final and binding.[11] The courts have a supervisory role over errors of jurisdiction and denials of natural justice.[12]

---

1 *Fawke* vs. *Holloway* [1986] VR 411.

2 Consumer Claims Tribunals Act 1973 (New South Wales), Section 3(1).

3 *Walsh* vs. *Palladium Car Park Pty. Ltd.* [1975] VR 949, at p. 955.

4 Section 18(2).

5 Small Claims Tribunals Act 1973 (Victoria), Section 31(3); Consumer Claims Tribunals Act 1987 (New South Wales), Section 22(1).

6 Small Claims Tribunals Act 1973 (Victoria), Section 31(1).

7 Consumer Claims Tribunals Act 1987 (New South Wales), Section 21.

8 Small Claims Tribunals Act 1973 (Victoria), Section 30; Consumer Claims Tribunals Act 1987 (New South Wales), Section 21.

9 Small Claims Tribunals Act 1973 (Victoria), Section 30.

10 Consumer Claims Tribunals Act 1987 (New South Wales), Section 21(2).

11 Small Claims Tribunals Act 1973 (Victoria), Section 16; Consumer Claims Tribunals Act 1987 (New South Wales), Section 34.

12 Consumer Claims Tribunals Act 1987 (New South Wales), Section 17; Small Claims Tribunals Act 1973 (Victoria), Section 12(2).

In New South Wales, the Building Disputes Tribunal is a specialist branch of the Consumer Claims Tribunal. It determines disputes concerning residential building work. The jurisdictional limit is also Aus. $10,000, and homeowners, licensed builders, or other building trades people can make claims. The Buildings Disputes Tribunal also has a debt collection function.

10.5 Technical and Material Support Groups

Consumers who seek to litigate their complaint face barriers, such as the cost of litigation (including the rule in courts that the losing party pay most, if not all, of the successful party's legal expenses) and the delay of the court hearings. As a consequence, it has been recognized by most Australian legislatures that, in the enforcement of consumer claims, some bureaucratic machinery is necessary in the interest of consumers.

In New South Wales, Community Justice Centres seek to resolve disputes, including some disputes between consumers and traders or suppliers within the local area in which they arise, by means of mediation and conciliation. They are voluntary, and no person can be compelled to take part in proceedings.

In Victoria, the government has established a Market Court under the Market Court Act 1979. The Victorian Market Court differs from the procedures available under the Trade Practices Act 1974 in that only the Minister or Director of Consumer Affairs has standing to seek relief from the Market Court. The Market Court has jurisdiction to make orders preventing conduct by traders which is unfair to consumers.[1] If the Market Court finds that conduct of the trader is unfair, it may make orders against that trader. Conduct is deemed by Section 15(2) of the Market Court Act 1979 to be unfair if:

(1) It is misleading;
(2) The trader takes advantage of the consumer; and
(3) It consists of entering into a contract with the consumer where the terms of the contract are such that no reasonable person would regard them as just.

The Market Court may make orders:

---

1 Market Court Act 1979 (Victoria), Section 15.

(1) Prohibiting the trader from entering into contracts with consumers;
(2) Prohibiting the trader from engaging in specified conduct;
(3) Setting aside contracts contravening or not in compliance with the Market Court's orders.

There are various other tribunals or authorities. For example, the Rental Bond Board is a New South Wales statutory body which provides an independent custodial service for rental bond monies. Landlords are protected against failure by tenants to comply with any terms or conditions of a residential tenancy agreement. The Board ensures that both parties have equal and fair access to claiming bonds on termination of tenancy.

The Residential Tenancy Tribunal has jurisdiction to hear and determine matters under the Residential Tenancy Act 1987 (New South Wales) and the Retirement Villages Act 1989 (New South Wales). The matters include requests to terminate tenancy agreements, payment of rental bonds on termination of tenancy, breaches relating to terms of tenancy agreements, and payment of compensation.

The Strata and Tenancy Commissioner's office is responsible for the investigation and resolution of complaints, distribution of information, research, and consultation with other bodies about residential and board and tenant matters.[1] The Fair Rent Board determines fair rents of prescribed premises and hears appeals against the Rent Controllers' determination of shared accommodation.

---

1 Residential Tenancy Act 1987.

Austria

Elisabeth Stern
Grohs-Hofer-Reiner
Vienna, Austria

Austria

Austria

Section 1

Introduction

1.1 Private Law, Administrative Law, and Self-Regulation

In Austria law, consumer protection is a topic which embraces various fields of law. For many years, it has been the declared aim of both the government and parliament to improve the legal and economic position of consumers in the market.[1] After there had been a certain amount of consumer protection for decades,[2] the main improvements started in the early 1970s.[3] The latest improvements have been induced by European Community (EC) regulations.

Since Austria has ratified the European Economic Area (EEA) Agreement and will become a Member State of the European Union (EU) in January 1995, EC Directives and standards on consumer protection are of growing importance for Austria. In some cases, Austrian legislation has already implemented EU standards by an "autonomous decision to adhere" to certain EC Directives, standards, and models. As from January 1995, Austria is under the obligation to transform the EC Directives in the area of consumer protection. Most of the transformation statutes have been already adopted.

A general survey of consumer protection law is an interdisciplinary task. In administrative and in private law, many statutes and decrees serve the purpose of consumer protection.[4] Consumer protection law is

---

1 Schuhmacher, in Krejci, *Handbuch des Konsumentenschutzgesetzes 1*; Governmental Communiqué 1970, 1971, 1975, 1979.

2 Vgl Ratengesetz 1896, "Protection of Hire-Purchase Sales etc.", Schuhmacher, *Verbraucher und Recht aus historischer Sicht, 1981.*

3 Kramer-Mayerhofer, *Konsumentenschutz im Privat- und Wirtschaftsrecht, 1977*, Krejci-Schilcher-Steininger, *Konsumentenschutz - ABGB und Verfahrensrecht, 1978.*

4 Wenger, Der Verbraucherschutz im österreichischen Verwaltungsrecht, *Juristische Blätter* 1970, at p. 231.

not a compact body of law like commercial law or tax law but rather a motive for legislative measures both in private and public law.[1]

The provisions on consumer protection are scattered over many statutes and decrees, making a systematic overview difficult. Consumer protection is by no means limited to private law.[2]

In general, the areas of consumer protection legislation cover the production of goods, advertising, distribution and information duties, use of unfair contract clauses and standard form contracts, individual sales and other contracts where one party is a consumer, and damages caused by the distributed products.

This survey does not attempt to establish a concept of Austrian consumer or consumer protection law, but rather follows a pragmatic approach, searching through Austrian private and public law for regulations which lead to consumer protection, leaving aside whether, according to Austrian legal doctrine, these provisions would be considered to be consumer protection provisions.[3] Especially as far as administrative law provisions are concerned, this approach often goes beyond the general meaning of consumer protection law in Austria.

While, in private law, it is a relatively easy task to establish which regulations are intended to protect certain consumer interests, this is rather more difficult in administrative law. Many statutes and regulations addressed to business activities serve the purpose of consumer protection, but only some statutes are explicitly addressed to this subject.

In administrative law, consumer protection is, in most cases, an indirect or reflexive protection because the consumer cannot directly enforce these regulations. The disregard of these regulations can only be prosecuted by public authorities. Only in some cases may such an administrative law provision influence the consumer's right to damages according to civil law, if it can be established that a certain provision is a special protective norm for consumers.[4]

---

1 *Schuhmacher in Krejci, Handbuch des Konsumentenschutzgesetzes*, at pp. 8 *et seq.*

2 Kramer, *Prinzipienfragen eines österreichischen Konsumentenschutzrechtes*, in Kramer-Mayerhofer, *Konsumentenschutz im Privat- und Wirtschaftsrecht*, at p. 10.

3 For the developing of a definition of consumer law, *see* Schuhmacher in Krejci, *Handbuch des Konsumentenschutzgesetzes*, at pp. 11 *et seq.*

4 Civil Code, Article 1311.

1.1.1 Consumer Protection in Private Law

The focal point of consumer protection in Austria is the Consumer Protection Act 1979.[1] Its main task is to strengthen the contractual rights of consumers. It applies to all contracts related to the business activity of one party but not the other. The first party is the "entrepreneur" and the second party the "consumer".

The entrepreneur and enterprise concept is a development of the Consumer Protection Act. "Enterprise" is defined as any permanent, independent business activity with at least a minimum organization, regardless of whether it is profit-oriented. "Entrepreneur" is a person who runs such a business in his own financial interest.[2]

The term entrepreneur has a wider meaning than the "merchant" concept according to the Commercial Code.[3] It is a functional approach which attempts to cover all kinds of business activities, regardless of the subject of the business or its size. In other aspects, it is a formal approach. To create and ensure certainty under which circumstances the of the Act are applicable, the Act does not require that there actually be a disturbance of balance of power between the entrepreneur and the consumer. This imbalance is irrefutably presumed.

As long as one party is a consumer and the other party is an entrepreneur, the Act applies. The qualification of whether a person is a consumer or entrepreneur and whether the contract is related to his business activities is solely based on objective criteria.

A subjective test of whether the entrepreneur knows or ought to know that the other party is a consumer and vice versa is unknown to the Consumer Protection Act.[4] Employment contracts are excluded from the application of the Act.

Finally, the Consumer Protection Act is only applicable to private law contracts. Legal relationships based on administrative law, even if they are contractual, are outside the scope of the Consumer Protection Act.

---

1 *Legal Gazette* 1979/840, Krejci (ed.), *Handbuch des Konsumentenschutzgesetzes*, 1981; Krejci, *Konsumentenschutzgesetz*, 1986; Doralt-Koziol, *Stellungnahme zum Ministerialentwurf des Konsumentenschutzgesetzes*, 1979; Koziol-Welser, *Grundriß des Bürgerlichen Recht I*, 9th ed., at pp. 505 *et seq.*, with further references.

2 Krejci, *Handbuch des Konsumentenschutzgesetz*, at pp. 209 *et seq.*; Krejci in Rummel, *Kommentar ABGB, 2nd ed.*, Paragraph 1, KSchG Rz 14 *et seq.*

3 *Handelsgesetzbuch, HGB*; Straube, in Straube, *Kommentar HGB*, vor Paragraph 1, Paragraph 1.

4 Krejci, in Rummel, *Kommentar ABGB, 2nd ed.*, Paragraph 1 Rz 25 *et seq.*

However, the Consumer Protection Act was only one step toward a concept of overall consumer protection. Other main areas are the Product Liability Act and the Unfair Competition Act. The Unfair Competition Act and other statutes, like the Banking Act, contain both private law and administrative law provisions which serve the purpose of consumer protection.

1.1.2 Consumer Protection in Administrative Law

In administrative law, statutes addressed to consumer protection are the Food Act and other food-related statutes, such as the Wine Act and the Quality-Class Act, the labeling provisions of the Unfair Competition Act,[1] the Electro-Engineering Act, the Product Safety Act, the Price Labeling Act, the Price Act, the Industrial Code, and the Cartel Code.

1.1.3 Consumer Protection by Self-Regulation

Direct consumer protection by self-regulation is more or less non-existent in Austria. Certain guidelines, such as the Code of Good Behavior of the advertising industry, can be regarded as further protection of consumers against offensive and indecent advertisements.

A special feature of the Austrian economic and legal system is the strong influence of the cooperation between management and labor, the so-called "Social Partnership". This system was established after World War II as a mechanism to avoid strikes and other conflicts between employers and employees. As a voluntary forum for cooperation, the Wage and Price Parity Commission[2] was established. Its members are the Federal Chancellor, certain Ministers, and the presidents of the trade associations. The Commission does not have executive power but, for decades, all important questions concerning the increase of prices and wages have been influenced by the Commission.

Starting with the Commission, the social partners have a strong influence on more or less all aspects of Austrian economic policy.[3]

---

1 Unfair Competition Act, Section 32.

2 Farnleitner, *Die Paritätische Kommission*, 1977; Marin, *Die Paritätische Kommission - aufgeklärter Technokorpratismus in Österreich*, 1982; Reiss (ed.), *Rechtsfragen des Sozialpartnerschaft*, 1987.

3 For their influence on price regulation, *see* the text below at Section 6.2.6.

1.2 Primary Interest Groups

As consumer protection can be seen as a natural conflict between the interests of entrepreneurs and of consumers, the primary interest groups are the representatives of these interests. This is the Austrian Chamber of Commerce and the Industry Association for the entrepreneurs, and the Austrian Chamber of Employees and the Austrian Confederation of Trade Unions for consumers.

Austria does not have any independent consumer-protection organizations, but consumer protection is linked to the trade associations.

There is only one organization directly addressed to the issue of consumer protection, the Association of Consumer Information.[1] It is organized as a cooperation between management and labor. Its headquarters are in Vienna, but there are regional offices all over Austria.

Originally, both the Austrian Chamber of Employees and the Austrian Confederation of Trade Unions had their own consumer organizations. In 1960, these organizations merged and, in 1961, the Association of Consumer Information was founded, and the Austrian Chamber of Commerce and the Austrian Chamber of Agriculture became members. The members established the VKI as an objective and politically-independent consumer information center. In 1975, the Austrian State became a supporting member of the association. The VKI is a member of the International Organization of Consumer Unions.

The cooperation of the social partners is institutionalized in certain advisory boards and commissions, such as the Consumer Policy Board at the Ministry of Health, Sport, and Consumer Protection, the Product Security Board under the Product Security Act, and the Advisory Board for Food Law.

1.3 Administrative Bodies and Public Law Structure

The Federal Ministry for Health, Sport, and Consumer Protection initiates and coordinates measures and projects in the area of consumer protection. The federal government has sole jurisdiction for consumer protection regulations as part of its general jurisdiction for civil law. In public law, there is no special jurisdiction for consumer protection but,

---

1 Verein für Konsumenteninformation, VKI.

as the federal government has jurisdiction for all trade matters, this is the basis for most consumer protection regulations.

There is no special public law structure for the implementation of consumer protection regulations. The authorities which supervise compliance with the regulations and procedures and sanctions are defined by individual statutes and general administrative law.

Section 2

Consumer Products and Service Standards

2.1 General Regime

Concerning the quality of goods and services, one must distinguish between general standards of quality and the special aspect of the safety of products and services.[1] The general standard of products and services is not regulated expressly for consumers.

2.1.1 Product and Service Quality

Consumer interests are protected by the general law of warranties and liability for sales and service contracts.[2]

Under Austrian law, goods are suitable according to the contract if they have the qualities expressly specified in the contract or commonly supposed to exist and they can be used and applied according to the nature of the contract or the express specifications.[3] This rule applies for services as well.[4] For consumer contracts, these provisions are mandatory,[5] and they also have a preventive function.[6]

2.1.2 Product Safety

In the area of product safety, a general standard is to be achieved by the Product Safety Act.[7]

According to the Act, all products sold must provide the security an average user of this kind of product expects. The aim of the Act is that

---

1 Schuhmacher, *Handbuch zum Konsumentenschutzgesetz*, at p. 47.
2 Schuhmacher, "Verbraucherschutz in Österreich", *Europäische Zeitschrift für Verbraucherrecht*, 1987, at p. 25.
3 Civil Code, Section 922.
4 Civil Code, Section 1167.
5 Consumer Protection Act, Sections 8 and 9.
6 Schuhmacher, in Krejci, *Handbuch des Konsumentenschutzgesetzes*, at pp. 47 *et seq.*
7 *Produksicherheitsgesetz, Legal Gazette* 1983/171.

only safe products reach the market and that dangerous products either do not reach the market or are at least removed as quickly as possible.[1]

For this purpose, the Ministry of Trade can take various actions to ensure product safety:

(1) It can order the introduction or modification of product instructions or the style of the product;
(2) It can issue orders and interdictions concerning advertising measurements;
(3) It can establish the characteristic properties of a product;
(4) It can issue sales and distribution prohibitions and restrictions; and
(5) It can oblige the producer to warn about dangers related to his product and to give instructions on how to avoid dangers.

The failure to obey such orders is an administrative law offense with a maximum fine of ATS 100,000. Products also can be foreclosed. If a manufacturer, importer, or dealer fails to obey such an order, he can be held liable by a victim of such a product according to the general law of liability.[2]

The Product Safety Act does not provide for recall of defective products. However, a Austria must implement the EC Directive on General Product Safety, the recall and withdrawal of unsafe goods will be included.

The Industrial Code also provides for the issuance of decrees concerning product safety.[3] It grants a wide competence; although not frequently used, it is the most general basis allowing the authorities to establish product safety standards.[4]

2.1.3 Product Liability

Another means of protecting consumers against unsafe products is to strengthen consumer remedies.[5] Until 1988, a consumer could claim

1 Posch, "Allgemeine Produktsicherheit und Produkthaftung", in Schuhmacher, *Verbraucherschutz in Österreich und der EG*, 1992, at pp. 33 *et seq.*

2 Civil Code, Section 1311; *see also* Posch, "Product Liability in Austria", *Comparative Law Yearbook of International Business* (1993), at n. 33.

3 Industrial Code, Section 69, Paragraph 1.

4 Schuhmacher, in Krejci, *Handbuch des Konsumentenschutzgesetzes*, at pp. 49 *et seq.*

5 Welser, *Produkthaftungsgesetz, Kurzkommentar*, 1988; Koziol-Welser, *Grundriß des Bürgerlichen Rechts I*, 9th ed., at pp. 491 *et seq.*; Posch, "Product Liability in Austria", *Comparative Law Yearbook of International Business* (1993), at p. 88.

damages from a defective product only under the general rules on civil liability.[1] As this system is based on the concept of default, a manufacturer was liable only if he at least negligently caused the defect in the product.

In cases where the injured person and the manufacturer had no contractual relationship, the manufacturer's vicarious liability was limited. The victim had to prove that the defect was caused by an employee unfit for the job.[2] To overcome these problems, legal doctrine and the courts developed the concept of contractual protective duties in favor of a third person. This means that, from the contract between the manufacturer and the dealer, mandatory protective duties arise in favor of the ultimate buyer. As this liability is a contractual liability, the manufacturer's vicarious liability is much stricter.[3]

The entrepreneur is liable for his employee's fault. Liability remains based on the concept of default but, in contractual liability cases, the burden of proof is on the manufacturer. By this judge-made concept, some of the problems of product liability were solved. However, certain problems remained, such as those related to the so-called innocent bystander. The *Produkhaftungsgesetz* 1990[4] now grants a consumer the right to damages against a manufacturer if the product has caused bodily injury or loss to the consumer. This Act follows, in general, the model of the EC Directive on Product Liability.

The manufacturer's liability is a strict liability. The sole criteria for liability is the defectiveness of the product. There is no distinction among design, manufacturing, or marketing defects. A product is deemed defective if it does not provide the safety which a person is entitled to expect under the specific circumstances.[5] To measure "reasonable exceptions", the following criteria must be taken into account:

(1) The presentation of the product;
(2) The possible intended purposes of the product; and
(3) The time when the product was put into circulation.

---

1 Civil Code, Sections 1295 *et seq.*
2 Civil Code, Section 1315.
3 Civil Code, Section 1313a.
4 Product Liability Act, *Legal Gazette* 1988/99.
5 Product Liability Act, Section 5.

Therefore, a product must be marketed together with the instructions and warnings necessary for proper use; otherwise, this lack in presentation is a defect of the product.[1]

The only defenses available to the manufacturer are set out by Section 8 of the Product Liability Act. The manufacturer can escape liability by proving that the defect is due to a mandatory legal rule or administrative order for the production of the product, or "the characteristics of the product could not, with regard to the state of scientific knowledge, have been discovered as defective at the time at which the defendant put the product into circulation".[2] This defense is available only if the defect was not discoverable, and not if the defect was discoverable but not solvable. The manufacturer is liable for accidental production defects, even if he was not able to prevent them. The exemption covers development risks.

The manufacturer of component parts also is under the strict liability of the Product Liability Act. He has one further exemption. He is not liable if he can prove that the defect was caused by the construction of the product into which the component part was fitted or resulted from instructions by the manufacturer of the finished product.[3]

If the manufacturer does not have his place of business in Austria, the liability shifts to the importer of the product to Austria. This ensures that the Austrian consumer can enforce his claim in Austria under Austrian law.

A person who presents himself as the manufacturer of the product or put his trademark on the product is treated as the manufacturer.[4]

In the case of damage caused by an "anonymous product", the dealers who sold it have the duty to disclose to the victim the manufacturer or the dealer from whom they acquired the product. If the dealer fails to disclose, he becomes liable as the manufacturer.

Not all damages are recoverable under the Product Liability Act. It only covers a minimum range of damages. The Act only provides for damages resulting from:

---

1 Posch, "Product Liability in Austria", *Comparative Law Yearbook of International Business* (1993), at p. 93.

2 An English translation of the Austrian Act on Product Liability by Posch was published in the *Comparative Law Yearbook of International Business* (1993), at pp. 109 *et seq*.; the citations of the Act follow this translation.

3 Posch, "Product Liability in Austria", *Comparative Law Yearbook of International Business* (1993), at p. 97.

4 "Would-be" manufacturer or quasi-manufacturer; *see* Posch, "Product Liability in Austria", *Comparative Law Yearbook of International Business* (1993), at p. 96.

(1) Personal injury - In this case, it does not matter whether the victim is a consumer. The damages include the expenses for the remedy, lost earnings, and compensation for pain and suffering.[1] If the victim was killed, the survivors entitled to support by the victim can claim these maintenance costs; and

(2) Property damage - The damages must be caused to an object other than the unsafe product. The damage caused to the unsafe product itself can be recovered only under the law of warranty and the general law of liability. The manufacturer is liable for property damages suffered by consumers. Liability for property damage is limited by Section 2 so that the manufacturer is liable only for property damage exceeding ATS 7,900. There is no compensation for pure economic loss.

2.1.3.1 Labeling

Based on Section 32 of the Unfair Competition Act, the competent Minister can issue detailed regulations concerning the labeling of goods and services.[2] For goods, the following information can be required:

(1) The name and address of the manufacturer or dealer;
(2) The quantity and characteristics of the goods;
(3) The necessary information for the use and maintenance of the product;
(4) The price in relation to certain quantities; and
(5) The product origin.

It also can be required that the goods be distributed only in certain amounts or in a certain type of packaging. Services also are subject to similar information requirements.

All labeling provisions serve the purpose to inform the consumer about the quality of the product and to prevent misleading impressions about the origin of a product.[3]

---

1 Civil Code, Sections 1325 *et seq.*

2 Schönherr-Wiltschek, *Wettbewerbsrecht*, at pp. 95 *et seq.*; Schuhmacher, *Verbraucherschutz bei Vertragsanbahnung*, 1983, at pp. 124 *et seq.*

3 Hanreich, in Wenger, *Wirtschaftsrecht*, at pp. 96 *et seq.*

2.2 Special Regimes

2.2.1 Food

The distribution of any kind of food, as well as slimming aids and food additives, is regulated by the Food Act 1975.[1] The regulation is intended to prevent health hazards and to ensure satisfactory information for consumers and other customers.

It is prohibited to market noxious, foul or unripe, or misleadingly labeled or described products. This prohibition includes food treated with radiation, hormones, and certain pesticides.

Section 10 of the Food Act is the basis for decrees to regulate minimum standards for product quality. The competent Minister can declare the conditions under which a product is deemed noxious or foul and can dictate in which manner products will be distributed.

Section 9 expressly prohibits health-related representations and advertisements in connection with food products. The use of additives is only allowed with permission of the authorities.

Anyone who offers food must take care that outside influences do not effect the hygienic standard of the product.

2.2.1.1 Labeling

To prevent deceptions and to ensure that consumers are sufficiently informed, labeling regulations can be issued.[2] The following information can be required:

(1) Usual characterization;
(2) Preservation method;
(3) Storing conditions;
(4) Time of packing;
(5) Recommended date of use;
(6) Ingredients;
(7) Nutrition value;
(8) Name and address of manufacturer; and
(9) Country of origin.

---

1 Lebensmittelgesetz, *Legal Gazette 86/1985*, Barfuß-Pindur Smolka, *Lebensmittelrecht*, looseleaf, 1975; Smolka-Blass, "Das Schicksal des österreichischen Lebensmittelrechts in der EG und im EWR", in Schuhmacher, *Verbraucherschutz in Österreich und der EG*, 1993, at pp. 77 *et seq*.

2 Food Act, Section 19.

Slimming products and food which is labeled as diet food can be marketed as such only if not prohibited within three months after the product has been notified to the authorities.

According to the Quality-Class Act, quality grades must be distinguished for certain products, and the products must be related to a certain class (for example, eggs, apples, pears, peaches, grapes, cucumbers, and tomatoes). The Quality-Class Act also contains packaging and labeling requirements.[1]

2.2.1.2 Standing

Consumers cannot directly enforce the standards ordered by the Food Act or the administrative decrees based on it. The violation of these regulations is sanctioned by penal and administrative law. In severe cases, the courts can revoke or restrict the trade license.

2.2.2 Drugs

The production and distribution of medical drugs is governed by the Drugs Act.[2] The Drugs Act ensures that only unobjectionable drugs reach the market. In general, only licensed products are allowed to be distributed. The development, production, and distribution of drugs are regulated.

There are specific restraints concerning advertising and detailed labeling and information provisions.

The distribution of "dubious" drugs is forbidden. A drug is dubious if, according to scientific and practical knowledge, it cannot be certain that the drug is not harmful.[3]

Drugs also must fulfill certain quality requirements according to the actual state of science, and there is a clear prohibition of misleading statements regarding drugs.

The detailed quality criteria are set out in the Drugs Code (*Arzneimittelbuch*). All drugs which are intended for consumers must fulfill the rules and regulations of the Drugs Code.[4]

---

1 Schuhmacher, "Verbraucherschutz in Österreich", *Europäische Zeitschrift für Verbraucherrecht* 1987, p 16.

2 *Arzneimittelgesetz, Legal Gazette* 83/1985, Mayer-Michtner-Schober, *Kommentar zum Arzneimittelgesetz*, 1987.

3 Drugs Code, Section 3.

4 *Legal Gazette* 1980/195.

All medicines which are consistently produced in the same composition and method and distributed to consumers under a brand name are so-called "drug-specialties". These drugs are only allowed to be distributed after they have been licensed by the Ministry of Health.

There are special constraints for advertising addressed to consumers. Advertising is only allowed for non-prescription drug specialties and other non-prescription drugs contained in the Drugs Code. The advertisements include a warning regarding the possible side effects of the medicine.

The Pharmacy Act (*Apothekengesetz*) states that only licensed pharmacists and doctors are allowed to sell drugs to consumers and then only in connection with their practices.

The consumer cannot directly enforce the above provisions. Only administrative law procedures and sanctions ensure the adherence.

2.2.3 Motor Vehicles

According to the Motor Vehicle Act,[1] all motor vehicles to be used on public roads must meet certain road-safety requirements. There is a mandatory inspection for all motor vehicles to obtain a road license. For mass-produced motor vehicles, this license is granted in form of a model license. The main object of the Motor Vehicle Act is road safety but, by introducing mandatory minimum standards for cars and other motor vehicles, the Act helps to protect consumers against unsafe new products.

2.2.4 Electrical Appliances

The Electro-Engineering Act[2] ensures that only technically safe products are released to the market. The Act applies to all types of electrical appliances. The general standard of safety is that appliances must be manufactured, produced, maintained, and operated or used in a way that does not endanger users. The competent Minister can issue regulations setting out safety security standards.[3] Products which are not in accordance with these standards may not be distributed in Austria. Rather than

1 *Kraftfahrgesetz, BGBl.* 1967/267.

2 *Legal Gazette* 1990/57, Elektrotechnikgesetz.

3 Electro-Engineering Decree 1990, *Legal Gazette* 1990/352.

setting out detailed security standards in the Decree, it refers to the regulations and standards elaborated by competent technical organizations.

The competent Minister can order that certain types of electrical appliances be tested to assure that they meet mandatory safety standards.[1] Tested products are identified with "safety labels". The tests must be requested by the manufacturer or by the importer.[2] The tests are carried out by state-authorized testing centers. The types of products that must be tested are regulated in mandatory-testing decrees (*Prüfungszwangsverordnungen*). The safety labels are known as "ÖVE testing certificates".

At present, there are no specific standards and regulations in Austria concerning tools, textiles, and toys.

2.2.5 *Insurance*

Insurance law has always been influenced by customer protection. However, the origin of the Austrian Insurance Contract Code 1958 dates to the beginning of this century. Thus, the Code is by no means a consumer-protection code according to modern standards. Its aim was always customer protection in general and not only consumer protection.[3]

The detailed regulation of the different types of insurance is achieved by general business conditions for all insurance contracts and for different types of contracts. They are supplemented by "special general conditions" for various types of insurance in each branch. The customer does not have any influence on the substance of these conditions. A certain control is exercised by the government because these conditions must be approved by the Insurance Supervisory Board.

By approving the general conditions, the state authorities can influence the terms of the insurance contract. However, this does not mean that the conditions are necessarily valid under contract law. Certain provisions can still be invalid because they violate provisions of mandatory private law.[4]

The general conditions only become part of the agreement because the parties include them in the contract. According to case law, it is well established practice that all insurance contracts are governed by general

---

1 Electro-Engineering Act, Section 8, Paragraph 5.
2 Electro-Engineering Act, Section 8, Paragraph 2.
3 Krejci, *Kundenschutz im Versicherungsrecht* 15.
4 Civil Code, Section 879, and Consumer Protection Act, Section 6.

conditions and, therefore, the customer must know that the insurance contract is concluded on the basis of the insurer's general conditions. There are no special regulations regarding the duty of the insurer and its agents to inform customers regarding the general conditions.

As with any other contracts between consumers and entrepreneurs, the Consumer Protection Act applies. However, this is more a theoretical aspect of consumer protection in insurance law as the issues regulated in the Consumer Protection Act do not have much practical importance in insurance contracts.

2.2.6 *Travel*

While Austrian law did not previously contain specific provisions on travel contracts, but such provisions were to come into force during 1994. The amendment of the Consumer Protection Act 1993[1] introduces new Paragraphs 31b-31f, which regulate tour-operator contracts in the interest of consumers in accordance with EU law. A tour-operator contract is defined as a contract which combines at least two of the following services: transportation, accommodation, and/or other tourist services for a lump-sum price.

A tour-operator is any person or organization offering organized travel arrangements on a regular basis.

The new regulations contain special provisions regarding the operator's right to alter his performance, the consumer's right to rescind the contract, and the consumer's right to claim damages.

The operator cannot reserve the right to increase the price within the twenty days before the start of the tour. Otherwise, a price increase clause is valid only if it also deals with the possibility of price reductions, as well, and if the change in price results from changes in transportation costs. The requirements of Section 6 of the Consumer Protection Act also must be observed.

If the operator changes essential parts of his performance, in cases where he is entitled to do so, the consumer can still rescind the contract without having to pay a contractual penalty or damages. The operator must inform the consumer about the changes and the option to rescind the contract. The consumer must inform the operator about his decision without delay.[2]

---

1 *Legal Gazette* 1993/247.

2 Consumer Protection Act, Section 31c, Paragraph 2.

The consumer has the right to transfer his contractual rights and duties to another person if he is unable to take part in the tour. However, he remains liable for the price, together with his substitute.

If the consumer rescinds the contract according to Section 31c of the Consumer Protection Act or if the operator cannot perform the tour, the consumer is entitled to require performance by taking part in an equivalent tour or to request the restitution of any payments already made. The consumer also is entitled to damages, unless the operator had to rescind the contract because the minimum amount of participants was not reached and such minimum subscription was a condition of the contract. *Force majeure* also operates as an exemption from liability. The liability of the operator remains based on the concept of fault as with any liability claim under the Civil Code.

The consumer must report any lack in performance immediately to the local representative of the operator if the operator has informed the consumer about this duty in writing. If the consumer fails to report in time, it does not effect his warranty rights, but it can reduce or preclude his right to damages. If the consumer does not give notice, he violates his duty to mitigate damages.

2.2.7 Correspondence Courses

The regulation of correspondence courses has been an issue before the legislature for more than ten years, but no action has been taken on the matter.

2.2.8 Mail Order

There are no specific statutes or decrees concerning mail-order contracts, but Section 8 of the Consumer Protection Act regulates the place of performance for warranty claims for consumer sales contracts involving the carriage of the goods. If the seller performed his obligation by sending or mailing the goods to a place in Austria, then this place of destination, which normally will be the consumer's home, is the place where the entrepreneur must remedy any defective performance.

According to the general contract law, the place of performance is the place from where the seller sent the goods.[1] There are no specific rights to rescind the contract in mail-order contracts.

1 Koziol-Welser, *Grundriß des Bürgerlichen Rechts*, 9th ed., at pp. 206 *et seq.*

Section 3

Testing

3.1 Mandatory Testing

As already pointed out, there are mandatory testing requirements for some electrical appliances, motor vehicles, and drugs. The so-called "food police" supervise the sale of foods. They can control all shops and enterprises selling food and take samples which are then tested. If the tests show that a product is a health hazard, the Minister of Health must warn the public. Administrative law sanctions also apply.[1]

3.2 Distribution and Effect of Test Results

The Association of Consumer Protection, the Austrian Chamber of Employees, and various organizations carry out comparative product tests and publish the results. The best-known magazine is the *Konsument*, published by the Association of Consumer Protection.

1 Walter-Mayer, *Grundriß des Besonderen Verwaltungsrechts*, 2nd ed., at p. 567.

Section 4

Advertising

The general regulation of advertising is set out in the Unfair Competition Act. Originally, the Unfair Competition Act was only regarded as protecting competitors, but the protection of consumer interests has emerged as an equally important purpose of the Unfair Competition Act.[1]

There are two main principles in advertising law, that of disclosure and that of truth.

4.1 Disclosure

The principle of disclosure means that everyone who is the addressee of an advertisement must be informed that the message is an advertising message. According to Section 26 of the Media Act (*Mediengesetz*), advertisements in newspapers and other periodicals or on radio and television must be clearly identified as such. Subliminal advertisements are prohibited.[2]

The non-disclosure of advertising activities to the addressee is a violation of the Unfair Competition Act.

4.2 Truth and Prohibition of Misleading and Deceptive Statements

Section 2 of the Unfair Competition Act prohibits misleading and deceptive statements regarding business circumstances made in the course of business for the purpose of competition. This includes misleading statements about the quality, the origin, and the price of the goods, price lists, the possession of awards, patents, and the reason or purpose for a special sale.

---

1 Hanreich, in Wenger, *Wirtschaftsrecht II*, 86 *et seq.*, with further references; Sack, "Schadenersatzansprüche wettbewerbsgeschädigter Verbraucher", in Kramer-Mayerhofer, *Konsumentenschutz im Privat- und Wirtschaftsrecht*, 1977, at pp. 99 *et seq.*

2 *See* Schuhmacher, *Verbraucherschutz bei Vertragsanbahnung*, at pp. 221 *et seq.*

To decide whether a statement is misleading, it must be considered whether the impression it is likely to make on an average customer would be misleading to him. It is not necessary that the entrepreneur have the intention to mislead; it is sufficient that the statement be objectively misleading. Boasting statements, which the average customer would not literally believe, are not treated as misleading statements. Various statutes, such as the Food Act, the Wine Act, and the Drugs Code, repeat and strengthen the prohibition of deceptive statements and advertisements for the products they regulate.

Some regulations prohibit certain conduct which could be misleading as such. In such cases, it is not necessary to decide whether the conduct is misleading in an individual instance. Such a regulation is Section 6a of the Unfair Competition Act, which prohibits the packaging of products in a way that the size of the package is out of proportion to the contents, if such a packaging is not justified by the nature of the product or the packing method.[1]

Section 30 of the Unfair Competition Act prohibits the public announcement that the goods offered are part of the assets of a bankrupt, if those goods only originally came from such assets but are no longer part of these assets. Section 31 of the Unfair Competition Act explicitly prohibits the assumption of marks of distinction and prizes and of certificates of qualifications issued by the authorities.

4.3 Unfair Advertising

According to Section 1 of the Unfair Competition Act, everyone must, in the course of business, refrain from acts which are considered *contra bono mores*. This includes all types of advertisements which are *contra bono mores*. The determination of which acts and advertising are *contra bono mores* is made by the courts. The following criteria have been established in case law:

(1) Canvassing of customers - Advertising measures which can influence the consumer to buy a product because of reasons which are not related to the product are unfair and *contra bono mores*. These include measures such as prize competitions with a direct or an

1 Schuhmacher, *Verbraucherschutz durch Vertragsanbahnung*, at pp. 258 *et seq.*; Unfair Competition Act, Sections 30 and 31.

indirect obligation to buy and offers where the purchase of a certain amount of the product is linked to a special offer for another product.

(2) Comparative advertisements - Comparative advertisements are generally prohibited, even if the statements are true and do not degrade the competitor. While it is clear that comparative advertising can influence the consumer to make an uninformed decision, there is no obvious reason why comparative advertisements necessarily harm the consumer. Therefore, the prohibition of comparative advertising can be justified only as a means of protecting competitors. There are two exceptions to the prohibition of comparative advertising. These are where only prices are compared without further advertising claims[1] and where types of products, production methods, or distribution systems are compared without reference to a specific competitor.

1 Unfair Competition Act, Section 2a.

Section 5

Standard Terms (Adhesive Contracts)

In Austrian contract law, consumer protection is not limited to standard terms or general business conditions. The Consumer Protection Act 1979 was intended to remedy the imbalance between consumers and entrepreneurs. Although the most basic principle of Austrian contract law is party autonomy, it had become obvious that party autonomy is only a justification for contract provisions if the parties are in state of equilibrium.

In reality, consumers do not have the option to vary provisions in a contract. They only have the option to enter into the contract or to leave it. In the case of essential commodities, they do not have even this option. Therefore, especially in the field of consumer protection, a formal understanding of party autonomy was replaced by the concept of substantial justice.

The Consumer Protection Act has implemented this principle by requiring that provisions on breach of contract, warranties, and liability (which are, according to the Civil Code, dispositive) be mandatory on behalf of the consumer. These provisions of the Civil Code cannot be modified to the disadvantage of the consumer.

Section 6 of the Consumer Protection Act provides a list of clauses which are invalid in consumer contracts. This list is supplemented by Sections 8 and 9 of the Act, regulating consumer warranty rights and permissible variations. In addition, Section 879 of the Civil Code deals with the problem of unjust and, therefore, immoral and void contracts and contract clauses. According to Section 879, Paragraph 3, of the Civil Code, an incidental contract provision not addressed to the essential obligations of the parties is void if it severely discriminates against one party. Only the clause is invalid, not the whole contract, and the invalidity must be invoked by the consumer.

Section 6 of the Consumer Protection Act is a concretization of the general clause of Section 879 of the Civil Code, which invalidates contract clauses which are *contra bonos mores*. Section 6 is only a demonstrative catalog.[1] Clauses not expressly mentioned by Section 6

---

1 For a detailed commentary on Section 6 of the Consumer Protection Act, *see* Krejci, in Rummel, *Kommentar ABGB*, 2nd ed., Paragraph 6, KSchG.

still may be invalid under Section 879 of the Civil Code due to the unbalanced positions between the entrepreneur.

Section 6 of the Consumer Protection Act distinguishes between the above clauses and certain clauses listed in Section 6, Paragraph 2, which are invalid only if the entrepreneur cannot prove that the terms were carefully explained to the consumer prior to agreement. These clauses are only invalid if the consumer was not aware of them.

A similar effect is reached on a more general level by Section 864a of the Civil Code, which states that unusual provisions in general business conditions are void if these provisions are detrimental to the interest of the other party and such party could not have expected the clause in the general conditions or at its specific place in the general conditions.

5.1 Delivery and Payment Terms

5.1.1 Limitation of Consumer's Commitment

Under Section 6, Paragraph 1, of the Consumer Protection Act, a clause is invalid if it allows the entrepreneur an unreasonably long or indefinite time to accept an offer of a consumer and states terms of unreasonable length before the consumer can remedy an entrepreneur's failure to deliver.

According to Austrian contract law, an offer is irrevocable after it has reached the offeree, and the offeror is bound for the time stipulated in his offer or, if no time is mentioned, for a reasonable time.[1]

For a reasonable time limit, it must be assumed that the period of time for the offeree may be only as long as, in the specific circumstances, he needs to decide to accept the offer. A significantly longer period without justified reason limits the consumer's scope of action and gives the entrepreneur the chance to speculate to find a better way of selling his products without economic risk.

Clauses extending the consumer's contractual commitment are invalid. This clause covers various aspects of contractual commitments. The terms of delivery may not be indefinite or unreasonably long without justification by the special circumstances of the contract.

A term of performance is indefinite if the consumer cannot know the date of delivery or, with some degree of certainty, establish it. The Act

1 Koziol-Welser, *Grundriß des Bürgerlichen Rechts I*, 9th ed., at pp. 105.

also embraces clauses limiting or impeding the consumer's rights to avoid, cancel, or rescind the contract.

Under Section 6, Paragraph 2, of the Act, clauses contained in general business conditions or standard form contracts, lessening the entrepreneur's contractual commitment, are void if they:

(1) Give the entrepreneur the right to cancel the contract without material grounds;
(2) Give the entrepreneur the right to transfer his contractual obligations to a third part not named in the contract with the effect that the former contract partner is released from his obligations; this does not effect cases where substitution is allowed by law; and
(3) Give the entrepreneur the right to vary or modify his performance, except where it is a reasonable modification.

5.1.2 Unilateral Price Increase

Price variation clauses, which allow the entrepreneur to demand a higher price than stated in the contract, are void, except where circumstances justifying a price increase are described in the contract and are independent of the entrepreneur's will and influence.[1]

Escalation clauses in long-term contracts, such as rental agreements where the amount of increase is linked to the index of living costs published by the Central Bureau of Statistics (*Verbraucherpreisindex*) are valid.

If a manufacturer or dealer makes his prices subject to the list price at the time for the delivery, the validity of the clause depends on whether the entrepreneur can influence the list price. Therefore, a manufacturer who determines his own prices cannot use this clause.

If the contract itself does not state a price, but the entrepreneur has the right to fix the price, Section 6, Paragraph 1, Number 5, of the Consumer Protection Act still applies. Although it does not expressly cover this case, the purpose of this provision requires that the entrepreneur state the relevant criteria for fixing the price.

---

1 Consumer Protection Act, Section 6, Paragraph 1, Number 5; and Section 6, Paragraph 2, Number 4.

5.1.3 Contractual Exclusion of Set Off

The entrepreneur's options to restrain or exclude the consumer's set off rights are limited if this would severely discriminate against the consumer with regard to his legal rights.[1]

The exclusion of set off is invalid if the entrepreneur becomes insolvent. Nor can it be excluded for accounts receivable which have a legal connection with the accounts payable, e.g., a consumer's liquidated warranty claim and the entrepreneur's claim for payment out of the same contract.

The other limitations are officially recognized claims and claims acknowledged by the entrepreneur.

5.2 Risk

In sales contracts, the seller bears the risk of loss or damage to the goods until the agreed time of performance or, if no time is agreed, until the time of the actual performance. If the seller is in delay with his performance, the risk does not shift to the buyer. Therefore, the risk normally passes to the buyer as soon as he is in possession of the goods. There are two exemptions:

(1) The buyer's delay in taking over the goods - In this case, the risk shifts to the buyer as soon as the seller offers his performance in accordance with the contract; in a sale of unascertained goods, the goods must be clearly identified to the contract at the time of performance; and

(2) Sales contracts to destination according to buyer's instructions - In cases where the contract involves carriage of the goods and it is agreed that the seller performs his obligation by sending them, the risk passes to the buyer as soon as the goods are handed over.[2]

These general regulations apply to consumer contracts.

---

1 Consumer Protection Act, Section 6, Paragraph 1, Number 8.

2 Civil Code, Section 429, ABGB, Article 8, Number 19, EVHGH.

5.3 Title

In general, the seller is obliged to transfer the title of the products to the buyer at the time of delivery. However, in cases where the buyer need not pay the full purchase price at that time, the parties can agree in the contract or later, but before the delivery, on retention of title. The seller then transfers the possession of the goods to the buyer, withholding ownership until the price has been fully paid. The retention of title serves as a security for the price. Clauses by which the seller attempts to withhold title until other possible claims against the buyer are settled are invalid.

There are no specific provisions concerning the transfer and retention of title for consumer contracts.

5.4 Conformity - Verification of Performance

A clause stating that the entrepreneur, or a person under his influence, has the power to decide with binding effect for the consumer whether the entrepreneur's performance is in accordance with the contract is void.[1]

5.5 Rejection, Right to Refuse Performance, Retention Rights

Austrian contract law gives the buyer the right to reject the goods at the time of delivery if they are not in accordance with the contract, even in cases of minor defects. If the buyer is entitled to reject the goods, he can refuse his own performance, under Section 1052 of the Civil Code, because contract obligations must be performed simultaneously if not otherwise agreed in the contract.

5.5.1 Right to Refuse Performance

For consumer contracts, Section 6, Paragraph 1, Numbers 6 and 7, of the Consumer Protection Act states that the consumer's rights of retention and his rights to refuse performance, under Section 1052 of the Civil Code, cannot be limited. Section 1052 of the Civil Code encompasses two cases.

---

1 Consumer Protection Act, Section 6, Paragraph 1, Number 10.

First, it establishes the general rule that a contract requires mutual simultaneous performance.

Second, if the parties have agreed to an advanced performance by one party, this party can suspend his performance and require a security before performance, if it becomes apparent that the other party cannot perform because of his financial situation.

The rights to withhold performance when the entrepreneur does not perform properly or his lack of creditworthiness becomes apparent cannot be excluded or restricted in consumer contracts.

This prohibition only applies to the consumer's statutory rights. Therefore, it remains generally possible that the parties agree to an advance performance by the consumer. Such a clause must be checked under the general rule of Section 879 of the Civil Code. If there is no reasonable justification for an advance performance by the buyer, such a provision could be *contra bono mores* because it only has the purpose of evading the law.[1]

5.5.2 Rejection

There are no regulations or court decisions relating to whether the right of rejection can be excluded in a consumer contract. The Consumer Protection Act does not expressly cover this case, dealing only with limitation or exclusion of warranty rights. Therefore, it is possible to vary this rejection right as long as this does not violate Section 879 of the Civil Code.

5.6 Warranty, Replacement, Refund

The Civil Code contains detailed provisions on warranties, but these provisions are, in general, not mandatory. The warranty liabilities are imposed by law and are independent of fault on the side of the seller. Austrian law does not distinguish between express and implied warranties or whether the warranty clause refers to merchantability or fitness of the goods for a particular purpose.

The main distinction is whether the defect is essential and whether it can be cured. Only if the defect is essential and cannot be cured may the buyer rescind the contract and require the refund of the price. In all cases where the defect can be cured, the buyer can require performance or

1 Krejci, in Rummel, *Kommentar ABGB*, 2nd ed., Paragraph 6, KSchG Rz 94.

reduce the price. If the defect is not essential and cannot be cured, the buyer can only demand a reduction of the price.

In general, warranty claims are for specific performance. As long as the defect is reparable, the buyer can choose whether he wishes the seller to remedy his performance or whether he wishes to reduce the price.

If the buyer requires performance, the seller can choose whether he wants to fulfill his duties by repairing the goods or, in the case of unascertained goods, by replacing them with other goods of the same species.

If the goods delivered are unreparable, but are items of unascertained goods, the buyer can require replacement with other goods of the same species. He can rescind the contract only if the seller does not replace the goods within a reasonable time.

The remedies do not extend to consequential damages. The buyer can claim damages only if the seller was at fault in selling defective goods, in which case he can claim consequential damages or he can seek damages instead of his warranty claims. This possibility to claim damages instead of warranty claims has only recently been granted by the courts, but it brings advantages for buyers because claims for damages come under the statute of limitations only three years after the damage has become apparent, while a warranty complaint must be filed within six months after the goods have been delivered.

For consumer contracts, Section 9 of the Consumer Protection Act makes these warranty provisions mandatory, except for two deviations which can be agreed on. The entrepreneur can fulfill his warranty obligation by delivering substitute new goods rather than paying back the price. In cases where the goods are reparable, the entrepreneur is entitled to demand that the goods be repaired rather than the purchase price reduced.

Other deviations and restrictions of the consumer's statutory rights are invalid. The warranty period of six months for goods and three years for real estate cannot be shortened; nor can the entrepreneur put the consumer under the obligation to examine the goods and to give notice of defects to preserve his warranty rights.

Furthermore, the consumer is entitled to request that repairs and completions be made at the place where the goods usually are located if this location is in Austria and if it is unreasonable for the consumer to transport the goods to the seller because of their bulk or weight.[1]

1 Consumer Protection Act, Section 8.

5.7 Liability for Damages

In Austrian law, contractual liability is based on a party's fault; it is not a strict liability. In consumer contracts, the entrepreneur cannot exclude or limit his liability in cases where he or persons he is responsible for have caused the damage willfully or by gross negligence. In general, liability for minor negligence can be excluded or limited.[1]

A clause excluding the entrepreneur s liability for goods which he has received for repair or other treatment or processing in general conditions is void. In this case even the liability for ordinary negligence can only be excluded if this was individually discussed and agreed on.[2]

5.8 Shift of Burden of Proof

Clauses which put the burden of proof on the consumer in cases where, pursuant to the law and general principles of burden of proof, the entrepreneur has this burden are invalid. The purpose is to ensure that the consumer can enforce his rights.[3]

5.9 Forfeiture

In service contracts, clauses that declare the goods handed over to the entrepreneur as forfeited after an unreasonably short time are void. What constitutes a reasonable period depends on the value of the goods, the cost, and any difficulties involved in storing the goods.[4]

The consumer may not have a disadvantage because of his minor negligence. Forfeiture means, in this context, the right of the entrepreneur to destroy, use, or sell the goods. If the goods are still there, the entrepreneur must give them back to the consumer even after the forfeiture period.

---

1 Consumer Protection Act, Section 6, Paragraph 1, Number 9.
2 Consumer Protection Act, Section 6, Paragraph 2, Number 5.
3 Consumer Protection Act, Section 6, Paragraph 1, Number 11.
4 Consumer Protection Act, Section 6, Paragraph 1, Number 12.

5.10 Statement Fictions

5.10.1 In General

The entrepreneur cannot require that a certain conduct of the consumer be deemed to be a statement or omission of a statement by the consumer, if this conduct would not have this meaning as a legal fiction or as an implied statement under Section 863 of the Civil Code.[1]

Under Section 863 of the Civil Code, conduct is an implied statement only if it reveals an intention beyond substantial doubt. Therefore, Section 6 prohibits the entrepreneur from creating statement fictions in a situation where, without this fiction, the meaning of the consumer's conduct does not show a clear intention.

In most cases, a point of reference for a deemed statement is the consumer's silence. However, this itself shows how dangerous such clauses can be for the consumer if he does not know about his obligation to answer.

5.10.2 Fiction that a Statement Has Reached the Consumer

Under Austrian law, generally, statements must reach the other party to be effective.[2] This rule cannot be changed to the disadvantage of the consumer.

5.10.3 Special Requirement for Consumer's Statements

A clause which requires the consumer to make his statements in a qualified form other than in writing and special communication requirements is void.[3]

5.11 Door-to-Door Sales

In door-to-door sales, Section 3, Paragraph 1, of the Consumer Protection Act gives the consumer the right to cancel the contract or his

1 Consumer Protection Act, Section 6, Paragraph 1, Number 2.

2 Civil Code, Section 862a, receipt principle; Consumer Protection Act, Section 6, Paragraph 1, Number 3.

3 Consumer Protection Act, Section 6, Paragraph 1, Number 4.

offer if the contract was concluded or the consumer's offer was made outside the entrepreneur's premises where he usually conducts his business.

The consumer may withdraw his offer at any time before he has received the acceptance. The right to cancel the contract must be exercised within one week after the contract has been concluded.

The entrepreneur has the duty to inform the consumer about the cancellation right and must hand over to the consumer a document stating the entrepreneur's name and address and the cancellation right. If the consumer is not informed concerning his right of cancellation, it ends one month after both parties have completely performed their obligations. The cancellation right in insurance contracts ends one month after the contract was concluded.

For door-to-door hire-purchase agreements[1] and sales of newspapers, periodicals, and magazines,[2] the cancellation right is unlimited if the notification document is not handed over to the consumer.

The consumer must cancel the contract in writing. The cancellation is effective if it is posted within the cancellation period. The cancellation right does not exist in the following situations:

(1) If the consumer initiated the business relationship; or
(2) If there were no negotiations between the parties prior to the conclusion, as is the case with contracts concluded by mail order.

The cancellation right does not apply to contracts with a price up to ATS 100 which usually are concluded outside of a business premises, such as a purchase of a newspaper or an ice cream on the street. If the type of business by its very nature is performed outside a permanent business premises, the cancellation right does not apply if the consideration is not more than ATS 300.

Section 54, Paragraph 3, and Section 60 of the Industrial Code give the consumer a similar cancellation right and make the violation of these information duties an administrative law offense.

1 Consumer Protection Act, Section 16.
2 Consumer Protection Act, Section 26.

5.12 Information Duties Concerning General Conditions of Sale

Section 73 of the Industrial Code obliges all entrepreneurs to display in their premises the general conditions they apply. This also applies to banks under Section 35, Paragraph 1, Number 1, of the Banking Act 1993.

Section 6

Reasonable Pricing and Price Controls

6.1 Price Information

As Austrian society is based on the concept of a free but social economy, the prices of goods are fixed via the market. However, a functioning market requires transparency of prices. The consumer only can make an informed choice if he has the information to compare products, and price information is of special importance.

The Price Information Act[1] obliges professional suppliers to show the prices for their goods and services. The Price information Act covers all offers of goods and services which are subject to the Industrial Code. The Industrial Code applies to the vast majority of trades, crafts, and industrial businesses. The Price Information Act also covers goods and drugs offered in pharmacies - except drugs which require a doctor's prescription - firearms, explosives, and tobacco products.

The Price Information Act does not apply to goods and services solely offered to other entrepreneurs and at auctions. Nor does it apply if the price information duty for a certain product or goods is more specifically regulated in another statute (e.g., banks). According to Section 35, Paragraph 1, of the Banking Act, banks must display in their premises the interest rates for savings accounts, the charges for services in connection with saving accounts and for other services, the effective interest rates for loans, and the general business conditions.

The Price Act requires that goods on display in a shop or offered for sale in another way in a shop be priced.

For services, the pricing obligation only exists after the Minister issues a decree naming the types of service businesses which have this duty and what it includes. Pricing for services is required only if necessary to enable the consumer to make price comparisons.

The price information must state the price including value added tax (VAT) and all other taxes and surcharges.

Violation of these duties and charging a higher price than the one marked on the product are administrative law offenses.

---

1 *Legal Gazette* 1992/14.

Based on Section 32, Paragraph 1, lit e, of the Unfair Competition Act, it can be ordered that, in addition to product price, the price per unit be made known.

Section 32 of the Unfair Competition Act gives authority to require price information in cases not covered by the Price Information Act.

6.2 Residual Control against Exorbitant Prices

In general, the question of price is left to party autonomy. Only if the relation of price and goods or services rendered is completely out of balance, or one party could not use his party autonomy, does the law provide remedies.

6.2.1 Indemnification

According to Section 934 of the Civil Code, a party can rescind a contract if it becomes apparent that he is receiving a consideration equal to less than half of what he must give.[1] The other party can uphold the contract, provided he makes up the deficiency according to common value. In consumer contracts, this provision is mandatory.[2] According to the Commercial Code, a merchant cannot invoke this remedy.[3]

6.2.2 Usury

A contract where one party exploits the improvidence, the strained financial situation, the lack of experience, or the frame of mind of the other party by causing him to promise or give a performance in exchange for a clearly disproportionate consideration is void.[4]

6.2.3 Partial Voidness

Section 917a of the Civil Code states that, if there exists a government-regulated minimum, maximum, or fixed price and the parties fix a

1 *Leasio enormis.*
2 Civil Code, Section 934a.
3 Commercial Code, Section 351a.
4 Civil Code, Section 879, Paragraph 2, Number 4.

price not in accordance with these provisions, such price fixing is invalid and the statutory price will apply.

6.2.4 Price Regulation by Administrative Law

The government's authority to regulate prices of goods and services is determined by the Price Act.[1] This regime applies as long as there are no special statutes for certain goods or services. The Price Act is part of an economic deregulation program of the Austrian government which reduces the state's regulating authority considerably.

Article 54 of the Constitution provides a regulation authority by the parliament for goods sold by a state-authorized monopoly.

According to the Industrial Code, as amended in 1992, the governor (*Landeshauptmann*) can fix maximum prices for certain products and services such as theater-ticket agencies,[2] chimney sweepers,[3] tourist guides,[4] and undertaker's establishments.[5]

6.2.5 Price Act

The Price Act 1992[6] in general gives authority to regulate prices only for crisis periods. Price regulation is allowed:

(1) For certain goods as a supplementary measure for trade guidance and rationing; and
(2) To overcome a lack of supply for goods which are not controlled or rationed.

The government in such cases can fix minimum and/or maximum prices. Apart from this price regulation in times of crises, there is only a general price regulation competence for certain drugs and medicines and for pipe-bound energy, electricity, gas, and municipal heating supply. The prices for all goods and services are subject to supervision to prevent abuse of market power.

---

1 Price Act, *Legal Gazette* 1992/145.
2 Industrial Code, Section 123.
3 Industrial Code, Section 177.
4 Industrial Code, Section 218.
5 Industrial Code, Section 239, and *see* Section 69.
6 *Legal Gazette* 1992/145.

6.2.6 *Price Regulation by Parity Commission*

The prices for eight product groups (milk and milk products; cereals, flour and semolina; brown bread; sugar; potato- and cornstarch; pipe-bound energy; cable television; and fuel oil and diesel) must be approved by the Parity Commission.

6.3 Estimates

The Consumer Protection Act provides that a consumer must pay for an estimate only if the entrepreneur informed him in advance regarding its cost.[1]

If the price for goods to be prepared or for services is based on an estimate, in consumer contracts, the entrepreneur must guarantee the price stated in the estimate. The entrepreneur and the consumer can agree otherwise.[2] According to general contract law,[3] an estimate is not binding; the entrepreneur only must notify the customer of the price increase. The customer can accept the higher price or rescind the contract but must pay for the work rendered up to that point.

6.4 Competition Law

The Austrian Cartel law can be regarded as a limited guarantee of justified prices. As both the abuse of monopolistic power and intended cartels are prohibited. A cartel can only be given consent by the Cartel Court, if it is politically or economically justified. One determining factor for this justification is how consumer interests are affected. Before taking its decision, the Cartel Court hears the Parity Cartel Board, whose members are nominated by the Chamber of Entrepreneurs and the Chamber of Employees.

Furthermore, if recommended retail prices for certain products exist but, in practice, these prices remain considerably under this limit, such a recommendation can be prohibited by a so-called net price decree.[4]

---

1 Koziol-Welser, *Grundriß des Bürgerlichen Rechts I*, 9th ed., at p. 509.
2 Consumer Protection Act, Section 5.
3 Civil Code, Section 1170a.
4 Hanreich, in Wenger, *Wirtschaftsrecht II*, 84.

In cases of misuse of dominant market power,[1] the procedure provided by the price Act can be applied.

6.5 Obligation to Contract

Retailers are obliged to sell to consumers usual quantities of essential goods. They are not allowed to hide their stock or to refuse to contract with a consumer.[2] Wholesalers are under an obligation to supply certain retailers if otherwise the local supply would be endangered. This also serves the purpose of consumer interests by preserving shopping facilities for necessary goods.

---

1 Cartel Code, Sections 34 and 35.
2 Local Supply Act, Section 5, *Nahversorgungsgesetz*.

Section 7

Installment Payments and Consumer Credit

7.1 Consumer Credit by Banks

On 1 January 1994, a new Banking Act[1] came into force. The consumer-oriented provisions of the Act are modified compared to the previous Banking Act.[2] In the following, only the regulations of the new Act are described. The amendments concerning consumer protection provisions were necessary to accord with the EC Directive on Consumer Credits,[3] although the Austrian Act contains some permissible deviations from the Directive.[4]

Section 33 of the Banking Act provides that consumer credits include all loans given by a bank and all building society loans to a consumer within the meaning of Section 1 of the Consumer Protection Act. There are no minimum or maximum limits for the amount of the loan.

The loan agreement must be concluded in writing, but it appears that this is not a validity requirement for the contract. At the conclusion of the loan agreement, the bank must inform the consumer in writing regarding the following details, and they must be part of the written contract:

(1) The total costs and the sum of public fees, taxes, and insurance fees in absolute figures;
(2) The effective yearly interest rate, as defined by Section 33, Paragraph 4, of the Banking Act, in digits;
(3) A reference to the fictive yearly interest rate and to the applicable interest rate on arrears;
(4) The terms of an interest adjustment clause, which must be based on objective criteria; and
(5) The number of payments, the amount of each payment, and the date of maturity of each payment.

Violation of this duty by a bank constitutes an offense under administrative law.

---

1 Banking Act, *Legal Gazette* 1993/532.
2 Banking Act 1979.
3 90/88/EWG, ABI 1990, Number L 61, 15.
4 Avancini, Iro, Koziol, *Bankvertragsrecht II*, at p. 105.

In civil law, it is quite difficult to asses the consequences of a bank's omission to inform. This omission to inform does not render the contract or its clauses void. Most likely, the consumer has the right to rescind the contract if he was mistaken regarding one of the facts for which the bank was obliged to provide inforamtion.[1] If the consumer rescinds the contract, he must pay back the loan. However, if without the mistake he would not have taken out a loan at all or would have been able to select a loan with better conditions, he can claim damages for the costs incurred by this mistake.[2]

A change in the interest rate must be notified to the consumer to become effective.[3] The Banking Act gives the consumer the right to pay back the loan earlier.[4] In this case, the bank must reduce the total costs by the interest and other costs which are not yet due.

At least once a year, the bank must send to the consumer a statement of account by 31 December. This statement must contain a detailed balance of the loan account.

Similar provisions apply to consumer current accounts, if the consumer is entitled to overdraw his account. To give the consumer the right to overdraw is a common practice of Austrian banks.[5]

According to Section 79 of the Insurance Supervision Act (*Versicherungsaufsichtsgesetz*), the provisions of Section 33 of the Banking Act also apply to loans granted to consumers by insurers.

7.2 Loans Arranged by Personal Loan Agents

According to Section 31 of the Consumer Protection Act, the personal loan agent loses his claim for commission if he does not inform the consumer about the name and the address of the credit grantor at the latest when the consumer receives the money. Notwithstanding the contract conditions, the consumer must pay an interest rate equivalent to only twice the bank rate of the Austrian National Bank if the agent acted not only on behalf of the consumer but also or only on behalf on the credit grantor. This is a rather strange provision, one without obvious justification.[6]

---

1 Consumer Protection Act, Section 872, Paragraph 2.

2 Avancini, Iro, Koziol, *Österreichisches Bankvertragsrecht II*, 1993, Rz 1/152 *et seq.*, with an overview of the possible solutions and with further references.

3 Banking Act 1994, Section 33, Paragraph 6.

4 Banking Act, Section 33, Paragraph 6.

5 Banking Act, Section 34.

6 Avancini, Iro, Koziol, *Österreichisches Bankvertragsrecht II*, 1993, Rz 1/154.

7.3 Hire-Purchase Contracts

7.3.1 Definition

The rules for hire-purchase contracts are established in the Consumer Protection Act. These special protection regulations apply to all sales of goods where the overall price is not higher than ATS 310,000 and the entrepreneur hands over the goods to the consumer before he has paid the price and where the consumer must pay the price in at least two installments. Service contracts are not covered; nor is the sale of investment products.[1]

7.3.2 Disclosure by the Entrepreneur

The entrepreneur must draw up a document called a *Ratenbrief* (Installment letter), which must contain the following details:

(1) The name, profession, and address of both parties;
(2) The date and place of the offer or the acceptance of the consumer;
(3) The total price, amount of the deposit, and number, amount, and due dates of the installments;
(4) The date of delivery; and
(5) A statement whether a bill of exchange or other securities for the payments were agreed.

For door-to-door contracts, the special consumer's right to rescind the contract applies.[2] The entrepreneur must give to the consumer a copy of the installment letter. If the entrepreneur does not follow these rules, he can be fined, but it does not effect the validity of the contract.

According to Section 73, Paragraph 8, of the Industrial Code, entrepreneurs offering their goods or services on a hire-purchase basis must display the yearly interest rate in their premises and state it in their catalogs, direct-mailing advertisements, and other leaflets. At the conclusion of the contract, the consumer must be informed about the yearly interest rate in writing. The latest amendment of the Industrial Code[3]

---

1 Krejci, in Rummel, *Kommentar ABGB*, 2nd ed., Paragraph 16, KSchG Rz 5.
2 Consumer Protection Act, Section 3.
3 *Legal Gazette* 1993/29.

provides that the government can issue a code of conduct for entrepreneurs offering or granting credits.[1]

The code can include information duties concerning the cost and payment moralities. This gives the government the necessary flexibility to adjust these rules to the EU Directives on consumer credits.

7.3.3 Consumer's Payment Obligations

In each hire-purchase contract, the consumer must make a minimum down payment. The down payment requirement is intended to prevent consumers from entering too easily into sales contracts for goods they cannot afford. The amount of the down payment is ten per cent of a price up to ATS 3,000 and twenty per cent of an amount exceeding ATS 3,000.

The entrepreneur loses his price claim, in the amount of the required down payment, if he delivers the goods without having received the down payment.

The maximum repayment period is five years, with effect from the date of delivery. If the contract states a longer repayment period, the entrepreneur is not entitled to the interest and other costs for the time after the five-year period, but the consumer can use the full period to pay back the loan.

7.3.4 Delay in Payment

In all cases where a consumer must pay the price in installments and is in delay, the entrepreneur must observe certain procedural regulations to terminate the credit. The entrepreneur and the consumer can agree on a clause to the effect that the whole obligation becomes due under the following conditions.

According to Section 13 of the Consumer Protection Act, the entrepreneur can terminate the credit and call for the full credited amount only if the consumer is in arrears with at least one payment for more than six weeks and the entrepreneur has warned the consumer about the consequences and has fixed an additional period of at least two weeks for the consumer to pay the money due. In addition, the entrepreneur must have performed his obligation completely.

---

1 Industrial Code, Section 73, Paragraphs 6 and 7.

7.3.5 Extension of Warranty Period

For all hire-purchase contracts, Section 23 of the Consumer Protection Act extends the warranty period for material defects until the maturity date of the final installment.

7.3.6 Premature Pay-Back of Loan

Like Section 33, Paragraph 8, of the Banking Act, Section 12a of the Consumer Protection Act gives the consumer the right to pay back a loan early and save the interest and other costs not yet due.

This right does not exist for certain real estate loans and, more importantly, for loans exceeding ATS 310,000 and for leasing contracts if they are more like rent contracts than financing agreements.

7.3.7 Other Contracts Equivalent to Hire-Purchase Sales

Section 17 of the Consumer Protection Act attempts to ensure that contract arrangements designed to circumvent the regulations applicable to hire-purchase sales are still governed by these regulations. The types of contracts equivalent to a hire-purchase sale are defined by case law and legal doctrine. These include, for example, a hire contract where, after a certain period, the consumer becomes the owner of the goods, and leasing contracts if the leasee has the same risks concerning the goods as an owner[1] and cash sales where the seller gives the buyer a loan to pay for the cash price.

Thus, the rules for hire-purchase sales apply to other contracts if the parties attempt to reach the same economic purpose as a hire-purchase sale, so long as such contract fulfills the other conditions of Section 16 of the Consumer Protection Act.

7.4 Sales Contracts Financed by a Third Party

Sales contracts as defined by Section 16 of the Consumer Protection Act, where the price is financed by a third party, are considered to be a

---

1 Krejci, in Rummel, *Kommentar ABGB*, 2nd ed., Paragraph 18, KSchG Rz 5; Krejci, in Egger-Krejci, *Das Leasinggeschäft*, 1987, at pp. 78 *et seq.*

special category of agreement.[1] Sales contracts and loan agreements together fulfill the same economic purpose as a hire-purchase agreement.[2] The loan agreement itself might be covered by the provisions for consumer credits, but those provisions do not cover the special problems of hire-purchase contracts.

For the consumer, the situation is the same as in a hire-purchase sale. He pays the price, plus interest, in installments and receives the goods at once. However, because the price is financed by a third party and not credited by the seller, the consumer would not have the protection of Section 16 of the Consumer Protection Act. More importantly, if the goods received are defective or if the seller commits another breach of contract, the consumer must repay the loan for the price back to the financier and cannot refuse performance as he could as to the seller.[3]

Therefore, it is the purpose of Sections 18 and 19 of the Consumer Protection Act to ensure that the consumer's protection in hire-purchase contracts is not undermined by splitting the hire-purchase sale into a sales contract and a financing agreement.

To protect the consumer's rights, therefore, Section 18 of the Consumer Protection Act states that the rules on hire-purchase sales[4] also apply to the contract between the consumer and the financier, if the sales contract and the financing contract are considered to be an economic unity, both for the seller and the financier and if the other conditions of Section 16 of the Consumer Protection Act are fulfilled.

Section 18 of the Consumer Protection Act states that there is an economic unity if there is a legal relationship between the seller and the financier in the handling of the sales and their financing or if they have a continuous business relationship in financing the entrepreneur's sales. The legal link can be based on a contract for financing or the fact that the seller assigns his claims and transfers the proprietary rights to the financier. A *de facto* business relationship is sufficient, even if the seller and the financier work together without a contractual framework. According to case law and legal doctrine, the sales contract and the financing contract form an economic unity if the seller and the financier work together.

In such cases, the consumer can refuse performance against the financier as long as he has this right to refuse performance against

---

1 Consumer Protection Act, Sections 18-19.

2 Krejci, in Rummel, *Kommentar ABGB*, 2nd ed., Paragraph 18, KSchG Rz 1.

3 Civil Code, Section 1052.

4 Consumer Protection Act, Sections 16-25.

the seller.[1] He must assert his right of refusal against the financier, but his claims arising out of the sales contracts (e.g., warranty claims, avoidance of the contract, and damages) must be asserted against the seller and not the financier. The consumer is not allowed to simply stop his payments.

Regulations regarding the minimum deposit and the maximum pay-back period apply to the financier.

The Consumer Protection Act does not provide specific rules for restitution in cases where the sales contract has been rescinded. The main question is whether the consumer must pay back the full loan to the financier, although he might not recover all his payments back from the seller.[2]

If the connection between the sales contract and the financing contract is not quite as close, so that the financier cannot be treated as the seller is, there may be cases where the seller induced the consumer to buy the goods on a credit and, therefore, the consumer will have the same rights against the seller as if the seller had financed the price himself.[3] These are cases where the sales contract and the financing contract form an entity for the seller but not for the financier.

If the consumer takes out a loan independently of the seller, Section 19 of the Consumer Protection Act does not apply.

The new provision of Section 26c of the Consumer Protection Act offers further protection of the consumer in contracts financed by a third party. Notwithstanding whether the conditions of a hire-purchase sale according to Sections 16 *et seq.* of the Consumer Protection Act are fulfilled, the consumer always has the same rights against the financier as against the supplier if there is an arrangement between the supplier and the financier regarding the financing of the supplier's contracts.

It also is required that the supplier has not performed his obligation to deliver or that the goods delivered or the services rendered are defective and that the consumer has attempted to enforce his rights against the supplier without success. The regulation does not apply to leasing contracts when the consumer does not, at the end of the contract, become the owner of the leased goods, but it applies to third-party-financed service contracts.

---

1 Consumer Protection Act, Section 18, Paragraph 2.

2 Krejci, in Rummel, *Kommentar ABGB*, 2nd ed., Paragraph 19, KSchG Rz 28.

3 Consumer Protection Act, Section 19.

Section 8

Trade Descriptions - Occupational Licensing

According to the Industrial Code, anyone who wants to carry out a trade in Austria must obtain a trade permit. For all crafts and for the so-called qualified trades, the issuance of a trade permit depends on a proof of qualification.

The proof of qualification is intended to secure a minimum standard of trade services offered. How the professional skills must be proven differs from trade to trade.[1]

Companies and other legal entities applying for a trade permit must have a manager or an employee who has the necessary qualifications. He is then the representative of the company.[2]

In civil law, the trade permit of a contract partner is of special importance in the law of misrepresentations. According to Section 873 of the Civil Code, a party to a contract who is mistaken about the other party's trade permit can rescind the contract.[3]

In addition to the general trade permit, the Industrial Code[4] gives the government the authority to issue codes of conduct (*Ausübungregeln*) for businesses covered by the Industrial Code. The last amendment of the Industrial Code[5] has widened this competence, but it will be exercised only where it is necessary for the protection of customers against financial loss and against harassment of their privacy. At present, there are codes of conduct for personal loan agents, estate agents, address agencies, chemical cleaners, and dating agencies.

---

1 Industrial Code, Sections 16-23.
2 Industrial Code, Sections 9 and 39.
3 Koziol-Welser, *Grundriß des Bürgerlichen Rechts I*, 9th ed., at p. 125.
4 Industrial Code, Section 69, Paragraph 2.
5 *Legal Gazette* 1993/29.

Section 9

Merchandise Classes

Except under the provisions of the Quality-Class Act, merchandise classes have no importance in consumer protection in Austria.

Section 10

Implementing Consumer Rights

10.1 Information

Information relating to consumer rights is mainly provided by the Association of Consumer Information, which has information centers throughout the country, and by the local departments of the Chamber of Employees and the Austrian Confederation of Trade Unions.

10.2 Material Incentives

Punitive awards or other material incentives in civil law actions are, in general, unknown to the Austrian legal system. In administrative law, the normal sanctions for the infringement of certain provisions are fines.

10.3 Class Actions

Austrian procedural law, in general, does not provide for class actions. In the area of consumer protection, there are two special class actions provided by Sections 28, 29, and 30 of the Consumer Protection Act and Section 14 of the Unfair Competition Act.

10.3.1 Class Action under the Consumer Protection Act

Certain interest groups, such as the Austrian Chamber of Commerce, the Austrian Chamber of Employees, the Austrian Chamber of Agriculture, the Austrian Confederation of Trade Unions, and the Association for Consumer Information, can sue entrepreneurs who use general sales conditions which contain illegal provisions. These actions can demand that the entrepreneur refrain from using such clauses.

10.3.2 Class Action under the Unfair Competition Act

In cases of violations of Sections 1 and 2 of the Unfair Competition Act and other special regulations of the Unfair Competition Act, the Austrian Chamber of Employees, the Austrian Chamber of Agriculture, and the Austrian Confederation of Unions can take actions against the entrepreneur to enforce general consumer protection interests.

10.4 Streamlined Procedures

Special procedures for litigation between consumers and entrepreneurs do not exist. For some branches and in certain counties, mediation committees exist, but they are of little importance.

The entrepreneur cannot restrict the consumer's rights and access to legal remedies in the contract. According to Section 14 of the Consumer Protection Act, the permissibility of a mutually agreed place of jurisdiction is restricted. Clauses to the effect that the consumer can be sued in a place different than his place of residence or domicile or place or work are void. The consumer's right to sue the entrepreneur at any of the entrepreneur's statutory venues cannot be excluded.

10.5 Technical and Material Support Groups

Consumers may receive free legal advice from the Association of Consumer Protection and the Chamber of Employees.

Belgium

Jules Stuyck and Chantal Goemans
University of Leuven
Leuven, Belgium

Belgium

Belgium

Section 1

Introduction

1.1 Private Law, Administrative Law, and Self-Regulation

Belgian consumer law is a mixture of private and public law rules. It is one of the areas of law where the borderline between private law and public law has become increasingly academic. Substantive provisions are very often enforced by penal sanctions while, at the same time, individual consumers who are prejudiced by the infringement, along with the Minister of Economic Affairs, and consumer organizations can bring an action for a cease and desist order before the Commercial Court. This action is provided for by the central piece of legislation in consumer matters: the Trade Practices and Consumer Protection Act 1991. The action for a cease and desist order also can be brought by competitors or trade organizations in the event that their interests (or those of their members) are affected by the wrongful act.

As a result, rules of consumer protection are often enforced by private actions from competitors who are put at a competitive disadvantage by infringements of these rules by their competitors. The very large scope of the action for a cease and desist order under the Trade Practices and Consumer Protection Act 1991 stems from the doctrine of "illegal competition", by virtue of which the infringement of any rule laid down by law or regulation may be considered as an act which is contrary to honest business practices within the meaning of the Trade Practices and Consumer Protection Act 1991, i.e., an act of "unfair competition". According to the Trade Practices and Consumer Protection Act an action for a cease and desist order can be brought against every infringement of that Act, including acts of unfair competition.

With regard to private law in the proper sense, the Code Napoleon, the French Civil Code from 1804 and still in force in Belgium, plays an important role. First, there are the still fundamental, general principles of contract law. One of these principles is that contracts must be concluded and executed in good faith. Before the entry into force of the Trade Practices and Consumer Protection Act 1991, with its specific rules on unfair contract terms and its general obligation for undertakings to inform consumers properly in the pre-contractual phase, the courts have construed the general principle of good faith in contractual matters in order to restore to a certain extent the imbalance between undertakings and consumers which is caused by the use of standard contract terms and adhesion contracts.

Moreover, in the area of consumer sales, the courts have interpreted the provisions of the Civil Code on the seller's liability for defective goods in such a way as to give consumers - even *vis-à-vis* producers with whom they have no contractual relationship - a fairly comprehensive protection in the event of accidents with unsafe consumer goods. Since the 1960s, the legislature has adopted a number of specific Acts, granting the consumer contractual protection in the following areas:

(1) The purchase of real property and construction contracts;
(2) Tenancy of primary residences;
(3) Installment sales; and
(4) Home party sales.

In these areas, the reciprocal obligations of the parties are fixed by mandatory rules, and contract clauses contrary to these rules are held null and void. Another technique of protection consists of providing for a trial period during which the consumer can withdraw from his or her contractual engagement. The nullity sanction and a trial period are also provided for in a number of provisions of the Trade Practices and Consumer Protection Act 1991, which introduced additional protection against sales concluded outside normal business premises, mail-order sales, and unfair contract terms (in general). Civil law sanctions are also contained in the Consumer Credit Act 1991, which contains a comprehensive set of rules for the different kinds of consumer credit (and not only installment sales and personal installment loans, as in the Installment Sales Act of 1957).

Finally, both the Trade Practices and Consumer Protection Act 1991 and specific consumer-protection statutes[1] impose formalities in the contractual field. The contract must be in writing and must comprise a certain number of specifications in order to inform the consumer properly about the nature of the product or service and the reciprocal rights and

---

1 Consumer Credit Act 1991, Land Insurance Act 1992, and Mortgage Credit Act 1992.

duties of the parties. Administrative sanctions are provided for in the Trade Practices and Consumer Protection Act 1991 and the Consumer Credit Act 1991 with regard to licensing and registration duties for the exercise of certain activities. The main administrative sanction consists of the withdrawal of the license or the authorization or the deletion of the registration. The exercise of the activity without license, authorization, or registration, where this is required, is a criminal offense.

In this way, penal sanctions come into play again. Many other licensing or authorization requirements are provided for in a significant number of statutes regulating the access to certain economic activities, such as banking, insurance, travel agencies, the manufacturing and distribution of medicines, and a considerable number of crafts and retail activities. One of the aims of these rules is to protect consumers against fraud, poor quality, or inexperienced professionals. These laws and regulations show the same mixture of administrative law and criminal law.

A great number of typical consumer protective rules, particularly in the areas of trade descriptions, safety, and foodstuff law, are primarily punishable with criminal sanctions, such as fines, imprisonment, and confiscation.

Criminal sanctions are seldom applied in consumer law. The reasons for this situation range from a lack of (specialized) inspectors to establish offenses and staff within the offices of the public prosecutors to the awareness of complainants that civil sanctions (in particular, periodic penalty payments) often are more effective.

1.2 Primary Interest Groups

1.2.1 Strictly Consumer-Oriented Organizations

The Consumer Union is the only organization in Belgium which can be qualified as a consumer organization in the real sense, as all its activities are directed toward informing consumers and defending their rights and interests.

The Consumer Union publishes a monthly consumer magazine, *Test Aankoop/Test-Achats*, and more specialized periodicals, as well as brochures and books on consumer affairs.

The Consumer Union is represented in the Consumer Council and is a member of the European Consumer Association (BEUC).

1.2.2 Other Organizations Representing Consumer Interests

Many other organizations are active in the field of consumer affairs and are recognized by the public authorities as representing consumers even though the protection of consumer interests is not their sole objective.

The most important of these organizations are the three trade unions (Christian, socialist, and liberal), the Christian and the socialist cooperative movement, and the family organization *Bond van Grote en Jonge Gezinnen/Ligue des Familles*. All these organizations also are represented on the Consumer Council.

1.2.3 The Research and Information Centre of Consumer Organizations

In 1975, the Minister of Economic Affairs launched several campaigns aiming to raise consumer awareness regarding the price of goods and services in a period of hyper-inflation. The consumer organizations convinced the minister that it would be better to replace the occasional campaigns by permanent consumer information.

It was then decided that part of the budget of the Ministry of Economic Affairs was to be allocated on a permanent basis to subsidize a Centre to be established and managed by the consumer organizations, the task of which would be to undertake research and provide information in consumer matters.

1.3 Public Law Structure for Consumer Protection

1.3.1 Government Level

Consumer protection is a national competence. Since there is no Ministry of Consumer Affairs, consumer matters fall under the jurisdiction of the Ministry of Economic Affairs or the Ministry of Justice, depending on whether it relates to market regulation, e.g., the Trade Practices and Consumer Protection Act, or civil law, e.g., product liability. The government which was formed in 1991 has one minister responsible for Justice and Economic Affairs. Consumers can file complaints about undertakings with the Ministry of Economic Affairs, more specifically with the Consumer Service established within the Ministry.

1.3.2 The Consumer Council

The Consumer Council is a consultative committee established within the Ministry of Economic Affairs by the Royal Decree of 20 February 1964.[1]

According to the Royal Decree of 9 December 1992,[2] which has modified the Council's existing composition, the Council consists of one president, two vice-presidents, and thirty-six ordinary members. All are appointed by the Minister of Economic Affairs. Eighteen members represent consumer organizations, ten represent trade associations in the production sector, three represent the organizations of distributors, two the organizations of farmers, and three represent small and medium-sized businesses. Finally, six members are chosen from experts in consumer matters, environment, and public health. They exercise the function of a permanent expert and have no voting rights.

The task of the Council consists of:

(1) Issuing, on its own initiative or at the request of the Minister of Economic Affairs, opinions expressing the different viewpoints of its members in relation to consumer affairs and proposals on actions which are taken or should be taken in the interest of consumers;
(2) Enabling the different interests groups it represents to discuss all matters relating to consumer affairs; and
(3) Implementing documentation on problems and matters addressing the interests of consumers and of coordinating and harmonizing consumer information initiatives.

The Consumer Council has played an important role in the preparation of recent major Acts in the area of consumer protection, such as the Trade Practices and Consumer Protection Act 1991 and the Consumer Credit Act 1991.

The Trade Practices and Consumer Protection Act 1991 established the Commission for Unfair Contract Terms within the Consumer Council.[3]

---

1 BS, 2 April 1964.
2 BS, 7 January 1993.
3 Trade Practices and Consumer Protection Act 1991, Article 35.

1.3.3 Consumer Representation in Consultative Committees

Consumers also are represented in a number of other consultative committees, such as the Commission for Price Regulation, the Central Economic Council, the Commission for Insurance, and the Commission for Unfair Contract Terms. In all these consultative committees, however, consumers are only represented by other (not strictly) consumer oriented organizations, such as cooperatives, family organizations, and the trade unions.

1.4 Market Regulatory Systems

Monopolies exist in the area of public utilities, such as postal services, telecommunications, railways, and the distribution of gas, electricity, and water, but have tended to disappear with the liberalization at the European Union (EU) level and the privatization wave of public enterprises which began in 1993 with the privatization of the state bank CGER. Monopolies have already disappeared in the areas of broadcasting and air transport. All the monopolies are state-owned or so-called "mixed" enterprises. Belgium has a mixed economy.

The state participates in the private economic sector, not only by exercising economic activities of its own, but also as a partner of private initiative. The national airline Sabena is a joint venture of the French state airline Air France and the Belgian state. In Distrigaz, the natural gas importer and distributor, the state has held (until now) fifty per cent of the shares, while the two most important shareholders are a private electricity company and an oil company.

Electricity distribution and cable re-transmission are also in the hands of private enterprises, who enjoy local (natural) monopolies.

Broadcasting is a somewhat special case since, both on the Dutch-Speaking and the French-Speaking regions of Belgium, one public television network (each with two to three channels) competes with a private one. The public stations are basically financed by a tax levied on the viewers, while the private stations receive their income from advertising.

Railway transport, telecommunications, postal services, air transport, and the distribution of energy are the subject of special regulations which aim at the continuity of the service in the general interest and, to a lesser but increasing extent, the protection of consumers against abuses.

Apart from special provisions in the different statutes on the establishment of the different utilities operators, protection of the public in general against monopolistic abuse is provided in three different ways. First, there is the control of the (federal and regional) parliaments over the (respective) governments. The government remains responsible for the management of public enterprises, even if they are given a certain autonomy. Second, there is the applicability of the Competition Act (including a prohibition of abuse of dominant positions) on the public sector. Third, there is a control by the federal Minister of Economic Affairs on price increases. Contrary to what is now (since the entry into force of the Competition Act on 1 April 1993) the case for most of the other products and services, price increases for oil, tele-distribution, gas, and electricity must be notified to the minister, who can oppose the increase.

In the area of consumer protection, attention also may be drawn to the creation of a Consumer Ombudsman for each public enterprise benefiting from management autonomy, pursuant to the Act of 21 March 1991 on public enterprises. The first example of application of this new status is the telecommunications operator, BELGACOM.

Section 2

Consumer Product and Service Standards

While the quality of services is ensured by rules governing the access to and the exercise of particular professions or economic activities, there are numerous statutory and regulatory provisions establishing a minimum quality standard for products or reserving the use of certain product names for products which comply with certain minimum quality requirements. More and more of these rules are the implementation of EU Directives.

2.1 General Regime

The general regime is based on two Acts: the Foodstuffs and Related Products Act of 24 January 1977[1] and the Trade Practices and Consumer Protection Act of 14 July 1991.[2]

2.1.1 The Foodstuffs and Related Products Act

2.1.1.1 Source of Rule

This is an Act of the national legislature (the King, in cooperation with the federal parliament). There are also numerous EU Directives regulating these matters.

2.1.1.2 Scope and Application

In principle, all foodstuffs fall within the scope of this Act, as well as a few other consumer goods which may endanger the health of consumers.

According to Article 1 of the Act, foodstuffs are all products and entities intended for human nutrition, including stimulants, salt, and spices.

---

1 BS, 8 April 1977, most recently amended by the Act of 22 March 1989, BS, 26 October 1989.

2 BS, 29 August 1991; err, BS, 10 October 1991, most recently amended by the Act of 5 November 1993, BS 11 November 1993.

The other products to which the Act applies are:

(1) Additives, aromatics, and technological catalysts;
(2) Objects or substances intended to be brought in contact with foodstuffs;
(3) Detergents, cleaning, and maintenance products;
(4) Tobacco, products with a tobacco base, and similar products;
(5) Cosmetics;
(6) Articles of use which may cause a physiological effect through absorption of parts of them, either through inhalation or through contact with the human body;
(7) Aerosols intended for foodstuffs and the products stated in items (1) through (6); and
(8) Products which are not what they seem and, therefore, may endanger the safety or health of consumers.

2.1.1.3 Substantive Provisions

The Act confers extensive powers on the King in matters relating to foodstuffs. The King can regulate and even prohibit, in the interest of public health or with a view of avoiding fraud or falsification, the production, the export, and the commerce of foodstuffs; production being not only the way of manufacturing but also packaging and labelling. This power includes the power to determine the composition of a foodstuff and the name under which it is placed on the market, and to prescribe the information which may or may not be delivered in connection with foodstuffs (e.g., labelling and advertising).

The King can also regulate and prohibit the marketing of diet foodstuffs, vitamins, and foodstuffs to which vitamins, oligo-elements, or nutrients have been added.[1] Moreover, in the interest of public health, the King can prescribe general labor hygiene measures and health regulations to be observed in the production and commerce of foodstuffs.[2] He also regulates the presence and labelling of additives[3] and contaminants in foodstuffs.[4] Finally, he can regulate and prohibit advertising pertaining to foodstuffs and relating to their composition, dietetic qualities or their effect on health.[5]

---

1 Foodstuffs and Related Products Act 1977, Article 2.
2 Foodstuffs and Related Products Act 1977, Article 3.
3 Foodstuffs and Related Products Act 1977, Article 4.
4 Foodstuffs and Related Products Act 1977, Article 5.
5 Foodstuffs and Related Products Act 1977, Article 7.

With regard to the other products encompassed in Article 1 of the Act, the King's powers differ depending on the product. Thus, the power to regulate and prohibit the production, the export, and commerce, including the power to determine the composition and the corresponding name of the products and to prescribe the information to be delivered applies to all these products, except for additives and products which are not what they seem. This also is the case with the powers conferred on the King by Article 3.[1] Tobacco, cosmetics, articles of use with a possible physiological effect, and aerosols are the only products for which the King can determine the substances they may contain.[2]

The King may regulate the registration of cosmetics[3] and advertising pertaining to additives, aromatics, and technological catalysts, detergents, cleaning and maintenance products, cosmetics, articles of use possibly having a physiological effect, and alcohol and alcoholic drinks.[4] He also can regulate the advertising regarding tobacco, products with a base of tobacco and similar products and limit or prohibit their use in public places and transport.[5]

2.1.1.4 Standing, Procedures, and Sanctions

According to Article 11 of the Act, and without prejudice to the competencies of the officers of the judicial police, the mayor and officials appointed by the King supervise the compliance with the Act and its implementing Decrees.

To this end, they may inspect business premises, storage rooms, and production facilities and examine all documents relating to the products to which the Act applies. Furthermore, since the Act is aimed at protecting public health against potentially dangerous products, these officials are not only allowed to take samples[6] but also to seize or remove harmful products from the market.[7]

They report offenses and send a copy of the report to the offender within ten days from the establishment of the offense. Three options are then open to them. They can inform the Public Prosecutor or notify the

---

1 Foodstuffs and Related Products Act 1977, Articles 3 and 6.
2 Foodstuffs and Related Products Act 1977, Article 6.
3 Foodstuffs and Related Products Act 1977, Article 6.
4 Foodstuffs and Related Products Act 1977, Article 7.
5 Foodstuffs and Related Products Act 1977, Article 7.
6 Foodstuffs and Related Products Act 1977, Article 12.
7 Foodstuffs and Related Products Act 1977, Article 18.

official appointed by the King within the Ministry of Public Health, or they can act according to the procedure of Article 11 bis. This procedure consists of warning the offender that, if he or she does not bring the infringements to an end within a specified period of time, the report shall be submitted to the said official, in which case the Public Prosecutor might be informed. When notified, the Public Health official may decide on an administrative fine to be paid by the offender. If he or she refuses to pay, the report will be sent to the Public Prosecutor.[1]

Non-observance of the Act and the Decrees implementing it also carries criminal sanctions. These sanctions differ depending on whether the offender merely places the products on the market, knowingly commits an infringement by trading in them, or is a manufacturer or importer.[2] The sanctions vary from eight days' to three months' imprisonment and/or a BF 26 to BF 300 fine for the first category, eight days' to six months' imprisonment and/or a BF 50 to BF 1,000 fine for the second, and one month to one year imprisonment and/or a BF 100 to BF 15,000 fine for the last category.

Without prejudice to Articles 269 and 274 of the Criminal Code (regarding resistance to public officials), Article 16 of the Act sanctions the refusal to comply with or the opposition to the inspection of the premises or the taking of samples by investigating officials with fifteen days' to three months' imprisonment and/or a BF 100 to BF 2,000 fine.

Refusing to submit to a medical examination or to comply with the prohibition of or the restraints to one's activity carries a prison sentence of one month to one year and/or a fine of BF 100 to BF 15,000.[3]

If the offenses are repeated within three years after conviction, the sentences will be doubled.[4]

The Criminal Code itself also contains sanctions in these matters. The sanctions range from six months' to five years' imprisonment with additional fines of BF 200 to BF 2,000 for mixing substances which can cause death or serious harm to the health with foodstuffs, as well as for consciously selling substances intended for the falsification of foodstuffs or foodstuffs which are mixed with the said substances.[5] Storing foodstuffs mixed with these substances with the intention of selling them carries three months' to three years' imprisonment and fines of

1 Foodstuffs and Related Products Act 1977, Article 19.
2 Foodstuffs and Related Products Act 1977, Articles 13-15.
3 Foodstuffs and Related Products Act 1977, Article 15.
4 Foodstuffs and Related Products Act 1977, Article 17.
5 Criminal Code, Articles 454 and 455.

BF 100 to BF 1,000.[1] Article 457 of the Criminal Code regulates the seizure, confiscation, and the rendering useless of the foodstuffs which are mixed with the harmful substances. The guilty party can furthermore be deprived of his or her rights, and the court will order the judgment to be made public. All fines must be multiplied by 100.

The Trade Practices and Consumer Protection Act 1991 extended the action for a cease and desist order to all acts of undertakings which are contrary to honest business practices and which are likely to prejudice the interests of one or more consumers.[2] According to well-established case law, infringements of legal provisions in the course of a business are contrary to honest business practices. This means that an action for a cease and desist order, pursuant to the Trade Practices and Consumer Protection Act 1991, can be brought in the event of infringement of the Foodstuffs and Related Products Act or other provisions of consumer law, and this in addition to the possibility for the Public Prosecutor to act on the basis of the criminal sanctions provided for in the relevant statute.

If the President of the Commercial Court establishes the existence of such an infringement of the Foodstuffs and Related Products Act, the court can order the offender to cease the infringement.[3]

Non-compliance with a cease and desist order is a criminal offense. More important is the frequently used possibility for the president to impose a periodic penalty payment for every day his order is not respected or for every new act (e.g., advertisement) in contravention of the order. The president also may order the publication of his judgment or a summary thereof.[4]

The action for a cease and desist order is brought forth as in summary proceedings (in essence, shorter time limits for summons and for the hearing of the case).

The action for a cease and desist order of the Trade Practices and Consumer Protection Act 1991 can be brought by every party who has a direct and individual interest, e.g., an individual consumer. In addition, in consumer matters, the action can be brought by the Minister of Economic Affairs and by consumer organizations represented in the Consumer Council.[5]

---

1 Criminal Code, Article 456.
2 Trade Practices and Consumer Protection Act 1991, Article 94.
3 Trade Practices and Consumer Protection Act 1991, Article 95.
4 Trade Practices and Consumer Protection Act 1991, Article 99.
5 Trade Practices and Consumer Protection Act 1991, Article 98.

2.1.2 Trade Practices and Consumer Protection Act 1991

2.1.2.1 Source of Rule

The origin of the law of unfair competition, which is now part of the Trade Practices and Consumer Protection Act 1991, goes back to the application of Article 1382, i.e., the provision on tort liability of the Civil Code of 1804, to the relationship between competitors. In the nineteenth century, the courts qualified certain commercial practices, such as the creation of confusion between one's business and the business of a competitor, and forms of advertising which misleads consumers to the prejudice of a competitor or denigrate a competitor, as unlawful acts within the meaning of Article 1382 of the Civil Code. Belgium adhered to the Paris Convention of 1883, which created a Union for the Protection of Industrial Property. In 1900, at the Brussels Conference, Article 10 bis was inserted into that Convention. This Article imposes an obligation on the Members of the Union to treat all citizens of the Union equally with respect to the protection against unfair competition. The Paris Convention (in force in Belgium in the Stockholm version of 1967),[1] approved by the Act of 26 September 1974,[2] defines unfair competition as an act which is contrary to honest business practices.

The prohibition of unfair competition, as defined by the Paris Convention, was a kind of extension of the protection of industrial property. Not only patents, trademarks, designs or models, and copyright, belonging to a trader's business should be protected against encroachment, but also the business name or goodwill, elements which are not specifically protected by an absolute right. In order to improve the enforceability of the prohibition of unfair competition contained in Article 1382 of the Civil Code and in the Paris Convention, which is directly applicable in Belgium, Royal Decree Number 55 of 23 December 1934 was introduced. This Royal Decree contained a general prohibition of acts of unfair competition as defined by the Paris Convention and introduced a new remedy: the action for a cease and desist order.

This action can be brought before the President of the Commercial Court by a competitor who suffers an actual or potential prejudice as a result of an act of unfair competition. The action can be brought forth

1 BS, 14 July 1967.
2 BS, 29 January 1975.

according to the procedural rules governing summary proceedings for interim measures - which means that a decision can be taken quickly - with the following two important exceptions:

(1) No urgency is needed for the admissibility of the action; and
(2) The decision taken by the President of the Commercial Court is not provisional but definitive (subject to appeal).

Compliance with the cease and desist order is ensured by making infringements of the order a criminal offense.

Beginning in the 1930s, the legislature also intervened to protect established merchants (small businesses, in particular) and sometimes consumers against certain sales methods and methods of sales promotion. Rules on premium offers, auction sales, seasonal sales, price indication obligations, and a licensing system for hawking were enacted in separate Acts which provided criminal sanctions.

The Trade Practices Act of 14 July 1971 had two main objectives. The first was to bring the different rules on advertising and sales promotion together into a single Act and to extend the scope of application of the action for a cease and desist order (until then, only available against acts of unfair competition) to the rules on sales methods and sales promotion. The second objective was to ensure better information and protection for consumers. The rules on the indication of prices and quantities were improved, the King was given new powers to establish rules with regard to labelling, misleading advertising was expressly prohibited, and consumer organizations were given the opportunity to bring an action for a cease and desist order against certain infringements of the Act (namely, those relating to advertising and sales methods).

The Act on Trade Practices and the Information and Protection of the Consumer 1991 maintains the system of the Act of 1971 but contains an important number of new rules aimed at strengthening the legal protection of consumers and improving the enforceability of the existing prohibitions and obligations. The new provisions include:

(1) The action for a cease and desist order was extended to all infringements of the Act;
(2) A new general clause prohibiting unfair conduct *vis-à-vis* consumers was introduced; and
(3) A prohibition of unfair contract terms was introduced.

The Trade Practices and Consumer Protection Act 1991 also implements EU Directives in the area of consumer protection.[1] The provisions on unfair contract terms contained in the Trade Practices and Consumer Protection Act 1991 also have been influenced by the proposal for a Directive on unfair contract terms in consumer contracts which was adopted on 5 April 1993.[2] Other Directives in the area of consumer protection (product liability and consumer credit) have been implemented by separate Acts: the Product Liability Act 1991 and the Consumer Credit Act 1991.

2.1.2.2 Scope and Application

Most of the provisions of the Trade Practices and Consumer Protection Act 1991 apply to sellers. This notion is broader than the notion of merchant used in the Commercial Code, but it is different from the notion of undertaking which determines the scope of application of the Competition Act 1991.

The seller is defined in Article 1(6) of the Trade Practices and Consumer Protection Act 1991 as:

> "(a) every merchant or craftsman and every natural or legal person who offers for sale or sells products or services in the exercise of a professional activity or with a view to realizing its articles of association;
>
> "(b) the public bodies or legal entities in which the public authorities have a predominant share and which exercise a commercial, a financial, or an industrial activity and which offer for sale or sell products or services;
>
> "(c) the individuals who, either in their own name or on behalf of a third party, which either has or does not have the legal personality, pursue, either with or without the intention of making a profit, a commercial, financial, or industrial activity and offer for sale or sell products or services."

Whether a person is a seller, to whom the provisions of the Trade Practices and Consumer Protection Act 1991 apply, depends on whether he or she offers for sale or sells "products" or "services" within the meaning of the Act.

---

1 Directive on Misleading Advertising of 10 September 1984, OJ 1984 L 250/17; Directive on Contracts Concluded outside Business Premises, OJ 1985 L 372/31.

2 Directive 93/13/EEC, OJ 1993 L 95/29.

A "product" is defined as a tangible, movable good. Therefore, the trade in securities and other intangible goods does not fall within the scope of the Act. Immovables also are excluded. The provisions on advertising, however, apply to all goods and obligations, i.e., intangible goods as well as immovables.

"Services" are all performances which constitute a commercial act or a craft activity. If craft activities can be disregarded here (they are not important in practice), this means that, for the services sector, the application of the Trade Practices and Consumer Protection Act 1991 is limited to merchants within the meaning of the Commercial Code and to parties who, although not merchants, occasionally perform a commercial act, e.g., a non-profit association in the educational or cultural field serving meals or organizing shows for remuneration, or a private individual earning an additional income by selling products or services.

It is clear that, if public undertakings, as well as the public authorities themselves, offer for sale or sell products or services as defined above, they must comply with the provisions of the Trade Practices and Consumer Protection Act 1991. Therefore, the Act applies to the public telecommunications operator BELGACOM, the public energy companies, and the public transport companies.

From the foregoing, it can be concluded that the Trade Practices and Consumer Protection Act 1991 does not apply to the professions, since their activities are not considered to constitute a commercial act. The sale of immovables also is excluded since the Act only applies to products (however, the provisions on advertising apply to all goods and obligations). It is uncertain whether the advertising provisions of the Act apply to securities and other financial instruments within the meaning of the Act on financial markets and financial transactions.

Although intangible goods do not fall under the definition of "product" and, therefore, do not fall within the general scope of application of the Act, Article 22 of the Trade Practices and Consumer Protection Act 1991 determining the scope of application of advertising provisions, refers to products, services, immovables, and all "rights and obligations", as provided for by the EU Directive on misleading advertising. "Rights and obligations" seem to include securities. Article 1, *in fine*, however, of the Act provides expressly that "this Act does not apply to securities and other financial instruments as determined by the legislation on financial transactions and financial markets". This question being resolved, however, it is noteworthy that the latter legislation contains comprehensive provisions against misleading advertising.

2.1.2.3 Substantive Provisions

Chapter II of the Trade Practices and Consumer Protection Act 1991 applies to the information of the consumer and contains provisions on price indication, on indication of the quantities, and on the denomination, the composition, and the labelling of products. Chapter III confers powers on the King in matters of designations of origin. Chapter IV contains very detailed advertising prohibitions. General provisions concerning the sale of products and services to the consumer can be found in Chapter V, which contains a general information duty, a regulation of unfair contract terms, and obligations for sellers to deliver certain documents to the consumer. Chapter VI of the Act regulates or forbids the following sales methods and methods of sales promotion:

(1) Sales at a loss;
(2) Announcement of price reductions and price comparisons;
(3) Clearance sales;
(4) Seasonal sales;
(5) Premium offers;
(6) Auction sales;
(7) Unsolicited sales;
(8) Distance sales;
(9) Pyramid sales; and
(10) Sales outside the business premises of the seller.

These provisions will be discussed in more detail in their respective sections below. Acts contrary to honest business practices, however, will be addressed here.

Acts of unfair competition are prohibited in Belgium, pursuant to Article 10 *bis* of the Paris Union Convention on industrial property, inserted into that Convention in 1900. Originally, the courts condemned acts of unfair competition, i.e., according to the Union Convention, acts which are contrary to honest business practices on the basis of the general provision of the Civil Code on tort liability.[1]

A Royal Decree of 1935 confirmed the unlawfulness of acts contrary to honest business practices and introduced the action for a cease and desist order, an effective means to combat unfair competition. The Trade Practices Act of 1971 maintained, in addition to many *per se* prohibitions (relating to misleading and comparative advertising and

---

1 Civil Code, Article 1382.

certain sales methods), the general prohibition of unfair competition. The Trade Practices and Consumer Protection Act of 1991 follows the same line. The general clause on unfair competition of Article 93 now reads:

> "Every conduct which is contrary to honest business practices by which a seller prejudices or may prejudice the professional interests of one or more other sellers is prohibited."

It is well-established case law that, apart from conduct which is contrary to commercial usages based on ethical rules governing industry and trade (e.g., the prohibition of industrial espionage, slandering or hindering a competitor, misleading the public, and exploiting a competitor), the general clause also covers any infringement, in the conduct of a business, of a legal or administrative provision, irrespective of the objectives of the provision in question.[1] At the request of competitors who were put at a competitive disadvantage, the courts have ordered undertakings to cease infringements of the law of establishment, tax law, social security, labor law, Sunday trading rules, price regulations, the law on lotteries, and antitrust law.

It is important to point out here that the Trade Practices and Consumer Protection Act 1991 also has introduced a new general clause of special interest to consumer protection matters. Article 94 reads:

> "Every conduct which is contrary to honest business practices by which a seller prejudices or may prejudice the interests of one or more consumers is prohibited."

Nearly two years after the adoption of this new provision, there is still no application.

2.1.2.4 Standing, Procedures, and Sanctions

The powers of the civil servants appointed by the Minister of Economic Affairs to investigate and establish infringements of the Act are similar to those of the inspectors who operate within the framework of the Foodstuffs and Related Products Act.[2] These powers also apply to investigations of possible infringements which, without being subject

1 Cass., 2 May 1985, [1985] Pas., I, 1081.
2 Trade Practices and Consumer Protection Act 1991, Articles 113 and 117.

to criminal sanctions, may be the object of an action for a cease and desist order initiated by the Minister of Economic Affairs.[1]

Where the investigators find that the Act has been violated, they have the same options open to them as the investigators under the Foodstuffs and Related Products Act. They can immediately report the offenses to the Public Prosecutor,[2] they can follow the warning procedure,[3] or they can offer the offender to settle out of court by paying an administrative fine.[4]

Pursuant to Article 101 of the Act, the Minister of Economic Affairs or a civil servant designated by him can issue a warning to any party who has infringed the provisions of the Trade Practices and Consumer Protection Act 1991. The warning, which must be issued within three weeks after establishing the offenses, consists of informing the offender that, if he or she does not cease the infringement of the Act within a specified period, one of the following measures will be taken:

(1) The minister will initiate an action for a cease and desist order;
(2) The investigators appointed by him will notify the Public Prosecutor; or
(3) The civil servants appointed by the Minister to this end will propose a settlement to the offender.

If the offender pays an administrative fine, criminal proceedings will not be initiated.[5]

Infringements of certain provisions of the Act (those concerning the information of the consumer and the prohibition of pyramid sales) are sanctioned with fines of BF 250 to BF 10,000.[6] In case of an infringement in bad faith of any provision of the Act (e.g., an offender who disregards the warning of Article 101 may be held to act in bad faith), the criminal courts may impose a fine of BF 500 to BF 20,000.[7] This provision is seldom applied, since bad faith is difficult to prove. A fine of BF 1,000 to BF 20,000 also may be imposed on those who do not comply with a cease and desist order of the president of the Commercial Court or on those who obstruct the investigation proceedings of Articles 113 *et seq.*[8] Presently, all fines should be multiplied by 100.

---

1 Trade Practices and Consumer Protection Act 1991, Article 114.
2 Trade Practices and Consumer Protection Act 1991, Article 113.
3 Trade Practices and Consumer Protection Act 1991, Article 101.
4 Trade Practices and Consumer Protection Act 1991, Article 116.
5 Trade Practices and Consumer Protection Act 1991, Article 116.
6 Trade Practices and Consumer Protection Act 1991, Article 102.
7 Trade Practices and Consumer Protection Act 1991, Article 103.
8 Trade Practices and Consumer Protection Act 1991, Article 104.

The President of the Commercial Court can establish the existence of an infringement of the Trade Practices and Consumer Protection Act 1991 (and, through the general clauses of Articles 93 and 94, also an infringement of any other Act, provided other sellers or consumers are prejudiced) and order the offender to cease the infringement.[1] Non-compliance with a cease and desist order is a criminal offense.

More important is the frequently used option of the President to impose a periodic penalty payment for every day his order is not respected or for every new act (e.g., advertisement) in contravention of his order. The president also may order the publication of his judgment or of a summary thereof.[2] The action for a cease and desist order is brought as in summary proceedings (in essence shorter time limits for summons and for the hearing of the case).

The action for a cease and desist order does not apply to acts of imitation or counterfeit which fall within the scope of the specific statutes on patents, trademarks, designs and models, and copyrights.[3] According to established case law, the action of Article 95 of the Trade Practices and Consumer Protection Act also is excluded against conduct which constitutes a violation of a contractual obligation (e.g., the non-observance of a non-competition clause in a contract for the transfer of a business).

The action for a cease and desist order of the Trade Practices and Consumer Protection Act 1991 can be brought by every party who has a direct and individual interest (e.g., a competitor or an individual consumer), the Minister of Economic Affairs (except in the case of infringement of Article 93), trade associations with legal personality (except in the case of an infringement of Article 94), and consumer organizations represented in the Consumer Council.[4]

2.2 Special Regimes

2.2.1 Food

The Foodstuffs and Related Products Act has been dealt with above. Numerous Royal Decrees have been made to implement it.

1 Trade Practices and Consumer Protection Act 1991, Article 95.
2 Trade Practices and Consumer Protection Act 1991, Article 99.
3 Trade Practices and Consumer Protection Act 1991, Article 96.
4 Trade Practices and Consumer Protection Act 1991, Article 98.

2.2.2 *Drugs*

2.2.2.1 *Source of Rule*

The rules governing these matters are found in the Drugs Act of 25 March 1964,[1] most recently amended by the Act of 29 December 1990.[2] This legislation implements EU Directives in this area.[3]

2.2.2.2 *Scope and Application*

Primarily, the Drugs Act applies to drugs and, according to Article 1, drugs are all substances which are presented as possessing therapeutic or prophylactic characteristics with regard to human or animal diseases. Also considered as drugs are all substances which are intended to be administered to humans or animals in order to establish a medical diagnosis or to remedy, improve, or modify organic functions. The drugs must comply with the provisions of the pharmacopoeia.[4]

Article 1 *bis* enables the King to extend the applicability of all or some of the provisions of the Act to objects, equipment and substances which are intended to be used in health care and which have diagnostic, preventive and therapeutic characteristics. When adding this Article in 1983 the legislature had several products in mind, such as magnetic bracelets, ultraviolet lamps, internal prostheses, pacemakers, artificial organs, cement or amalgams to be used in dentistry, surgical materials, substances which can provide indications of diabetes and pregnancy, and contraceptives.

In the interest of public health, the King can determine the professional qualifications which the retailers of these products must possess.[5]

2.2.2.3 *Substantive Provisions*

Article 6 empowers the King to regulate and supervise, in the interest of public health, the import, export, manufacture, preparation, transportation, distribution, possession, retention, offer for sale, sale, transfer for

1 BS, 17 April 1964.

2 BS, 9 January 1991.

3 *See*, for example, Council Directive 92/28/EEC of 31 March 1992, on advertising for drugs for human consumption, OJ 1992 L 113/13.

4 Drugs Act of 25 March 1964, Article 2.

5 Drugs Act of 25 March 1964, Article 6 *ter*.

consideration or for nothing, packaging, packages, denomination, content and labelling of the packages, and delivery of drugs. To this end, every drug must be registered with the Ministry of Public Health before it can be brought on the market.[1]

A prescription is required for the sale of these registered drugs to the public, until such time as the Minister of Public Health decides to lift this restriction. The King can prohibit the stated activities completely or partially where they involve a drug which is considered to have a harmful effect or if its effect is insufficiently established.[2] If there are reasons to believe that the effect of a drug can be harmful or if it is not sufficiently established that the drug is therapeutically ineffective, the Minister of Public Health can suspend the delivery of that drug or attach special conditions to it, such as a prescription.[3]

Article 9 regulates the advertising of drugs. Primarily, it prohibits all advertising for unregistered drugs or for drugs the delivery of which is suspended or prohibited according to Articles 7 and 8. It empowers the King to prohibit all advertising aimed at the public involving prescription drugs or drugs intended for treatment of diseases or conditions. The King can, in the interest of public health, regulate or subject to selective prohibitions the advertising aimed at the public and at professionals.

It is prohibited to offer, directly or indirectly, premiums or benefits at the time of the delivery of drugs. Manufacturers, importers, and wholesalers of drugs are prohibited from, directly or indirectly, offering or giving premiums or benefits to parties authorized to prescribe drugs. It is, furthermore, prohibited to request or accept premiums or benefits.[4]

Article 11 of the Drugs Act empowers the King to regulate the information to be given to the public and to professionals. This power includes the possibility to impose informative texts, the content of which can be determined for each drug by the Minister of Public Health. The information aimed at the public must at least be formulated in the language(s) of the area in which the drug is distributed. The information principally targeted by Article 11 are the instructions delivered with drugs, and these instructions are regulated by Royal Decree.

The King also can establish the general conditions under which manufacturers, importers, and wholesalers may effect or encourage

---

1 The registration of drugs is regulated by Royal Decree of 3 July 1969, BS, 10 July 1969, most recently amended by Royal Decree of 27 November 1992, BS, 12 December 1992.

2 Drugs Act of 25 March 1964, Article 7.

3 Drugs Act of 25 March 1964, Article 8.

4 Drugs Act of 25 March 1964, Article 10; *see* the Trade Practices and Consumer Protection Act 1991, which prohibits joint offers, as discussed below.

clinical tests with drugs. The Minister of Public Health can prohibit the parties from effecting or encouraging tests which do not comply with these conditions.[1]

The King can exempt pharmacists and other parties who are entitled to distribute drugs from complying with their obligation to guarantee the quality and conformity of the drugs delivered by them. The Minister of Public Health can recognize laboratories which conduct quality and conformity checks on behalf of the pharmacists and other authorized persons without, however, relieving the latter from their responsibilities.[2] Finally, the King is responsible for establishing the content and publication of the pharmacopoeia. A copy of the latter must be present in pharmacies at all times.[3]

2.2.2.4 Standing, Procedures, and Sanctions

The King appoints civil servants within the Ministry of Public Health who are responsible for the supervision of the compliance with this Act and its implementing Decrees. They may inspect the relevant premises and examine all documents. If the drugs are found to be counterfeit or falsified, they will be seized, and samples of them will be taken. If drugs are decayed, expired, or not in compliance with the Act and its implementing provisions, the civil servants may destroy the drugs with the assent of the parties concerned. Failing such assent, the drugs will be seized.

Within three days after establishing the offenses, a copy of the report will be sent to the offender.[4] The Public Prosecutor also is informed. Some infringements are sanctioned with criminal prosecution; for others, the Public Prosecutor may decide not to prosecute and to instead notify the civil servant appointed by the King. In this case, the civil servant determines the administrative fine to be paid by the offender, who is notified by registered mail. This notification renders a criminal suit impossible. Payment of the fine settles the claim of the administration, and failure to pay the fine within the specified period of time will result in court action brought by the civil servant.[5]

Criminal prosecution excludes administrative fines, even if the criminal prosecution results in acquittal.

---

1 Drugs Act of 25 March 1964, Article 6 *bis*.
2 Drugs Act of 25 March 1964, Article 13.
3 Drugs Act of 25 March 1964, Article 2.
4 Drugs Act of 25 March 1964, Articles 14, 15, and 16.
5 Drugs Act of 25 March 1964, Article 17.

Selling, offering for sale, or distributing counterfeit, decayed, or expired drugs, and drugs which do not conform with the registered formula carries fines of BF 26 to BF 500. Infringements of Articles 3 and 6, Paragraph 3, of the Drugs Act and their implementing Decrees, and of the implementing Decrees of Articles 6 *bis*, and 6 *ter*, Paragraphs 2, 11, and 13 are sanctioned with fines of BF 100 to BF 1,000 and/or imprisonment of eight days to one month. Infringement of Article 9 and its implementing Decrees or of the implementing Decrees of Articles 7 and 8 is sanctioned with fines of BF 500 to BF 15,000 and/or one month to one year imprisonment. The refusal or obstruction of investigative measures, sample taking, and seizing of drugs carries the same penalty as does the counterfeiting of drugs and the sale, offer for sale, and distribution of counterfeit, decayed, or expired drugs, and drugs which do not conform with the pharmacopoeia or the registered formula, as well as storing these products with the intention to sell or distribute them.

Finally, non-observance of the implementing Decrees relating to drugs containing sedatives, narcotics, or psychotropic substances which can lead to dependence, the list of which is established by the King, is sanctioned with fines of BF 1,000 to BF 100,000 and/or three months' to five years' imprisonment.[1] All fines must be multiplied by 100.

If the offenses are repeated within three years after conviction for infringement of the Act and its implementing Decrees, the sentences can be doubled.[2] As stated previously, an action for a cease and desist order can be brought against any act which is contrary to honest business practices.

2.2.3 Motor Vehicles

2.2.3.1 Source of Rule

The technical requirements with which cars, their trailers, their parts, and their safety accessories must comply are regulated by the Royal Decree of 15 March 1968.[3] The most recent Act regulating these matters is the Act of 21 June 1985.[4]

This legislation implements numerous EU Directives in this area.

---

1 Drugs Act of 25 March 1964, Article 16.

2 Drugs Act of 25 March 1964, Article 18.

3 BS, 28 March 1968, err., BS, 24 April 1968, most recently amended by Royal Decree of 12 December 1991, BS, 24 December 1991.

4 BS, 13 August 1985.

2.2.3.2 Scope and Application

The Act applies to vehicles for transportation on land, including their parts and safety accessories, which are intended to be used in Belgian traffic.[1] Not only is the Act not applicable to trailers; there is a discrepancy between the notions used in the Act and in the Royal Decree. The former refers to "vehicle", whereas the latter uses the term "car". According to Article 1 of the Royal Decree, a car is a motor vehicle weighing more than 400 kilograms, with the exclusion of motorbikes and motorcycles. Article 1 also contains an extensive list of very detailed definitions of different types of cars, their parts, and definitions of mass and loading capacity.

2.2.3.3 Substantive Provisions

In the interest of traffic safety and to promote rational energy consumption, the King establishes:

(1) The technical requirements to be met by vehicles for transportation by land, by their parts, and by the safety accessories designated by him, such as requirements relating to their construction, assembly, recognition, homologation, and repair and maintenance;
(2) The measures to control whether the regulations which are referred to in item (1) are applied; and
(3) The conditions under which the constructors or manufacturers must prove that the vehicles, their parts, and safety accessories, intended for Belgian traffic, comply with the regulations referred to in item (1).

The King may entrust the control of vehicles which are brought into circulation to bodies recognized by him. The King also is empowered to take all measures necessary to implement international obligations, in these matters, primarily EU law.[2]

Detailed technical requirements for the different parts of the vehicles, conditions for recognition as a constructor, homologation procedures, and the detailed rules on the technical inspection can be found in the Royal Decree. With regard to the periodical technical inspections, it must be noted that they apply not only to vehicles used for commercial

---

1 Act of 21 June 1985, Article 1.
2 Act of 21 June 1985, Article 1.

purposes, but also to vehicles for private use. Generally, all vehicles are inspected by the officially recognized service for automobile inspection before they are introduced on the market for the first time or before they are brought on the market again. After that, they are inspected every three or six months or every one or two years, depending on the type of car and its use. For passenger cars, a yearly inspection is imposed as of the fourth year after the car was initially brought into circulation although, in certain cases, exemptions are provided. A certificate is delivered after inspection.[1] Vehicles without a valid inspection certificate or with a non-compliance certificate prohibiting it for traffic are not allowed on public roads, unless in exceptional cases provided by the Royal Decree.[2]

2.2.3.4 Standing, Procedures, and Sanctions

According to Article 2 of the Act, the King establishes the rules concerning administrative control for examination of the compliance of vehicles, their parts, and safety accessories with the recognized or homologated type. He can, with due consideration for the right of defense, determine the administrative measures for implementation of these rules. Those measures include the withdrawal of the recognition or the homologation. An appeal can be lodged with the Minister of Transport who makes a decision after consulting with the competent consultative committee in which administration and industry are equally represented. He also can bring legal action to obtain the removal of vehicles, their parts, and safety accessories from the market, or he can institute legal proceedings aimed at taking vehicles, their parts, and safety accessories off the market or removing them from use in traffic.

The King appoints civil servants, qualified police officers, and officers of the judicial police who are charged with the investigation of infringements of this Act and Decrees relating to the technical requirements regarding vehicles for transportation on land, their parts, and their safety accessories. The civil servants have access to all business premises (except for laboratories and test and research centers) and to the vehicles, their parts, and safety accessories. They may examine all business documents directly relating thereto. They may take copies of those documents and ask for explanations. They also may test the vehicles, their parts, and safety accessories, or have them tested pursuant to Article 2 of the Act.

---

1 Royal Decree of 15 March 1968, Article 23.
2 Royal Decree of 15 March 1968, Article 24.

The undertaking must pay for and bear the risks of the tests. These measures can only be taken if they are deemed necessary for the investigation of crimes and with due respect for the confidentiality of manufacturing secrets. All qualified parties (i.e., civil servants, police officers, and officers of the judicial police) are empowered to report infringements of the Act and the Decrees. Infringements can be committed by parties who manufacture, assemble, repair, sell, exhibit, lend, or lease the non-complying products and also by individuals who use these products. A copy is sent by registered mail to the offender within eight days from the establishment of the infringement.[1]

Without prejudice to possible damages to be paid, non-observance of the Act and the Decrees relating to the technical requirements regarding vehicles for transportation on land, their parts, and their safety accessories carries a fine of BF 10 to BF 10,000 and/or eight days' to three months' imprisonment. If the same offense is repeated within two years after the previous conviction, the sentence will be at least doubled. The competent courts to hear these cases are the police courts, i.e., magistrate courts for all criminal offenses.

The courts may prohibit natural or legal persons who have infringed the rules about construction and recognition of vehicles, their parts, and safety accessories from selling or leasing out, personally or through an intermediary, the same category of products for use in Belgium during a period of one to twelve months. This also applies when these parties are only civilly liable. The prohibition can become permanent if the same offense is repeated within five years following the previous conviction.[2] The limitation period for the public prosecution of these offenses is five years from the day on which they took place.[3] All fines are multiplied by 100.

If the conditions are applicable, the action or a cease and desist order also can be brought forth in the event of infringement of the Act.

2.2.4 Electrical Appliances

2.2.4.1 Source of Rule

These matters are regulated by the Act of 11 July 1961, relating to the indispensable safety guarantees for machines, parts of machines, materials,

1 Act of 21 June 1985, Article 3.
2 Act of 21 June 1985, Article 4.
3 Act of 21 June 1985, Article 5.

tools, appliances, and recipients,[1] most recently amended by the Programme Act of 22 December 1989,[2] and by the Royal Decree of 23 March 1977,[3] implementing it with regard to the safety guarantees of electrical machines, appliances, and wires. The Royal Decree implements Council Directive 73/23/EEC of 19 February 1973 on the harmonization of the laws of EU Member States relating to electrical equipment designed for use within certain voltage limits.[4]

2.2.4.2 Scope and Application

The Act enables the King to impose safety requirements for machines, parts of machines, materials, tools, and appliances. Article 2 of the Royal Decree defines "electrical machine and appliance" as every device designed to produce, transform, distribute, or use electrical energy and "wire" as single or assembled conductors with their individual or common mantle. The Royal Decree does not, however, apply to the following categories:

(1) Electrical equipment for radiology and medical purposes;
(2) Electrical parts of goods and passenger lifts;
(3) Electricity meters;
(4) Electrical equipment with regard to its radio-electrical interference;
(5) Specialized electrical equipment for use on ships, aircraft, or railways which comply with the safety provisions established by international bodies in which the EU Member States participate.

The Royal Decree also does not apply to electrical equipment intended for export to non-EU countries and, in part, to plugs and socket outlets for domestic use.[5]

2.2.4.3 Substantive Provisions

Article 1 of the Act empowers the King to establish the safety requirements with which machines, parts of machines, materials, tools, and

---

1 BS, 24 July 1961.

2 BS, 30 December 1989; *see also* Council Directive 89/392/EEC of 14 June 1989 on the approximation of the laws of the Member States relating to machines, OJ 1989 L 183/9, amended by Council Directive 91/368/EEC of 20 June 1991, OJ 1991 L 198/16.

3 BS, 31 March 1977.

4 OJ 1973 L 77/29.

5 Royal Decree of 23 March 1977, Article 1.

appliances of a dangerous nature must comply to be imported, manufactured, stored, offered for sale, disposed of, delivered after repair, leased, lent, handled, exported, transported, or used. Article 3 of the Royal Decree states that the electrical equipment must be constructed in accordance with sound engineering practice and that it may not endanger the safety of individuals, domestic animals, or property when properly installed and maintained and used in applications for which it was intended.

The principal elements of the safety objectives consist of three parts:

(1) General conditions;
(2) Protection against hazards arising from electrical equipment; and
(3) Protection against hazards which may be caused by external influences on the electrical equipment.

It is prohibited to deal in electrical equipment which does not comply with the provisions of Article 3.[1] Plugs and socket outlets for domestic use must comply with standards relating to them. These standards must be homologated by the King or registered by the Belgian Institute for Standardization.[2]

2.2.4.4 *Standing, Procedures, and Sanctions*

Within one month from notification, the party concerned may request, by registered mail, that the Minister authorize a new test. Based on the results of this new test, or where such a test was not requested within the period, the Minister, advised by the competent consultative committee, can, for safety reasons, prohibit the equipment in question from being brought onto the market.[3]

Without prejudice to the powers of the officers of the judicial police, the King appoints civil servants within the Ministries of Economic Affairs and of Employment and Labor charged with supervising the compliance with the Act and its implementing Decrees.[4] They must act in accordance

1 Royal Decree of 23 March 1977, Article 4.
2 Royal Decree of 23 March 1977, Article 10 *bis*.
3 Royal Decree of 23 March 1977, Article 11.
4 Programme Act of 22 December 1989, Article 2, and Royal Decree of 23 March 1977, Article 14.

with the provisions of the Act on Labor Inspection[1] and are also empowered to enter all business premises, make inventories, take samples, and seize or seal the equipment which is the object of the infringement.[2]

The limitation period for the public prosecution of an infringement of the Act and its implementing provisions is three years from the day on which the offense took place.[3] An action for a cease and desist order can be brought against any act which is contrary to honest business practices.

2.2.5 *Tools*

The Act of 11 July 1961, relating to the indispensable safety guarantees for machines, parts of machines, materials, tools, and appliances,[4] most recently amended by the Programme Act of 22 December 1989, also regulates these matters. Apart from the Act, there are no provisions specifically regulating the safety of tools in the interest of the general public. The safety of tools, however, is regulated in the interest of specific categories of parties.[5]

2.2.6 *Textiles*

Textiles fall within the scope of application of the Foodstuffs and Related Products Act. More specifically, they are considered articles of use which may cause a physiological effect through contact with the human body.[6] Some aspects (e.g., designations), however, are regulated by the Trade Practices and Consumer Protection Act 1991.

The Royal Decree of 22 May 1984,[7] which implements Article 6, Paragraph 1(b) of the Foodstuffs and Related Products Act and Council

---

1 Act of 16 November 1972, BS, 8 December 1972, Article 2.

2 Programme Act of 22 December 1989, Article 3.

3 Programme Act of 22 December 1989, Article 9.

4 BS, 24 July 1961.

5 *See*, e.g., the General Regulation for Labor Protection, approved by Regency Decrees of 11 February 1946 and of 27 September 1947, BS, 3 April 1946 and 3 and 4 October 1947, most recently amended by Royal Decree of 14 September 1992, BS, 20 September 1992.

6 Foodstuffs and Related Products Act of 24 January 1977, Articles 1, 2; (f).

7 BS, 14 July 1984.

Directive 76/769/EEC[1] and its amendments[2] prohibit the marketing of textiles intended for contact with the human body and which contain tris, dibromopropyl, phosphate, tris-(aziridinyl) phosphinoxide, and polybrominatedbiphenyls. Textiles which satisfy the conditions established in Article 1 of the Royal Decree are declared harmful and can be seized according to the provisions of Article 18 of the Foodstuffs and Related Products Act.

2.2.7 Toys

2.2.7.1 Source of Rule

The Act of 29 June 1990[3] and its implementing Decree of 9 March 1991[4] regulate the safety of toys. The Act and the Royal Decrees were made pursuant to EU Council Directive 88/378/EEC of 3 May 1988 on the approximation of the laws of the Member States concerning the safety of toys.[5]

2.2.7.2 Scope and Application

Article 1 of the Act defines "toy" as any product or part thereof designed or clearly intended for use in play by children of less than fourteen years of age. Article 1 of the Royal Decree excludes twenty-one items from the scope of application. These items are listed in Annex I of the Royal Decree and include Christmas decorations, scale models for adult collectors, sports equipment, and video toys.

---

1 Directive of 27 July 1976 on the approximation of the laws, regulations, and administrative provisions of the Member States relating to the restrictions on the marketing and use of certain dangerous substances and preparations, OJ 1976 L 262/201.

2 In particular, those introduced by the Council Directives 79/663/EEC and 83/264/EEC, OJ 1979 L 197/37 and OJ 1983 L 147/9.

3 BS, 18 July 1990, most recently amended by Royal Decree of 22 March 1993, BS, 24 April 1993.

4 BS, 14 May 1991, most recently amended by Royal Decree of 22 March 1993, BS, 24 April 1993.

5 OJ 1988 L 187/1.

2.2.7.3 Substantive Provisions

Toys may be placed on the market only if they do not jeopardize the safety or health of users or third parties when they are used as intended or in a foreseeable way, bearing in mind the normal behavior of children. In the condition in which it is placed on the market, taking into account the period of foreseeable and normal use, a toy must meet the safety and health requirements established in Annex II of the Royal Decree.[1]

Annex II, which states the essential requirements, mainly describes three general principles. The first principle to be observed is that the users of toys, as well as third parties, must be protected against health hazards and risk of physical injury when toys are used as intended or in a foreseeable way, bearing in mind the normal behavior of children.

Second, the degree of risk present in the use of a toy must be commensurate with the ability of the users and, where appropriate, their supervisors, to cope with it. This applies in particular to toys which, by virtue of their functions, dimensions, and characteristics, are intended for use by children under thirty-six months of age. To observe this principle, a minimum age for users of toys, as well as the need to ensure that they are used only under adult supervision, must be specified where appropriate.

Finally, labels on toys and/or their packaging and the instructions for use which accompany them must draw the attention of users or their supervisors fully and effectively to the risks involved in using them and the ways of avoiding such risks.

The Annex also imposes requirements aimed at avoiding particular risks relating to physical and mechanical properties, flammability, chemical properties, electrical properties, hygiene, and radioactivity.

Toys which comply with Article 2 of the Act of 29 June 1990 are provided by the manufacturer (i.e., the producer, the importer, or the distributor[2]) with an EU mark.[3] This mark denotes conformity with the relevant national standards which transpose the harmonized standards. The Belgian standards must be published in the Belgian State Gazette and the harmonized standards in the Official Journal of the EU. Toys bearing the mark are presumed to comply with the provisions of Article 2

---

1 Royal Decree of 22 March 1993, Articles 2 and 3.

2 Act of 29 June 1990, Article 1.

3 Act of 29 June 1990, Article 3.

of the Act.[1] Toys, for which no particular requirements are provided or for which these requirements cannot be met or can be met only in part, nevertheless may be provided with the EU mark if they are in conformity with an approved model which has been subjected to an EU-type examination, carried out by an officially recognized body.[2]

The EU mark, together with the name and/or the company name and/or the mark and the address of the manufacturer, the authorized representative, or the importer into the EU, must be affixed to the toy or to the packaging in a visible, legible, and indelible manner. If the toys are small or consist of small parts, the information may be provided in the same manner on the packaging, on a label or on a enclosed leaflet. If the particulars are not affixed to the toy itself, the consumer's attention must be drawn to the advisability of retaining the necessary information for future reference.[3]

The King designates the toys which may be placed on the market only when accompanied by the necessary warnings and indications of precautions to be taken when using the toys.[4] Article 10 of the Royal Decree refers to its Annex III, which states that toys must be accompanied by appropriate clearly legible warnings to reduce inherent risks in their use as described in the essential safety requirements. The Annex lists more specifically the warnings relating to:

(1) Toys not intended for children under thirty-six months of age;
(2) Slides, suspended swings and rings, trapezes, ropes, and similar toys attached to a crossbeam;
(3) Functional toys;
(4) Toys containing inherently dangerous substances or preparations and chemical toys;
(5) Skateboards and skates for children; and
(6) Toys intended for use under water.

2.2.7.4 Standing, Procedures, and Sanctions

If it is determined that a toy bearing the EU mark jeopardizes the safety and health of consumers and third parties, the Minister of Economic Affairs can take all appropriate measures to remove the toy from the

1 Act of 29 June 1990, Article 3.
2 Act of 29 June 1990, Article 4.
3 Act of 29 June 1990, Article 8, and Royal Decree of 22 March 1993, Article 11.
4 Act of 29 June 1990, Article 7.

market or to prohibit or restrict its introduction onto the market. He or she can require the manufacturer to inform the consumers, to recall the toys, to exchange them, or to modify them. The Minister also can impose a complete or partial refund of the price of the toy and determines how and to what extent the manufacturer must bear the costs resulting from the measure taken.

With respect to electrical toys or toys which endanger the health of the consumer, the Minister of Economic Affairs requires the advice and consent of the Ministers of Energy and of Public Health, respectively.[1] Every decision restricting the introduction of a toy on the market must be reasoned and notified without delay to the manufacturer concerned. It must specify the right and the time limit for appeal. The King determines how the public should be informed of the decision.[2]

Without prejudice to the powers of the officers of the judicial police, the King appoints civil servants within the Ministries of Economic Affairs and of Public Health charged with supervising the compliance with the Act and its implementing Decrees. They act according to the procedures provided for by the Trade Practices and Consumer Protection Act 1991.

Parties will be subject to fines of BF 500 to BF 20,000 if they:

(1) Unduly affix the EU mark to toys;
(2) Affix marks or inscriptions to the products which can create confusion with the EU mark; or
(3) Infringe on the provisions of the implementing Decrees of the Act.[3]

All fines are multiplied by 100. An action for a cease and desist order can be lodged where the conditions for it are satisfied.

2.2.8 *Insurance*

2.2.8.1 *Source of Rule*

The private law aspect is regulated by the Act of 25 June 1992 (Land Insurance Act)[4] which replaced the Act of 11 June 1874.

---

1 Act of 29 June 1990, Article 5.
2 Act of 29 June 1990, Article 6.
3 Act of 29 June 1990, Article 9.
4 BS, 20 August 1992.

The public-law aspect of insurance is regulated by the Act of 9 July 1975 on the control of insurance companies.[1] The Act of 9 July 1975 implements EU Directives in this area of insurance.

2.2.8.2 *Scope and Application*

The Land Insurance Act applies to all land insurance agreements to the extent that no specific Acts apply to them (the *lex specialis* principle). This is the case with the Act of 21 November 1989,[2] relating to the mandatory liability insurance for motor vehicles. The Land Insurance Act contains general provisions relating to all land insurances and specific provisions distinguishing between indemnity insurances and personal insurances, and indemnity insurances and lump sum insurances. It also contains specific provisions for some sub-categories.

Regulated sub-categories of indemnity insurances are fire insurance, harvest insurance, credit insurance, and liability insurance. Personal insurances are life insurance and non-life personal insurances, such as birth and dowry insurances, health and accident insurances, and collective accident insurances. The Act also applies to mutual insurance associations. It does not, however, apply to re-insurance or to insurance of transport of goods not mainly conducted on land.[3]

The Control Act applies to Belgian undertakings, foreign undertakings with an establishment in Belgium, and foreign undertakings which perform insurance activities in Belgium without an established office there.[4] Article 2 of the Control Act also contains a list of undertakings to which the Act does not apply and also a list of undertakings to which the Act will apply only three years from its entry into force.

2.2.8.3 *Substantive Provisions*

The Land Insurance Act contains many mandatory provisions and is much more detailed than the Act of 1874. Whereas the Act of 1874 originated in merchant law, the new Act is consumer friendly.

---

1 BS, 29 July 1975, most recently amended by the Royal Decree of 8 January 1993, BS, 9 February 1993.
2 BS, 8 December 1989.
3 Act of 25 June 1992, Article 2.
4 Act of 9 July 1975, Article 2.

The Land Insurance Act regulates certain contract documents emanating from the insurer. The first is the insurance proposal to be completed by the policyholder to inform the insurer about the risk to be insured. The second is the pre-signed policy which contains an offer to contract, signed by the insurer. The third is the insurance application in which the insurer offers to bear the risk temporarily at the request of the policyholder.[1]

An important innovation is the generalization of the distinction between the insurance proposal and the insurance application, previously only known in the areas of life insurance, fire insurance, and motor vehicle liability insurance. Even after signing an insurance application or a pre-signed policy, the polifcyholder and the insurer have the right to terminate the contract within thirty days after the insurer has received the documents.[2]

At the time of entering into a contract, the policyholder is required to disclose all information known to him which should reasonably be considered relevant for the assessment of the risk by the insurer. No disclosure is required for genetic data or for circumstances of which the insurer knows or of which the insurer reasonably should have known. If the insurer performs a contract with a policyholder who did not answer all questions, the insurer has no recourse based on this omission, except in case of fraud.[3] Where the old Act sanctioned every concealment of relevant information with nullity of the contract, the new Act distinguishes between intentional and unintentional omission. The former is sanctioned with nullity and the latter with modification or termination of the contract.[4]

Related to the obligation of Article 5 is the obligation of the policyholder to notify the insurer of all new or modified circumstances which are likely to result in a considerable and durable increase of the insurer's risk.[5] However, this provision does not apply to life, health, and credit insurances.

The Act also strictly regulates the payment of the premium in case of termination of the contract and the sanctions in the event of non-payment, thus ensuring legal security and consumer protection.[6]

---

1 Land Insurance Act 1992, Article 1.
2 Land Insurance Act 1992, Article 4.
3 Land Insurance Act 1992, Article 5.
4 Land Insurance Act 1992, Articles 6 and 7.
5 Land Insurance Act 1992, Article 26.
6 Land Insurance Act 1992, Articles 14-18.

An important change in favor of the consumer is that the duration of an insurance contract may no longer exceed one year.[1] The contract is tacitly renewed for consecutive one-year periods unless three months notice is given by one of the parties. It also should be noted that the Act extends to policyholders the same possibilities that the insurer has to terminate the contract, thus strengthening their position.[2]

The Act prohibits arbitration clauses entered into before a dispute arises[3] and exclusivity clauses.[4] In matters of liability insurance, it prohibits double evaluation[5] and extends an autonomous right of recourse against the insurer to the victim.[6]

The purpose of the Control Act is to protect policyholders and third parties affected by the execution of insurance contracts. The Act establishes the main conditions with which insurance undertakings must comply and the specific rules relating to liquidation of insurance operations.

Undertakings require an approval from the King in order to conclude or offer insurance contracts relating to risks which are located in Belgium.[7] Contracts concluded with undertakings which have not been approved or which have not been exempted from approval are null and void. The conditions for approval are contained in the Act and its implementing Decrees. Important in the approval procedure is the Control Office for Insurances. It is to this Office that all requests for approval must be sent[8] and which advises the King in granting approvals.[9]

Chapter III regulates the exercise of the insurance activities. It contains rules on solvency margins, accounting, information to the Control Office, maintaining of documents, investigating powers of the Control Office, and civil and criminal liability of administrators, managers, and general representatives to the policyholders and third beneficiaries. Article 20 contains provisions relating to the information to be issued to the policyholder. All proposals and policies and, in general, all documents intended for the Belgian public, must state that the undertaking has received approval for particular insurance activities, which also must be specified. These documents also must contain the identification

---

1 Land Insurance Act 1992, Article 30.
2 Land Insurance Act 1992, Articles 4, 29, 30, and 31.
3 Land Insurance Act 1992, Article 36.
4 Land Insurance Act 1992, Article 65.
5 Land Insurance Act 1992, Articles 82-83.
6 Land Insurance Act 1992, Article 86.
7 Control Act 1975, Article 3.
8 Control Act 1975, Article 5.
9 Control Act 1975, Article 4.

number the Control Office has issued to the undertaking. Foreign undertakings must state the country in which they are established, if they are not established in Belgium, the address of the establishment granting coverage, and the registered office.

Article 14 of the Control Act differentiates between activities in the non-life insurance sector and those in the life insurance sector. However, in both cases, the general rule is that Belgian law applies.

2.2.8.4 Standing, Procedures, and Sanctions

The Control Office for Insurances is charged with supervising the observance of the Land Insurance Act and its implementing Decrees.[1]

Under the Control Act, undertakings and agents, brokers, and intermediaries are obligated to submit to the Control Office all information it requests. The Control Office can inspect all documents in the offices of the undertaking and can appoint civil servants within its own administration or independent experts who report to it.[2] Without prejudice to the powers of the judicial police, the King appoints members of the Control Office who are charged with investigating and establishing infringements of this Act and its implementing Decrees. These civil servants can be assisted by experts designated by the Control Office.[3]

The Control Office can issue warnings and impose deadlines for compliance with the Control Act and its implementing Decrees. If they are not complied with within a specified period of time, the Control Office can publish these warnings in the *Belgian State Gazette* and impose administrative fines of a minimum of BF 1,000 and a maximum of three per cent of the technical and financial proceeds up to BF 50-million. If the offense is repeated within five years, this maximum amount will be increased to five per cent of the technical and financial proceeds up to BF 75-million.[4]

The Land Insurance Act provides for criminal sanctions only for infringements resulting in nullity of the insurance contract by virtue of Article 43 (over-insurance in bad faith), Article 51 (the principle of indemnity), and Article 96 (insurance for young children). The sanctions consist of one month to five years' imprisonment and/or fines of BF 1,000 to BF 10,000.[5] All fines are multiplied by 100.

---

1 Land Insurance Act 1992, Article 140.

2 Control Act 1975, Article 21.

3 Control Act 1975, Article 21.

4 Control Act 1975, Articles 51 and 52.

5 Land Insurance Act 1992, Article 139.

Under the Control Act, administrators, directors, managers, or mandataries who conclude or attempt to conclude insurance contracts before the company has approval from the King are sanctioned with one month to five years' imprisonment and/or fines of BF 1,000 to BF 10,000.[1] The same sanction is provided for agents, brokers, or intermediaries who mediate in the conclusion of insurance contracts which do not comply with the Control Act and for administrators, managers, or mandataries who deliberately give false statements to the Control Office, its civil servants, or its mandataries or refuse to disclose requested information and generally for non-performance of obligations imposed by the Control Act and its implementing Decrees.[2] All fines are multiplied by 100.

An action for a cease and desist order also can be brought against acts contrary to honest business practices committed in the framework of the Land Insurance Act and the Control Act. Nullity also is provided for in both the Land Insurance Act and the Control Act to sanction certain types of non-compliance.

2.2.9 Travel

2.2.9.1 Source of Rule

The applicable law consists of the Act of 21 April 1965 on the status of travel agencies[3] and its implementing Royal Decree of 30 June 1966.[4] Belgium also is a party to the Convention on Travel Contracts of 23 April 1970.[5]

As with the Convention on Travel Contracts, the EU Council Directive 90/314/EEC of 13 July 1990 on package travel, package holidays, and package tours[6] is aimed at consumer protection and information.

The Directive was to be incorporated into Belgian law in 1994. The government proposed a bill on 22 July 1993, regulating organized travel contracts and intermediary travel contracts. This bill is in a very large part inspired by the Convention on Travel Contracts, but attempts to

1 Control Act 1975, Article 53.

2 Control Act 1975, Articles 54 and 55.

3 BS, 10 June 1965.

4 BS, 27 July 1966, most recently amended by the Royal Decree of 22 September 1988, BS, 28 October 1988.

5 Approved by the Act of 30 March 1973, BS, 17 May 1973.

6 OJ 1990 L 158/59.

adapt it to the obligations imposed by the Directive. The bill, nevertheless, has a larger scope of application than the Directive in that it is aimed not only at package deals but also at the activities of travel organizers and travel intermediaries. If the bill is passed, it will replace the Convention on Travel Contracts rules which Belgium denunciated.[1]

Test Aankoop/Test-Achats, together with the Association of Flemish Travel Agencies, has established a model contract for use by travel organizers. Since the Directive, the government bill, and the model contract do not differ essentially from the Convention on Travel Contracts, the following discussion will focus on the Convention on Travel Contracts.[2]

2.2.9.2 Scope and Application

The Act of 21 April 1965 applies to parties who organize or sell journeys or sojourns for a fixed price, including accommodations, or to intermediaries who sell such journeys and sojourns, transportation tickets, and accommodation or meal vouchers. To fall within the purview of the Act, these activities should be performed as a chief occupation, with a view to making a profit, and on a permanent basis. Exceptions are made, however, for touring-car operators who do not perform these activities as a chief occupation and on a permanent basis and for non-profit associations which perform them on an accessory basis.[3]

The Convention on Travel Contracts applies to travel contracts concluded by a travel organizer or intermediary, where the principal place of business or, failing any such place, habitual residence, or the place of business through which the travel contract has been concluded, is located in a Contracting State.[4] A travel organizer is a person who habitually or regularly undertakes in his own name to provide for another, for an inclusive price, a combination of services comprising transportation, accommodation separate from the transportation, or any other service relating thereto. A travel intermediary (travel agent) is an individual who habitually or regularly undertakes to provide for another, for a price, either an organized travel contract or one or more separate services rendering possible a journey or sojourn. For both categories of

1 BS, 6 January 1994.

2 It should be noted that the bill had not yet passed. In the meantime, however, the Directive has been implemented by the Act of 16 February 1994 (BS, 1 April 1994), which was to enter into force on 4 October 1994.

3 Act of 21 April 1965, Article 1.

4 Convention on Travel Contracts of 23 April 1970, Article 2.

persons, it is unimportant whether such activities are their main business or whether or not they exercise them on a professional basis.[1]

It is noteworthy that Article 1 of the government bill specifies that travel organizers and intermediaries are sellers within the meaning of the Trade Practices and Consumer Protection Act 1991.

2.2.9.3 Substantive Provisions

Under the Act of 21 April 1965 and its implementing Decree, a license is required in order to perform the said activities.[2] Exemptions, however, are provided for certain categories of operators who satisfy certain conditions stated in Article 1 of the Act. No one is allowed to use the title of travel agent or the designation of travel agency or similar terms without holding a license delivered according to Article 1 of the Act.[3] The Royal Decree provides for three categories of licenses (A, B, and C)[4] and imposes the conditions to be met[5] and the procedures to be observed[6] to obtain the authorization. It also contains the procedures for withdrawal and suspension of the license and for appeal[7] and the obligations imposed on the holders of a license.[8]

The conditions to be met to obtain a license are divided into two categories, one relating to the individuals performing the activities and the other relating to the undertakings. The first category contains conditions pertaining to the age, nationality, and professional competence of the applicant.[9] The second category contains conditions relating to the financial means, the supplemental guarantee, funds, and the technical equipment of the undertaking.[10]

The licenseholder receives a shield which must be installed in a place easily visible to the public, close to the entrance to the establishment(s).[11] The licenseholder also must state the name of the undertaking and the category and number of the license on business

---

1 Convention on Travel Contracts of 23 April 1970, Article 1.
2 Act of 21 April 1965, Article 1.
3 Act of 21 April 1965, Article 2.
4 Royal Decree of 30 June 1966, Article 2.
5 Royal Decree of 30 June 1966, Articles 3-12.
6 Royal Decree of 30 June 1966, Articles 13-17.
7 Royal Decree of 30 June 1966, Articles 18-19.
8 Royal Decree of 30 June 1966, Articles 20-33.
9 Royal Decree of 30 June 1966, Articles 3-7.
10 Royal Decree of 30 June 1966, Articles 8-12; *see also* Articles 3-7 of the Act.
11 Royal Decree of 30 June 1966, Article 20.

documents and in advertisements.[1] Finally, the licenseholder has a duty to his clientele consisting of:

(1) Giving them the correct necessary information relating to the prices and conditions of the journey;
(2) Providing the agreed services in the agreed conditions;
(3) Maintaining the confidentiality of the conditions of a journey even if reservations are cancelled, unless the client gives written permission to release the information or the licenseholder is called on to testify in court or is obligated by law to disclose these conditions;
(4) Using the funds deposited by the client exclusively for purposes related to the undertaking and refunding the money due without delay; and
(5) Avoiding professional contact with suppliers or subcontractors who do not offer reliable professional and ethical guarantees.[2]

The Convention on Travel Contracts contains provisions on the information to be given to the traveler in the travel document or contract. This information includes:

(1) The signature or the stamp of the travel organizer or intermediary;
(2) Place and date of issue;
(3) Name and address of the travel organizer and/or intermediary;
(4) Name of the traveler(s);
(5) Places and dates of the beginning and end of the journeys and sojourns;
(6) All necessary specifications concerning transportation, accommodation, and ancillary services included in the price;
(7) The inclusive price covering all services provided for in the contract;
(8) Circumstances and conditions under which the traveler may cancel the contract;
(9) Any other terms the parties may agree on; and
(10) Any modification of the particulars of the prospectus supplied to the traveler.[3]

---

1 Royal Decree of 30 June 1966, Article 21.

2 Royal Decree of 30 June 1966, Article 22; Article 22 also contains a duty toward suppliers and the duty toward colleagues to abstain from acts contrary to honest business practices.

3 Convention on Travel Contracts of 23 April 1970, Articles 5, 6, and 18.

The traveler may cancel the contract at any time, in whole or in part, provided the traveler pays compensation to the travel organizer or intermediary.[1] The traveler may cancel the contract without compensation or reimbursement if the travel organizer increases the inclusive price more than ten per cent, due to changes in the exchange rates or in carrier tariffs and only if this possibility was expressly stated in the travel contract. In that event, the traveler is entitled to a refund of all sums paid to the travel organizer.[2]

The travel organizer may cancel the contract, in whole or in part, without indemnity if, before or during the transaction, exceptional circumstances arise which the travel organizer could not have known at the time of the conclusion of the contract and which, had they been known at that time, would have given valid reason not to conclude the contract. In the event of cancellation of the contract before its completion, the travel organizer must refund in full any payments received from the traveler. In the event of cancellation of the contract during its performance, the travel organizer must take all necessary measures in the interest of the traveler. Furthermore, the parties must compensate each other, as required, in an equitable manner.[3]

The travel organizer and intermediary are responsible for the acts and omissions of their employees and agents when acting in the course of their employment or within the scope of their authority.[4]

The travel organizer is liable for any loss or damage caused to the traveler as a result of non-performance, in whole or in part, of obligations, unless it can be proven that he or she acted as a diligent and conscientious travel organizer. This liability is limited for each traveler to Gold francs 50,000 for personal injury, Gold francs 2,000 for damage to property, and Gold francs 5,000 for any other damage. The King can increase these amounts.

The travel intermediary is liable for wrongful acts or default committed in performing his or her obligations. These wrongful acts or defaults will be assessed with regard to the duties of a diligent travel intermediary. The liability is limited to BF 10,000 for each traveler. The King also can increase these amounts. The travel intermediary is not liable for non-performance, in whole or in part, of journeys, sojourns, or other services governed by the contract.[5]

---

1 Convention on Travel Contracts of 23 April 1970, Articles 9 and 20.

2 Convention on Travel Contracts of 23 April 1970, Article 11.

3 Convention on Travel Contracts of 23 April 1970, Article 10.

4 Convention on Travel Contracts of 23 April 1970, Articles 12 and 21.

5 Convention on Travel Contracts of 23 April 1970, Article 22.

The traveler is liable for any loss or damage, caused by his or her wrongful acts or default to be assessed with regard to a traveler's normal behavior, as a result of non-compliance with obligations to the travel organizer, an intermediary, or parties for which they are responsible.[1]

2.2.9.4 Standing, Procedures, and Sanctions

Under Act of 1965 and its implementing Decree, if Article 1 of the Act or the conditions of Articles 3-12 of the Royal Decree[2] or the obligations of Articles 20-33 of the Royal Decree[3] are not or are no longer complied with, the license can, depending on the circumstance be refused, suspended, or withdrawn. The same sanctions apply where the applicant, the licenseholder, an administrator, a manager, or one of the parties charged with daily management was declared bankrupt in an undertaking which performed the activities as described in Article 1, Paragraph 1, of the Act of 1965 or where he or she was an administrator, a manager, or a person charged with daily management of such an undertaking at the time it was declared bankrupt. Finally, this sanction applies in the event the amount of the contested debts of the licenseholder reaches the amount of the security guaranteeing the debts.[4]

Without prejudice to the powers of the officers of the judicial police, the state police, the local police, and the civil servants appointed by the King within the Ministry of Tourism are charged with the investigation, establishment, and reporting of infringements of the Act of 1965 and its implementing Decree. The reports are sent to the Public Prosecutor's Office and copies are sent, within four days from determination of the infringement, to the offender or, as the case may be, to the owner of the travel agency and to the Minister of Tourism.[5]

By applying for the license, the applicant allows the necessary unannounced inspections or investigations by the civil servants within the Ministry of Tourism. The investigations may take place only during normal business hours and are restricted to the rooms reserved for the completion of business transactions. They must be discrete and may not interfere with business or disturb clients.[6]

---

1 Convention on Travel Contracts of 23 April 1970, Articles 16 and 23.
2 Implementing Article 4 of the Act of 21 April 1965.
3 Implementing Article 5 of the Act of 21 April 1965.
4 Act of 21 April 1965, Article 6.
5 Act of 21 April 1965, Article 10.
6 Act of 21 April 1965, Article 11.

It is prohibited to perform the activities of a travel agency without an authorization,[1] as are using the title of travel agent or the designation of travel agency or similar terms without holding a proper authorization[2] and unlawfully displaying a shield.[3] Infringements of these prohibitions are sanctioned with eight days to one month of imprisonment and/or with a fine of BF 26 to BF 1,000.[4]

The courts also can prohibit the offender from, personally or through an intermediary, carrying out the activities of a travel agency for a period of one to twelve months. If the offense is repeated, this prohibition can become permanent.[5] All fines are multiplied by 100.

An action for a cease and desist order can be brought against all acts contrary to honest business practices, e.g., carrying out the activities of a travel agency without authorization.

The Convention on Travel Contracts contains chapters on legal proceedings and on the nullity of stipulations contrary to the Convention. According to Article 29 of the Convention, the travel contract may contain an arbitration clause, provided it stipulates that the arbitration tribunal will apply the Convention. Article 30 fixes a two-year period of limitation for an action originating from a travel contract subject to the Convention and based on death or injury, either bodily or mental, caused to a traveler. This period runs from the contractual date of termination of the service giving rise to the dispute. It will begin to run on the date of the death of the traveler if the death resulted from a travel-related injury which occurred within three years from the date of termination of the service. The period of limitation for other actions originating from a travel contract subject to the Convention is one year from the contractual date of termination of the service.

Any stipulation which would directly or indirectly derogate from the provisions of the Convention is null and void, insofar as it would be detrimental to the traveler. This is the case with clauses shifting the burden of proof or assigning the benefit of insurance taken out by the traveler to the travel organizer or intermediary. The nullity only effects the clause in question and not the contract as a whole.[6]

---

1 Act of 21 April 1965, Article 1.

2 Act of 21 April 1965, Article 2.

3 Act of 21 April 1965, Article 5, and Royal Decree of 30 June 1966, Article 20.

4 Act of 21 April 1965, Article 9.

5 Act of 21 April 1965, Article 9.

6 Convention on Travel Contracts of 23 April 1970, Article 30.

The action for a cease and desist order also can be lodged against acts contrary to honest business practices relating to the matters regulated the Act of 21 April 1965 and by the Convention on Travel Contracts.

The government bill provides for an action for a cease and desist order and also contains the same administrative measures and criminal sanctions as the Trade Practices and Consumer Protection Act 1991.

2.2.10 Correspondence Courses

2.2.10.1 Source of Rule

The applicable law in this case is the Act of 5 March 1965 on correspondence education[1] and its many implementing Decrees. The French community in Belgium has instituted its own regulation of these matters by the Decree of 18 December 1984.[2]

2.2.10.2 Scope and Application

Article 1 of the Act of 5 March 1965 defines correspondence education as education through the periodical exchange between the student and the organizing body of instructions for work completed pursuant to the instructions and corrections of this work. A correspondence course is the whole of the subject matter preparing for examinations, whether or not competitive, organized or recognized by the state, and to be taken before an Examination Committee instituted by the King.

2.2.10.3 Substantive Provisions

Chapter II of the Act regulates the education organized, subsidized, or recognized by the state to the extent that it prepares for examinations to be taken before an Examination Committee instituted by the King.[3] These courses are free, and books and other materials may not be sold by the organizing body without the permission of the Minister of Education.[4] This Chapter also contains provisions relating to the organization of state education and to the qualifications teachers must

---

1 BS, 23 March 1965.
2 BS, 2 February 1965.
3 *See*, for example, Royal Decree of 13 April 1965, BS, 26 May 1965.
4 Act of 5 March 1965, Article 3.

have in order to be appointed by the Minister, and indicates the conditions for state subsidies and recognition.

Chapter III contains the prohibition of certain practices. The first Article of this Chapter regulates correspondence courses for which the student must pay. It provides that, for such courses, a contract must be drawn up of which every party concerned must receive a copy. It also prescribes the content of the contract (e.g., the manner in which the education will be organized, the duration of the courses, the registration fee, the tuition fees, and all the other costs the student must bear) and renders null and void all clauses obligating the student to follow courses of more than one year or to pay for more than three months of lessons in advance.[1]

Article 24 of the Act provides that all documents (e.g., contracts, publications, and advertisements) issued by bodies which organize correspondence courses must state legibly and in full the specification "correspondence education" and the corporate name, if applicable. Article 25 of the Act contains a general prohibition of all misleading practices with regard to the quality and significance of the courses. Article 26 of the Act states that the advertising for correspondence courses may not promise advantages such as premiums, gifts, or rebates, and may not result from the intervention of recruiters and touts. Finally, Article 25 of the Act allows registrations on a trial basis only if they are completely free of charge and if they are not a determining factor for establishing the number of students.

2.2.10.4 Standing, Procedures, and Sanctions

The King appoints inspectors within the Ministry of Education. The inspectors are charged with controlling whether the courses are given in accordance with the curriculum and with controlling the educational level of the courses organized by the state or by subsidized or recognized organizations.[2] Inspection is regulated by the Royal Decree of 15 April 1965 on the inspection of correspondence education[3] and by the Royal Decree of 11 May 1965 on the inspection of subsidized or recognized correspondence courses.[4]

---

1 Act of 5 March 1965, Article 23.
2 Act of 5 March 1965, Article 4.
3 BS, 26 May 1965.
4 BS, 15 October 1965.

The inspectors can observe teachers and students and examine all relevant documents, such as the texts of the lessons and assignments, the completed assignments and their corrections, student evaluation reports, registration files and contracts, and publications and advertisements issued by the correspondence education organization. Individual reports, evaluating teachers they observed, are communicated to the teachers concerned and sent to the Office for Correspondence Education, which retains a copy for the minister, responsible for appointing the teachers.

The inspectors also draw up general reports regarding every subsidized or recognized correspondence course. These reports are communicated to the director of the course and are also sent to the Correspondence Education Office and must enable the minister to evaluate whether the courses still satisfy the conditions for granting subsidies and recognition. If not, the subsidies or recognition can be withdrawn.

Finally, the inspectors investigate organizations which apply for subsidies or recognition and report their findings to the minister.

Article 27 of the Act sanctions infringements of Articles 23-26 with eight days' to three months' imprisonment and/or with fines of BF 26 to BF 1,000. These fines are multiplied by 100. Where the conditions are met, an action for a cease and desist order can be brought.

2.2.11 Regulated Trade Practices

Chapter VI of the Trade Practices and Consumer Protection Act 1991 regulates or forbids the following sales methods and methods of sales promotion.

2.2.11.1 Sales at a Loss

A merchant may not sell a product at a loss. Sale at a loss is any sale at a price which is not at least equal to the price at which the merchant has purchased the product or at which he could purchase it in case of repurchase. The law also prohibits sales with an extremely low profit margin (after deduction of general costs).[1] This prohibition does not apply to:

1 Trade Practices and Consumer Protection Act 1991, Article 40.

(1) Products which are sold out;
(2) Products which are sold in seasonal clearance sales;
(3) Products the value of which can diminish quickly and which can not be preserved any longer;
(4) Products offered to satisfy a specific temporary need when this need has disappeared and the products can apparently no longer be sold under normal conditions;
(5) Products the commercial value of which has substantially decreased as a result of damage, a decrease in their possibilities of use, or a radical change in the technique; and
(6) When, for imperative competition reasons, a seller is compelled to adjust his prices to those generally charged by his competitors.[1]

2.2.11.2 Announcements of Price Comparisons and Discounts

When a seller announces a price reduction or makes a price comparison, he or she may refer only to a price which was charged - except for goods the value of which can rapidly decrease - during a period of at least one month or a price which is regulated by virtue of the Price Regulation Act. The date from which the reduced price is valid will be announced during the entire period of the offer. Except for clearance sales, this period may not be longer than one month.[2]

2.2.11.3 Clearance Sales

A clearance sale is one made as a liquidation for the purpose of an accelerated sale of a stock or assortment of goods, in one of the following cases:

(1) The sale takes place pursuant to a judicial decision (e.g., bankruptcy);
(2) The heirs of a deceased offer for sale the stock which they have acquired;
(3) The seller offers for sale the stock which he has acquired after a transfer of business;
(4) A seller who terminates his business offers for sale his entire stock, provided he or she has not, during the last three years, sold out similar goods for the same reason;

---

1 Trade Practices and Consumer Protection Act 1991, Article 41.
2 Trade Practices and Consumer Protection Act 1991, Article 43.

(5) Rebuilding or renovation on the sales premises takes more than forty working days and makes sales during that period impossible, provided the seller has not, during the last three years, sold out similar products for the same reason;
(6) Transfer or cessation of the establishment renders the sale of the products necessary, provided the seller has not, during the last year, sold out similar products for the same reason;
(7) Serious damage to the stock or an important part of it has been caused by a disaster;
(8) The commercial activity is seriously impeded by *force majeure*.[1]

2.2.11.4 Seasonal Clearance Sales

Sales under the name of *Soldes*, *Solden*, *Opruiming*, *Schlussverkauf*, or under any other name suggesting the accelerated sale at a reduced price at the end of a season may take place only on the premises where the seller usually offers identical products for sale. Only those products which the seller had in stock at the beginning of the seasonal sale may be cleared. Every product cleared will be reduced in price.[2] Seasonal clearance sales of articles of dress, leather goods, and shoes may only take place in the period from 3 to 31 January and from 1 to 31 July.[3] Moreover, from 15 November to 2 January and from 15 May to 30 June, a seller may not announce or give discounts.

2.2.11.5 Joint Offers

Article 54(2) prohibits so-called joint offers to consumers. A joint offer exists if the acquisition, free of charge or otherwise, of products, services, or all other advantages or titles with which these can be obtained is linked to the acquisition of other, or even identical, products or services.[4] The definition of joint offer, and hence the scope of the prohibition of Article 54, includes premium offers (a present, whatever its form, is offered to consumers purchasing a good or a service) and combination sales. Even the sale of two or more identical products for one price is covered by the prohibition.

---

1 Trade Practices and Consumer Protection Act 1991, Article 46.
2 Trade Practices and Consumer Protection Act 1991, Article 51.
3 Trade Practices and Consumer Protection Act 1991, Article 52.
4 Trade Practices and Consumer Protection Act 1991, Article 54(1).

Articles 55 through 57 of the Trade Practices and Consumer Protection Act 1991, however, contain a number of exceptions to the prohibition of all joint offers. Pursuant to Article 55 of the Trade Practices and Consumer Protection Act 1991, it is permitted to offer jointly for one total price products or services forming one whole (e.g., cups and plates of one dinner set) and identical products or services, under the following conditions:

(1) Each product or service must be available separately at its usual price in the same establishment;
(2) The purchaser must be clearly informed about this possibility and about the separate price of each product or service; and
(3) The discount granted, if any, may not exceed one-third of the added prices.

Pursuant to Article 56 of the Trade Practices and Consumer Protection Act 1991, one may offer, free of charge, together with the main product or service:

(1) Accessories of the main product which are specifically adapted to the main product by the manufacturer;
(2) The packaging and the recipients, the nature and value of which are reasonably related to the product;
(3) Small products and services accepted by commercial custom, as well as the delivery, the installation, and the maintenance of the goods delivered;
(4) Samples in quantities which are strictly necessary to appraise the qualities of the product;
(5) Chromos, vignettes, and pictures with a small commercial value;
(6) Participation forms in authorized lotteries; and
(7) Objects with clearly visible and indelible commercial inscriptions, which are not sold as such, provided the price at which the offeror has purchased them does not exceed five per cent of the selling price of the main product or main service.

It also is permitted to offer, free of charge, together with a main product or service,[1] a number of titles which amount to a discount on further purchases or which, after collection of a certain number of them, give right to restitution in cash.

---

1 Trade Practices and Consumer Protection Act 1991, Article 57.

2.2.11.6 *Gift Coupons*

Gift coupons are documents which a manufacturer, an importer, or a retailer distributes, free of charge, and which give the acquirer the possibility to obtain an advantage in the form of a cash discount at the time of the purchase of a product or a service.[1] Within the meaning of Article 54 of the Trade Practices and Consumer Protection Act 1991, a joint offer exists when a gift coupon is not distributed freely but is offered to consumers who acquire a product or a service.

Such a coupon can only be delivered according to the provisions of Article 57. When there is no such link, the distribution of coupons is totally free, provided they contain a number of specifications (e.g., the nominal value they represent).[2]

2.2.11.7 *Auction Sales*

Sales by auction are regulated as indicated, except in the following cases:

(1) Sales of a non-commercial nature;
(2) Sales exclusively addressed to individuals doing business in the goods concerned;
(3) Sales of objects of art, collectors' items (with the exception of carpets and jewelry), and antiques, provided they take place in locations which are usually used for that purpose;
(4) Sales implementing a judicial decision or a legal provision; and
(5) Sales in the event of judicial composition with assignment of business.[3]

In all other cases, auctions are permitted only if they relate to used products. A used product is a product which shows clear signs of use, unless those signs are exclusively the result of an artificial aging process.[4] The prohibition against auctioning new products does not apply in the instance of a clearance sale which takes place in accordance with the regulation on clearance sales.

---

1 Trade Practices and Consumer Protection Act 1991, Article 63.
2 Trade Practices and Consumer Protection Act 1991, Article 64.
3 Trade Practices and Consumer Protection Act 1991, Article 69.
4 Trade Practices and Consumer Protection Act 1991, Article 70.

2.2.11.8 Unsolicited Sales

The sending of a good or the performance of a service without prior request is prohibited. The minister may grant an exemption for sales with a charitable purpose. In any case, the addressee is under no obligation whatsoever to return the product or to pay for the product or service.[1]

2.2.11.9 Distance Sales

A "distance sale" is a sale which is concluded without the simultaneous physical presence of the seller and the consumer and which takes place within the framework of a sales method in which a recourse is made to a technique of distance communication, such as mail-order sales.[2] A distance sale becomes final only after a trial period of seven days from the day of delivery of the goods.[3]

Offers of distance sales also must contain a number of specifications and at the latest, at the time of the delivery of the goods, the consumer must receive a contract document with a number of specifications, including his right to a trial period.[4]

2.2.11.10 Pyramid Sales

Pyramid sales are a form of swindling. The Trade Practices and Consumer Protection Act 1991 contains criminal sanctions for those organizing a pyramid sale system, described as a sale consisting of building up a network of professional or non-professional sellers in which each participant is hoping to win more by an extension of the network than by the sale of products to the consumer. The participation in a pyramid with knowledge of its function also is prohibited.[5]

A particular form of pyramid selling is mentioned in Article 84(2), the so-called "snowball sale", which consists of offering the consumer goods by raising the expectation that he or she will be able to acquire the goods either free of charge or at reduced prices, provided that the consumer places, for remuneration, tickets or coupons with third parties or that he or she recruits members or collects subscriptions.

---

1 Trade Practices and Consumer Protection Act 1991, Article 76.
2 Trade Practices and Consumer Protection Act 1991, Article 77.
3 Trade Practices and Consumer Protection Act 1991, Article 78.
4 Trade Practices and Consumer Protection Act 1991, Article 79.
5 Trade Practices and Consumer Protection Act 1991, Article 84(1).

2.2.11.11 Sales Outside Business Premises

Sales outside business premises are those which take place at the residence of the consumer or of another consumer or at his place of business, during an excursion organized by the seller, or during an exhibition or a fair.[1] The following are not considered as sales outside business premises:

(1) Auction sales;
(2) Distance sales;
(3) Sale of insurance policies;
(4) Under certain conditions, sales during events without a commercial character or with a charitable aim;
(5) Consumer credit transactions falling within the scope of the Consumer Credit Act 1991; and
(6) Sales occurring at the time of a visit of the seller which the consumer has expressly and specifically requested.[2] For every sale outside business premises, the seller must supply the consumer with a document containing a number of specifications, including the right to a trial period of seven working days.[3]

1 Trade Practices and Consumer Protection Act 1991, Article 86.
2 Trade Practices and Consumer Protection Act 1991, Article 87.
3 Trade Practices and Consumer Protection Act 1991, Article 88.

Section 3

Testing

3.1 Voluntary and Mandatory Testing

Comparative tests are completed on a voluntary basis by the Consumer Union (*Test Aankoop/Test-Achats*). There is no mandatory testing in Belgium.

3.2 Distribution and Effect of Test Results

The results of the comparative tests of *Test Aankoop/Test-Achats* are published in its monthly magazine of the same name. There are also special consumer programs on television which discuss the results of these tests. Comparative tests by consumer organizations, however, may not be referred to in advertisements.[1]

1 Trade Practices and Consumer Protection Act 1991, Article 23.

Section 4

Advertising Claims

4.1 Comparisons

The Trade Practices and Consumer Protection Act 1991 contains detailed advertising prohibitions. For the application of the Trade Practices and Consumer Protection Act 1991, advertising means every communication which has as its direct or indirect purpose to promote the sale of products or services, irrespective of the place and the medium.[1]

Article 23 of the Act prohibits advertising containing comparisons which are deceptive or denigrating or which make it possible, without necessity, to identify one or more other sellers.

With regard to comparative advertising, it is obvious that Belgian law is very restrictive. Article 23 not only prohibits comparisons which denigrate competitors or which are false or misleading, but also prohibits truthful, moderate, and objective comparisons between competing products. The words "which make it possible to identify one or more other sellers" has even led the courts to condemn comparisons in which a group of competitors can be recognized (e.g., the hauliers in general in an advertisement for transport by rail or the importers of wood in an advertisement for aluminum profiles). In fact, every express or implied reference to competitors is prohibited, unless there is a specific necessity. The grounds of necessity which have been accepted until now by the courts are limited to:

(1) Legal self-defense;
(2) Request by the customer (a request which may not be provoked); and
(3) Introduction of new products or systems (in particular, in the pharmaceutical sector).

The Court of Appeal of Brussels has accepted that an implied comparison was necessary to allow a new entrant to penetrate a market on which a competitor had a dominant position.[2] An advertisement of Pepsi Cola

1 Trade Practices and Consumer Protection Act 1991, Article 22.
2 Court of Appeal Brussels, 7 June 1983, [1983] JT 717.

(with a very low market share in Belgium) claimed that, in a blindfold test, its cola had been found more tasty by a majority of consumers than another comparable drink which, of course, was recognizable as Coca Cola (with a market share of more than eighty per cent).

4.2 Media Channels

4.2.1 Applicable Law

Advertising and sponsoring through media channels is a competence of the Communities in Belgium. This means that the Flemish, the French, and the German-Speaking communities each enacted their own Decrees regulating these matters. The Act of 6 February 1987 on radio distribution and television distribution networks and on commercial advertising on radio and television[1] has been amended by Decrees of the Communities.[2] These Decrees also contain provisions on advertising and sponsorship,[3] which implement the television broadcasting Directive of 3 October 1989.

4.2.2 Substantive Provisions

Radio and television broadcasting organizations may transmit advertisements only if they are authorized to do so by the government.

Advertisements may not present political, religious, or ideological views; nor may they discriminate on the grounds of race, sex, nationality, philosophical or political conviction, or prejudice human dignity. They may not encourage behavior prejudicial to health or safety of the environment.

Advertising may not directly or indirectly relate to:

---

1 BS, 3 April 1987, err., BS, 25 April 1987.

2 For the Flemish-Speaking Community, by the Decrees of 13 June 1990 (BS, 18 July 1990) and of 12 June 1991 (BS, 14 August 1991), most recently amended by Decrees of 15 December 1993; for the French-Speaking Community, by the Decrees of 4 July 1989 (BS, 31 August 1989) and of 19 July 1991 (BS, 2 October 1991); for the German-Speaking Community, by the Decree of 19 February 1990 (BS, 19 May 1990).

3 *See*, for the Flemish-Speaking Community, the Decree of 12 June 1991 (BS, 14 August 1991), most recently amended by the Decree of 15 December 1993; for the French-Speaking Community, the Decree of 17 July 1987 (BS, 22 August 1987), amended by the Decree of 19 July 1991 (BS, 2 October 1991).

(1) Cigarettes and tobacco products;
(2) Medicines and medical treatments which are only available with a prescription;
(3) Other goods and services which the government designates; and
(4) Statements of price.

Advertising pertaining to alcoholic beverages must comply with the following criteria:

(1) It may not be aimed specifically at minors and, in particular, depicting minors consuming these beverages;
(2) It may not link the consumption of alcohol to enhanced physical performance or to driving;
(3) It may not create the impression that the consumption of alcohol contributes toward social or sexual success;
(4) It may not claim that alcohol has therapeutic qualities or that it has a stimulating, calming, or stress-reducing effect;
(5) It may not encourage over-consumption of alcohol or present abstinence or moderation in a negative light; and
(6) It may not place emphasis on high alcoholic content as being a positive quality of the beverages.

Advertising also may not cause moral or physical detriment to minors and must comply with the following criteria for their protection:

(1) It may not directly exhort minors to buy a product or a service by exploiting their inexperience or credulity;
(2) It may not directly encourage minors to persuade their parents or others to purchase the goods or services being advertised;
(3) It may not exploit the special trust minors place in parents, teachers, or other individuals; and
(4) It may not unreasonably show minors in dangerous situations.

Advertising may not use subliminal techniques, and surreptitious advertising is prohibited. Advertising must be readily recognizable as such and kept separate from other parts of the program service. Provisions also regulate the way in which advertisements must be inserted in and between programs and the amount of advertising per day and per hour.

Sponsoring is regulated in a manner similar to advertising. The conditions as established above for advertising also must be met with regard to sponsoring. Additional requirements for sponsored programs are that the content and scheduling of these programs may not be influenced by the sponsor in such a way as to affect the responsibility and editorial independence of the broadcaster with respect to programs. Sponsors may not encourage the purchase or rental of the products or services of the sponsor or a third party, in particular by making special promotional references to those products or services. Finally, sponsored programs must be clearly identified as such by the name and/or logo of the sponsor at the beginning and/or the end of the program and news and current affairs programs may not be sponsored.

4.3 Target Audiences

Special provisions protect minors against advertising through media channels, as discussed above.

Section 5

Unfair Contract Terms

5.1 Source of Rule

Articles 31-36 of the Trade Practices and Consumer Protection Act 1991 regulate these contract terms.

5.2 Scope and Application

Articles 31-36 apply to terms in consumer contracts, as well as to the supply conditions of the public authorities.

5.3 Substantive Provisions

Contract terms and conditions which create an obvious imbalance between the rights and obligations of the parties can be declared null and void by the court.[1]

In addition to the general clause of Article 31, a number of terms and conditions are black-listed.[2] If they appear in a consumer transaction, they are automatically null and void. The twenty-one black-listed terms and conditions are not only void, they also are "prohibited", which means that an action for a cease and desist order is possible against the use of such terms and conditions. The black-list includes terms which confer on the seller the right to unilaterally change the price, the terms of delivery, or the characteristics of the product or the service, exclusion of liability for intent or gross negligence, exclusion of legal redress, and the right of unilateral termination without compensating the consumer.

In order to ensure the balance between the rights and obligations of the parties to a contract of sale of products or services, the King may, for the sectors of economic activity or the categories of products or

1 Trade Practices and Consumer Protection Act 1991, Article 31.
2 Trade Practices and Consumer Protection Act 1991, Article 32.

services he designates, prescribe or prohibit the use of certain terms in contracts with consumers. He also can impose the use of model contracts.[1]

Before taking one of these measures, the King must consult the Commission for Unfair Terms[2] and the High Council for Small and Medium-Sized Undertakings.

5.4 Standing, Procedures, and Sanctions

The issues relating to standing, procedures, and sanctions were addressed in the general overview of the Trade Practices and Consumer Protection Act 1991.

1 Trade Practices and Consumer Protection Act 1991, Article 34.

2 Established by virtue of the Trade Practices and Consumer Protection Act 1991, Articles 35-36.

Section 6

Reasonable Pricing and Price Controls

6.1 Price Information

Price information is regulated by the Trade Practices and Consumer Protection Act 1991.

6.1.1 Products

Except in the case of auction sales, a seller must indicate in writing and in an unambiguous manner the price of the products offered for sale to the consumer. In addition, if the products are displayed, the price indication must be legible and clearly visible.[1]

6.1.2 Services

A seller must indicate in writing and in a legible, clearly visible, and unambiguous manner the tariff of the services offered to consumers.[2]

6.1.3 General Rules

The price or tariff indicated will be the total price or total tariff, including value added tax, all other taxes, and the costs of all services which the consumer will be required to bear.[3]

All prices and tariffs must be indicated initially in Belgian francs.[4] This means that the indication of prices and tariffs in another currency is allowed, provided it is accompanied by an indication in Belgian francs.

---

1 Trade Practices and Consumer Protection Act 1991, Article 2, Paragraph 1.
2 Trade Practices and Consumer Protection Act 1991, Article 2, Paragraph 2.
3 Trade Practices and Consumer Protection Act 1991, Article 3.
4 Trade Practices and Consumer Protection Act 1991, Article 4.

6.1.4 *Indication of Price Comparisons and Price Reductions*

Price comparisons with other sellers or with the prices imposed or recommended by the manufacturer are prohibited, and reference to prices established by the public authorities may not be presented in the same manner as price reductions.

A seller who announces a price reduction must refer to the price formerly applied to the same products or services in the same establishment.[1] The price reductions announced will be genuine. Except for products whose value can quickly diminish, no price or tariff can be considered usual if it has not been applied during a continuing period of one month preceding the date from which the reduced price is applied. The date from which the reduction applies will be indicated during the entire sale period at the reduced price. With the exception of clearance sales, this period may not exceed one month and, except for the products the value of which can quickly diminish and which cannot be preserved any longer (e.g., fresh food), it may not be shorter than one business day.[2]

A seller also may refer in a legible, clearly visible, and unambiguous manner to prices regulated pursuant to the Price Regulation Act 1945. In this case, however, he may not use the techniques for announcing price reductions as stated in Article 5 of the Trade Practices and Consumer Protection Act 1991.[3]

Merchants cannot announce a price reduction or a price comparison if they cannot give evidence that the price referred to complies with the conditions established hereabove.[4]

Every indication of a price or tariff reduction which is expressed by an amount or a discount percentage will be limited to one of the following techniques:

(1) Indication of the new price next to the crossed-out old price;
(2) Statement of "new price" and "old price" next to the corresponding figures;
(3) Announcement of a discount percentage and the new price next to the crossed-out old price; and
(4) Announcement of a uniform discount percentage granted for the products and services or the categories of products and services to

1 Trade Practices and Consumer Protection Act 1991, Article 43, Paragraph 1.
2 Trade Practices and Consumer Protection Act 1991, Article 43, Paragraph 1.
3 Trade Practices and Consumer Protection Act 1991, Article 43, Paragraph 4.
4 Trade Practices and Consumer Protection Act 1991, Article 43, Paragraph 5.

which this indication applies; in both cases, the announcement shall state whether or not the price reduction has been applied.

In no case may the indication of a price reduction be presented to the consumer as a free offer of a certain quantity of the product or part of a service.[1]

When a price reduction which is limited in time is announced outside the sales premises and the seller has run out of the products concerned, he must deliver to the consumer, for each product which value exceeds BF 1,000 and is no longer in stock, a voucher which gives the right to purchase that product within a reasonable period of time and at the terms of the offer, except where it is impossible to restock the products under the same conditions.[2]

6.2 Residual Controls against Extortionate Prices

6.2.1 Legislative Framework

During World War II, the government enacted, on the basis of special powers conferred on it by Parliament, several *arrêtés-lois* containing measures to ensure the normal supply of the country and imposing criminal sanctions on abuses in trade in basic necessities. They contained price-fixing powers for the government. The *arrêté-loi* of 22 January 1945,[3] "concerning the repression of infringements of the regulation of the supply of the country", is still in force. It provides for two kinds of government intervention in the economic market. The Minister of Economic Affairs and the Minister of Agriculture may prohibit, regulate, or control the importation, production, manufacture, possession, processing, use, distribution, purchase, sale, exhibition, offer for sale, and transport of commodities, goods, and animals. They also may reserve the exercise of certain activities to certain individuals or undertakings they designate and close undertakings whose activities are deemed superfluous or harmful. They also may requisition, for consideration, any goods, commodities, or animals with a view to placing them at the disposal of the public authorities or of private individuals or

1 Trade Practices and Consumer Protection Act 1991, Article 5.
2 Trade Practices and Consumer Protection Act 1991, Article 45.
3 BS, 24 January 1945, err., BS, 11 February 1945.

institutions and impose, for remuneration, on parties subject to the requisitions all obligations deemed necessary.

According to the Council of State, the highest administrative court, the general power to prohibit or regulate trade in certain products is no longer applicable. The power to requisition, while still valid, has rarely been used in recent years.

The Minister of Economic Affairs can take a number of measures in order to ensure that a certain price level is not exceeded. The powers in this respect have even been extended by amendments of the *arrêté-loi* of 22 January 1945 by Acts of Parliament in 1969 and 1971. The Act of 1971 also confirmed the enforceability of the *arrêté-loi* of 1945 and changed its title to the Act of 22 January 1945 concerning economic regulation and prices. The Act of 22 January 1945 contains criminal sanctions, including the closing of the premises, and special powers for the investigation, establishment, and prosecution of infringements, a general prohibition against selling commodities, goods, or animals at a price higher than the "normal price"[1] and a general prohibition against refusal to sell.[2] The latter prohibition has seldom been applied, and it is questionable whether it is significant since the entry into force on 1 April 1993 of the Competition Act of 5 August 1991.

In recent years, with a low inflation rate, price regulation has been relaxed. In many sectors, price liberty has been effective since 1986. Since 1 May 1993, the obligation of prior declaration of price increases has been abolished for practically all sectors of the economy. Only the tariffs for energy, water distribution, cars, tele-distribution, mandatory insurances, rest homes, and waste processing are subject to price regulation. For some other products, such as bread and medicines, the Minister has fixed maximum prices. Nevertheless, the legal instruments for a strict and comprehensive price policy still exist and could be used more intensively in times of higher inflation. The margin of intervention of the Belgian authorities, however, has become limited in the context of European integration. In a series of judgments in the 1970s and the 1980s, the EU Court of Justice declared a number of national price-fixing measures, including elements of Belgian price regulation, contrary to the principle of free movement of goods within the Common Market.

---

1 Act of 22 January 1945, Article 1, Paragraph 2.
2 Act of 22 January 1945, Article 4.

6.2.2 *Price Regulation*

6.2.2.1 *Scope and Application*

The provisions of the Price Regulation Act apply to all products (movable goods) and services performed on a self-employment basis which are not subject to specific legislation.[1] The Price Regulation Act does not apply to the renting of motion pictures and intellectual property. The Minister of Economic Affairs, however, has been empowered by a special Act of 30 July 1963[2] to establish maximum prices for the renting of films. The Price Regulation Act applies to the public authorities and public undertakings, such as water and electricity distribution and transport,[3] and to bank services which are not directly related to monetary policy.[4]

6.2.2.2 *Prohibition of Abnormal Prices*

In the absence of a maximum price established by the Minister of Economic Affairs or of a program contract, it is an offense to sell at a price which is higher than the "normal price". It also is an offense to make an exorbitant profit (even by selling at or below the maximum price).

It is for the courts to determine whether a price is excessive or gives rise to an abnormal profit. To determine whether a price is unusually high, the courts have regard to the profit made, the market conditions, and the costs of the undertaking. According to the Court of Cassation,[5] the courts, although deciding independently to what extent they take into consideration each of the three criteria mentioned, must have regard to market conditions. Cases in which the sale at an excessive price were established are exceptional. In most of these cases, sale at an unusual price was only one of the charges.

6.2.2.3 *Price Interventions of the Government*

The Minister of Economic Affairs is competent to establish prices. However, before taking any of the general measures of price policy

---

1 The most important example is the special price regulation for pharmaceutical products which are reimbursed by social security, contained in Articles 313 *et seq.* of the Programme Act of 22 December 1989, BS, 30 December 1989.

2 BS, 16-17 August 1963, err., BS, 9 October 1963.

3 Council of State, 14 March 1980, Number 20.193.

4 Court of Appeal Brussels, 17 November 1988, [1989] RDC/TBH, 373.

5 Cass., 13 April 1948, [1948] Pas., I, 558.

(such as the establishing of maximum prices), the minister must consult the Commission for Price Regulation, created in 1969 and composed of representatives of industry, agriculture, distribution, trade unions, consumer cooperatives, family organizations, and several ministers of the national government.

The Minister of Economic Affairs can establish a maximum price for any given product. It is an offense to sell above the maximum price. Presently, maximum prices only exist for a few products and services, such as bread, taxi fares, electricity, gas, and pharmaceutical products.

The prior requirement of an advance declaration of price increases has been abolished by the Ministerial Decree of 20 April 1993, 28 April 1993. Pursuant to this Decree, which became effective on 1 May 1993, an undertaking with a turnover of more than BF 300-million must notify every change in its sale prices to the Price Service of the Ministry of Economic Affairs no later than the day of its application. The notification states the existing prices, the new prices, the changes in percentage, and the exact date of application.[1]

However, undertakings in a limited number of sectors must, irrespective of their turnover, apply for approval of a price increase with the Price Service of the Ministry of Economic Affairs. The sectors include those related to petroleum products, waste processing, rest homes, gas and electricity, water distribution, medicines, motor vehicles of less than 3.5 tons, tele-distribution, and certain mandatory insurances.[2] The application must state the name and address of the applicant, nature and specifications of the products concerned, and the turnover, existing prices, and the prices applied for and their exact date of application. Sales conditions, market and competition conditions, a justification in figures of the increase and the evolution of cost price elements, the annual accounts of the undertaking for the last three years, and the trading account of the division concerned must be included in the application.[3]

Within sixty days of the application, the Minister of Economic Affairs must advise the applicant of the decision. As soon as the undertaking has received the decision, it may apply the price increase which has been authorized. In the absence of a decision within that time limit, the undertaking has the right to apply the proposed price increase.[4] Prices of new products in the sectors mentioned in Article 3 must be notified

1 Ministerial Decree of 20 April 1993, Article 2.
2 Ministerial Decree of 20 April 1993, Article 3.
3 Ministerial Decree of 20 April 1993, Article 4.
4 Ministerial Decree of 20 April 1993, Article 5.

to the Price Service not later than ten days before their application. In the absence of an answer by the minister within ten days, the product will be considered as a new product (for which an application for an authorization of price increase is not required).

Since 1969, the Minister of Economic Affairs can conclude so-called program contracts with individual undertakings or associations of undertakings. These contracts may contain obligations in the area of prices.[1] With regard to the remaining areas, the Price Regulation Act is vague on the nature and scope of these contracts. The program contract for petroleum products, which is still effective, is undoubtedly the most significant. This program contract exempts petroleum companies from price increase declarations and the imposition of maximum prices, provided they adhere to the program contract concluded between the Minister of Economic Affairs and the Belgian Petroleum Federation. This program contract provides for a flexible adaptation of the price of fuel at service stations, but with a number of obligations for the suppliers *vis-à-vis* the retailers (in respect of margins).

6.3 Competition Law

Belgian competition law is basically structured after EU competition law. The Act of 5 August 1991 on the protection of economic competition (Competition Act 1991)[2] is a transcription of Articles 85 *et seq.* of the Treaty of Rome and the EU Merger Regulation.[3] The EU provisions are adapted to the Belgian situation (e.g., with respect of the definition of the market on which the restrictive practice must take place).

In view of the similarity of the concepts and the wording of the prohibitions in the Belgian Act and in EU law, the case law of the Court of Justice, as well as the regulations, decisions, and notices of the European Commission in competition matters have a genuine interpretative value for the application of the provisions of the Belgian Act. With regard to consumer interests, it may be noted that, as in EU competition law, an exemption from the prohibition of restrictive agreements may be granted only if a fair share of the benefit resulting from the agreement (e.g., improvement of distribution) is passed to the consumer.

---

1 Price Regulation Act 1945, Article 1, Paragraph 3.

2 BS, 11 October 1991.

3 Regulation 4064/89/EEC on the control of concentrations between undertakings, OJ 1989 L 257/14, entered into force on 21 September 1990.

With the entry into force of this Competition Act, price controls have been relaxed. Indeed, the Competition Act 1991 is devised as an alternative for a direct means of price control, in the general interest and in the interest of consumers in fair prices.

Section 7

Consumer Credit

7.1 Applicable Law

To implement EU Council Directive 87/102/EEC of 22 December 1986 for the approximation of the laws, regulations, and administrative provisions of the Member States concerning consumer credit,[1] the Belgian legislature approved the Act of 12 June 1991 on consumer credit (Consumer Credit Act 1991).[2]

The Act includes a general section which applies to all credit agreements and a special section with provisions respectively relating to installment sales, finance lease, installment loans, and the opening of lines of credit.

7.2 Information

7.2.1 Advertisement

Chapter II of the Consumer Credit Act 1991 regulates the advertising of credit. Article 5 of the Act states that any advertisement which has as its object or which may result in the granting of credit must specify in a legible, clearly visible, and unambiguous manner:

(1) The identity, address, and quality of the advertiser;
(2) The credit form concerned; and
(3) The particular or restrictive conditions under which the consumer credit can be submitted.

Any advertisement which indicates an interest rate or any figures relating to the costs of the credit must, in a clearly visible manner, state the annual percentage rate of charge as well.[3]

---

1 OJ 1987 L 42/48.
2 BS, 9 July 1991.
3 Consumer Credit Act 1991, Article 5, Paragraph 2.

The annual percentage rate of charge consists of the total cost of the credit to the consumer expressed as an annual percentage of the amount of the credit granted.[1] The calculation of the annual percentage rate of charge is regulated by the Royal Decree of 4 August 1992 on the charges, percentages, duration, and conditions of repayment.[2] This Royal Decree was made pursuant to the Consumer Credit Act 1991 and implements EU Council Directive 90/88/EEC of 22 February 1990, amending Directive 87/102/EEC.[3] If the precise calculation of the annual percentage rate of charge is impossible, the advertisement must state the total cost of the credit by means of a representative example, which also is determined by the Royal Decree of 4 August 1992.[4]

Any advertisement containing the statement "free credit" or a similar statement other than the indication of the annual percentage rate of charge is prohibited.[5]

The Act also contains strict regulations regarding hawking credit agreements.[6]

With regard to advertising, the Consumer Credit Act is, in relation to specific problems in matters of consumer credit, a *lex specialis* with respect to the Trade Practices and Consumer Protection Act 1991, which is the *lex generalis*.

7.2.2 Information Obligation

The provisions relating to advertising cannot be separated from the broader information obligation the Consumer Credit Act 1991 organizes in favor of the consumer. The credit institution or the credit intermediary must supply the consumer, in an exact and complete manner, with all necessary information regarding the credit agreement in view. It also is required to search for the credit which, with respect to its type and its amount, is best suited, having regard for the financial situation of the consumer at the time of the conclusion of the credit agreement.[7]

---

1 Consumer Credit Act 1991, Article 1.
2 BS, 8 September 1992.
3 1990 L 61/14.
4 Consumer Credit Act 1991, Article 5, Paragraph 2.
5 Consumer Credit Act 1991, Article 6.
6 Consumer Credit Act 1991, Articles 7-9.
7 Consumer Credit Act 1991, Article 11.

Conversely, the consumer is required to supply, at the request of the credit institution or credit intermediary, the correct and complete information in order to enable it to assess his or her financial situation and means of repayment.[1]

The credit institution or credit intermediary wishing to conclude a credit agreement must present the consumer with a free written offer. This offer must contain a number of specifications, such as information relating to the credit institution or credit intermediary, the amount of the credit granted, the annual percentage rate of charge, conditions of repayment, and the text of Article 18, which conveys the consumer the right to renounce the agreement within seven working days from signing the agreement when it was concluded on the day the offer became valid.[2]

The credit institution may present an offer only when, based on the information it possesses or should possess, it must reasonably assume that the consumer will be able to perform the obligations arising from the agreement.[3] If the credit institution infringes this obligation, the court can relieve the consumer, in whole or in part, from paying the interest for default and reduce his or her obligations to the price which would have applied in a cash payment for the goods or services or to the amount borrowed.[4]

As with regard to advertising, the Consumer Credit Act 1991 also is a *lex specialis* as far as unfair contract terms in credit agreements are concerned,[5] the *lex generalis* being the Trade Practices and Consumer Protection Act 1991.

7.3 Repayment Terms

The Royal Decree of 4 August 1992 imposes maximum terms for installment sales, finance lease, installment loans, and all credit agreements for which the terms for repayment and the installments generally remain the same for the entire duration of the agreement (e.g., for credit amounts between BF 8,600 and BF 20,000, the maximum term for repayment is

1 Consumer Credit Act 1991, Article 10.
2 Consumer Credit Act 1991, Article 14.
3 Consumer Credit Act 1991, Article 15.
4 Consumer Credit Act 1991, Article 92.
5 Consumer Credit Act 1991, Articles 28-33.

eighteen months; for amounts between BF 20,001 and BF 100,000, twenty-four months; for amounts between BF 300,001 and BF 400,000, forty-eight months; and for amounts higher than BF 1,500,000, 240 months).[1]

For credit agreements for which the terms for repayment generally remain the same for the entire duration of the agreement, and for which the installments are allowed to vary, including the opening of lines of credit, the Royal Decree imposes minimum installments.[2]

7.4 Termination of the Credit Agreement

7.4.1 Trial Period

As mentioned above, the consumer has the right to renounce the agreement within seven working days from signing the agreement when it was concluded on the day the offer became valid.[3] The same right is extended to the consumer, but now also for installment sales and for finance leases where the agreement was concluded in the presence of both parties outside the business premises of the credit institution or the credit intermediary.[4] If the credit agreement is concluded in the absence of both parties, i.e., by long-distance correspondence, the Trade Practices and Consumer Protection Act 1991 applies.

The Trade Practices and Consumer Protection Act 1991 also provides the consumer with the right to renounce the agreement within seven working days.[5]

The consumer does not have the right to renounce an installment sale if the agreement was not concluded by long-distance correspondence or outside the business premises. The lack of a trial period, however, is largely compensated by the requirement that the seller, by the time the agreement is signed, receive an advance from the consumer of at least fifteen per cent of the purchase price in the instance of a cash payment.[6]

If the consumer renounces the agreement, he or she must inform the credit institution by registered mail and return the amounts received or used in virtue of the conditions of the agreement, *pro rata temporis*. No

---

1 Consumer Credit Act 1991, Article 8.
2 Consumer Credit Act 1991, Article 9.
3 Consumer Credit Act 1991, Article 18, Paragraph 1.
4 Consumer Credit Act 1991, Article 18, Paragraph 2.
5 Trade Practices and Consumer Protection Act 1991, Article 88.
6 Trade Practices and Consumer Protection Act 1991, Article 45.

indemnity may be demanded pursuant to the renunciation, and the advance paid by the consumer within the framework of the agreement must be returned to him within thirty days from renunciation of the agreement.[1]

7.4.2 Accelerated Reimbursement

The consumer has the right at any time to accelerate the satisfaction of his or her obligations under the agreement. In case of a complete accelerated payment, the consumer has the right to a reduction of the total amount to be paid or to an equivalent restitution, provided that he or she declares the intention to the credit institution by registered mail one month before the total reimbursement.

The amount of the reduction or of the restitution consists of at least seventy-five per cent of the total cost of the credit which has a bearing on the accelerated payment. The manner in which these amounts are calculated is regulated by the Royal Decree.

7.4.3 Payment Facilities

Pursuant to Article 38 of the Consumer Credit Act 1991, the Justice of the Peace can grant payment facilities to a consumer whose financial situation has deteriorated.

If the granting of payment facilities raises the costs of the credit agreement, the Justice of the Peace determines the part the consumer must bear.

---

1 Consumer Credit Act 1991, Article 18, Paragraph 3.

Section 8

Trade Descriptions and Occupational Licensing

8.1 Trade Descriptions

Trade descriptions are governed by the Trade Practices and Consumer Protection Act 1991. It contains provisions on price indication, indication of the quantities, denomination, composition, and labelling of products, and designations of origin.

8.1.1 Price Indication

Price indication is discussed above.

8.1.2 Indication of Quantity

Each product which is conditioned and destined for sale must bear on the package, or if there is no package on the product itself, in a clearly visible and unambiguous manner, the nominal quantity expressed in the unit of measure. There are a number of exceptions to this principle. Additional obligations also have been introduced for foodstuffs and prepackaged products.[1]

8.1.3 Denomination, Composition, and Labelling of Products and Services

Article 13 of the Trade Practices and Consumer Protection Act 1991 contains the following general obligations:

---

1 Trade Practices and Consumer Protection Act 1991, Article 8; *see also* Royal Decree of 26 January 1976, BS, 5 February 1976 and Royal Decree of 28 December 1979, BS, 1 January 1980, err., BS, 11 July 1980, implementing Directive 76/221/EEC concerning prepackaged goods.

(1) The labelling indications imposed by this Act, by its implementing provisions or by the implementing provisions of the Trade Practices Act 1971, as well as the directions for use and the warranties must be made at least in the language or the languages of the region in which the products are put into circulation;

(2) The indications on the label must be clearly visible and legible and must be clearly distinct from advertising; and

(3) In no case may the labelling be presented in such a way that it may be confused with a quality label.

The language of the region is either Dutch (for Flanders), French (for Wallonia), German (for the German-Speaking Community of Belgium), or Dutch and French (for Brussels). It should be stressed that the language obligation with respect to directions for use and warranties is not limited to the case that such documents are imposed by law (as a general rule, they are not). The requirement that the label should be, in all circumstances, at least in the language of the region is contrary to Article 30 of the Treaty of Rome (and Directive 79/112/EEC on the labelling of foodstuffs) if it is applied to products originating in another EU Member State. According to EU law, the Member States must accept that the labelling requirements are met by the use of another language which is easily understood by the consumers or that the information is guaranteed in some other way.[1]

Notwithstanding the powers conferred on him in the area of public health, the King can, with the intention of guaranteeing fairness in commercial transactions or the protection of consumers, take a number of measures relating to the composition, labelling, and denominations of products.

8.1.4 Designations of Origin

Belgium has not ratified any of the international conventions on the protection of designations of origin (for wine and cheese). By virtue of the Act of 18 April 1927, however, concerning the protection of designations of origin of wine and spirits, foreign denominations of origin for wine and spirits are protected in Belgium if they are notified by the

1 CJEC, 18 June 1991, Case C-369/89, *Piageme* vs. *Peeters*, [1991] ECR I-2971.

interested government to the Belgian government. These denominations are published in the Belgian State Gazette.

The Trade Practices Act 1971 introduced the possibility for the King to recognize Belgian designations of origin. The Trade Practices and Consumer Protection Act 1991 contains the same rules. A designation of origin is the geographical name of a country, a region, or a place, which designates a product which originates from that area and the quality and characteristics of which are exclusively or substantially due to the geographical environment which includes natural and human factors.

A designation of origin is recognized by Royal Decree on a proposal by the Ministry for Small and Medium-Sized Undertakings. The Royal Decree establishes the conditions which products must fulfill to be marketed under the protected designation.[1] The King also may make the production and sale of products under a protected designation of origin dependent on the possession of a collective or individual certificate of origin.[2] It is prohibited to use a protected designation of origin for products which do not comply with these conditions even when it is accompanied by expressions such as "type", "method of", or "similar to".[3] It also is prohibited to produce or sell products under a designation of origin without the possession of a certificate of origin where such a certificate is required or to use a designation which is presented as a designation of origin where such designation is not recognized as a designation of origin.[4]

The Decree of 7 September 1989 of the Regional Council of Wallonia[5] created the possibility for the protection of Walloon designations of origin and quality labels.

8.1.5 Sanctions

The sanctions of the Trade Practices and Consumer Protection Act are discussed above.

---

1 Trade Practices and Consumer Protection Act 1991, Article 17.
2 Trade Practices and Consumer Protection Act 1991, Article 19.
3 Trade Practices and Consumer Protection Act 1991, Article 21.
4 Trade Practices and Consumer Protection Act 1991, Article 20.
5 BS, 28 November 1989, on which date it also entered into force.

8.2 Occupational Licensing

8.2.1 The Establishment Act for Small and Medium-Sized Undertakings

8.2.1.1 Source of Rule

The Act of 24 December 1958 (Establishment Act)[1] introduced the possibility for the King to impose, at the request of the representative association of small and medium-sized undertakings of the sector concerned, establishment requirements relating to a minimum knowledge of business management and specific professional education for small and medium-sized undertakings wanting to exercise the activity concerned. Pursuant to the Act, establishment requirements were established by Royal Decree for twenty different sectors (e.g., hairdressers, photographers, butchers, watchmakers, electricians, and a number of activities relating to the construction industry).

The Act of 1958 was replaced by the Act of 15 December 1970 on the exercise of professional activities in small and medium-sized commercial and craft undertakings,[2] but the Royal Decrees taken pursuant to the Act of 1958 remained in force. They were consecutively amended to bring them in line with the provisions of the Act of 1970, which has basically maintained the system of 1958. The King can impose requirements as to professional qualifications at the request of the sector concerned. The Act of 1970 has been amended several times, most recently in 1987.[3] It has given rise to nineteen new Royal Decrees (e.g., garagekeepers, trade in secondhand cars, plumbers, restaurants and catering, and undertakers).

8.2.1.2 Scope of Application

An establishment regulation pursuant to the Establishment Act of 1970 only applies to small and medium-sized undertakings as defined by the King. The Royal Decrees all define small and medium-sized undertakings by reference to the yearly average number of employees, usually less than fifty, sometimes less than twenty, or even less than five.

---

1 BS, 11 January 1958.

2 BS, 20 March 1971.

3 *See* van Gerven and Stuyck, *Wetboek Economisch en Financieel Recht- Economisch Recht/1* (Story-Scientia, Brussels), B.I.3.

Every individual who has the daily management of the undertaking must comply with the establishment requirements. He or she may be the self-employed head of the undertaking, but also, in the case of a company, an employee designated for that purpose. It is not necessary that one and the same person fulfills all establishment requirements. One person can have knowledge of business management while another (who is the actual head of the workshop) has the required professional knowledge. These possibilities are important for those undertakings that exercise different regulated activities. Finally, the establishment requirements also apply to independent (not to employed) managers of branches of the undertaking.

8.2.1.3 Establishment Certificates

Before being allowed to exercise one or more of the thirty-nine activities regulated by virtue of the Acts of 1958 and 1970, a small or medium-sized undertaking must be in the possession of the appropriate establishment certificate(s) delivered by the competent Chamber of Craft and Industry. An establishment certificate for a specific profession will be delivered only if the applicant can prove knowledge of business management and the professional knowledge as required by Royal Decree.

The required knowledge of business management has been established in a uniform manner, for all regulated activities, by the Royal Decree of 25 February 1971, as amended,[1] which contains general implementing provisions of the Establishment Act 1970. In contrast, the Royal Decrees regulating professional activities contain the requirements concerning specific professional knowledge.

With regard to the activities of retail and wholesale trade, the King is empowered to impose knowledge of business management (only) without a request by the representative associations.[2] The Royal Decree of 12 June 1989[3] made the requirements relating to knowledge of business management contained in the Royal Decree of 25 February 1971 applicable to the retail trade.

---

1 *See* van Gerven and Stuyck, *Wetboek Economisch en Financieel Recht - Economisch Recht/1* (Story-Scientia, Brussels), Bb II.1.

2 Establishment Act 1970, Article 4.

3 BS, 24 January 1990.

8.2.1.4 Professional Knowledge

The Royal Decrees list the diplomas, certificates, and other verification of professional qualification. In addition to a diploma, professional experience of a maximum of two years may be required. Individuals who do not fulfill the formal qualification requirement may be admitted to the professional activity, provided they show evidence of sufficient practical experience, the nature and duration of which will be established by the Royal Decree. The exercise of activities in a neighboring professional field also may be accepted as evidence of professional qualification.

8.2.1.5 Exemptions

The following parties are definitively exempted from the obligation to obtain an establishment certificate:

(1) Individuals who previously exercised the regulated activity (on a self-employed basis) at the time the regulation entered into force;
(2) The surviving husband or wife who continues the business of the deceased, provided the latter complied with the establishment requirements; and
(3) Persons wanting to exercise a regulated activity in a commune of less than 2,000 inhabitants, when this is justified by local circumstances and subject to a favorable opinion of the Chamber of Craft and Industry and the assent of the Ministry of Small and Medium-Sized Undertakings.

The following parties are provisionally exempted from obtaining the certificate:

(1) For one year, the purchaser of an undertaking and the person succeeding an independent branch manager;
(2) For three years, the children of the deceased head of an undertaking who complied himself with the establishment requirements (for infants, the three years begin to run when they reach the age of maturity); and
(3) For six months, the parties who, in a company, succeed the person who complied with the establishment requirements after that person has left the company.

8.2.1.6 *Sanctions*

The exercise of a particular activity which is regulated without the required certificate is an offense. Moreover, this will be considered as an act contrary to honest business practices against which any competitor (or trade association) can bring an action for a cease and desist order pursuant to the Trade Practices and Consumer Protection Act 1991.

8.2.2 *The Professions*

The exercise of the traditional professions, such as notaries public, lawyers, architects, doctors, dentists, pharmacists, veterinarians, and more recently company controllers, is organized by separate statutes, some of which date to the French Revolution. Apart from the professional qualifications required for their establishment (a specific diploma of higher education and/or training under the supervision of an established member of the profession), the members of these professions must join a professional organization in which the law has vested the power to ensure that its members comply with the rules of professional conduct.

8.2.3 *The Establishment of Aliens*

According to an Act of 19 February 1965[1] which was amended in 1977 and 1984[2] an alien who wants to exercise an independent activity of a lucrative nature in Belgium must possess a professional card provided by the Ministry of Small and Medium-Sized Undertakings. There are many exceptions to this obligation, relating to the person wanting to exercise the activity and to the nature of the activity. The most significant category of aliens exempt from the obligation are citizens of EU Member States. Other categories of individuals exempt from this requirement are:

(1) Women whose professional activity is limited to helping their husband in the exercise of his profession;

---

1 BS, 26 February 1965.

2 *See* van Gerven and Stuyck, *Wetboek Economisch en Financieel Recht, Economisch Recht/1* (Story-Scientia, Gent), Bd II.1.

(2) Ambulant merchants;
(3) Refugees having obtained a permit to reside in Belgium;
(4) Artists and musicians performing in a circus or theater, provided their presence in Belgium does not exceed fifteen days per semester;
(5) Sportsmen who exercise their activity not more than sixty days a year; and
(6) Businessmen who stay in Belgium for not more than three months per semester.[1]

The professional card determines precisely the nature of the activity for which it is delivered. The card is personal, cannot be transferred, and is valid for five years. Renewal of the card is possible.

The minister can refuse the card only after having obtained the opinion of the Council for Economic Investigation of Aliens, an administrative court. The applicant must be heard by the Council. Decisions which depart from the opinion of the Council must be made by the minister personally. The Council has the power to withdraw the card in instances where it is used unlawfully.

8.2.4 The Establishment of Large Sales Surfaces

By virtue of an Act of 29 June 1975 on the establishment of shops,[2] a license is required for the operation of a retail shop with a large sales surface, i.e., a gross built-up surface of more than 3,000 square meters and a net built-up surface of more than 1,500 square meters in "Zone I" (urban regions) and a gross built-up surface of more than 1,000 square meters and a net built-up surface of more than 750 square meters in "Zone II" (rural regions). A license also is required for the expansion of an existing shop when these thresholds are exceeded.

8.2.5 Licensing Requirements in Various Sectors

The exercise of a number of economic activities is subject to an authorization imposed by specific legislation: tourism (tour operators, travel agents, camp sites, hotels), transport, the manufacture of and trade in medicines, and mining activities. The granting of the authorization is

---

1 Royal Decree of 11 December 1980, BS, 10 January 1981.
2 BS, 1 July 1975.

generally made dependent on the fulfillment of conditions relating to the quality of the services (e.g., accommodation standards for hotels and camp sites), professional qualifications, and financial guarantees.

8.2.6 Supervision of Insurance Companies and Credit Institutions

Insurance companies and credit institutions, such as banks, are subject to an authorization and a permanent supervision by a specialized government body. The supervision relates to prudential rules. The minimum requirements for the granting of an authorization as well as the essential prudential rules have been harmonized at the EU level by EU Directives.[1] The supervisory authority for banks is the Commission for Banking and Finance; the supervision of insurance companies is exercised by the Control Office for Insurance.

The EU Directives for banking and insurance have introduced the principle of "home state control" and "single license". Supervision of a bank or insurance company is the (quasi-) sole responsibility of the Member State in which that bank or insurance company has its head office. Once the bank or insurance company has obtained an authorization by the authorities of that Member State, it can exercise its activities throughout the European Union by establishing branches or agencies in other Member States or by providing cross-border services. As a result, the Belgian banking and insurance authorities will only supervise EU companies which have their head office in Belgium.

Belgium is presently gradually adapting its legislation in order to implement said Directives. In the area of insurance, the Act of 9 July 1975 on the control of insurance companies[2] has been amended by the Act of 19 July 1991,[3] implementing the "second generation" Directives. The implementation of the third-generation Directives constituting the ultimate stage of the liberalization process is forthcoming. The Act of 22 March 1993[4] has amended Royal Decree Number 185 on the control of banks and the emission of securities[5] to bring it in line with the Second Banking Directive.

---

1 *See* the Second Council Directive 89/646/EEC on credit institutions, OJ 1989 L 368/1 and Third Council Directive 92/49/EEC on direct insurance other than life insurance, OJ 1992 L 228/1.

2 BS, 29 July 1975.

3 BS, 9 August 1991.

4 BS, 19 April 1993.

5 BS, 10 July 1935.

Section 9

Merchandise Classes as Applied to Bulk Products

9.1 Applicable Law

Bulk products are addressed in Chapter II of the Trade Practices and Consumer Protection Act 1991, specifically in its Section 2, which regulates the indication of quantity. Some Royal Decrees implementing the Trade Practices Act 1971 still apply as well.[1] They are often the result of the implementation of EU Directives.[2]

9.2 Classes

Article 7 of the Trade Practices and Consumer Protection Act 1991 defines the different classes in which bulk products can be sold.

Products which are sold loose are those which are measured or weighed only by the customer or in his presence.

Products sold by the piece are those which cannot be fractioned without changing their nature or properties.

Conditioned products are products which were fractioned, weighed, counted, or measured, even during the production process, and are then packed, or not, and this with the intention of rendering these operations unnecessary at the time they are sold.

Prepacked products are conditioned products which are packed before being offered for sale, regardless of the nature of the package, which covers the product entirely or partly, but in such a manner that the

1 For example, regulating indications of quantity, Royal Decree of 4 September 1972, BS, 28 September 1972, amended by Royal Decree of 30 January 1975, BS, 21 February 1975, and Royal Decree of 26 January 1976, BS, 5 February 1976; regulating prepacking, Royal Decree of 28 December 1979, BS, 1 January 1980, err., BS, 11 July 1980, most recently amended by Royal Decree of 6 August 1990, BS, 4 September 1990, and Royal Decree of 16 February 1982, BS, 12 March 1982, amended by Royal Decree of 6 August 1990, BS, 4 September 1990.

2 For example, regulating prepacking, Council Directive 75/106/EEC of 19 December 1974, OJ 1975 L 44/1, amended by Council Directive 89/676/EEC, OJ 1989 L 398/18; Council Directive 76/211/EEC of 20 January 1976, OJ 1976 L 46/1, amended by Council Directive 78/891/EEC, OJ 1978 L 311/21, and Council Directive 80/232/EEC of 15 January 1980, OJ 1980 51/1, amended by Council Directive 87/356/EEC, OJ 1987 L 192/48.

content cannot be altered without opening or changing the package. This definition encompasses prepacked products in pre-established quantities and prepacked products in variable quantities.

9.3 Indication of Quantity

Article 8, Paragraph 1, of the Trade Practices and Consumer Protection Act 1991 provides that each product intended for sale must state on the package, or failing such package, on the product itself, in a legible, clearly visible, and unambiguous manner, the nominal net quantity expressed in a unit of measure.

For products conditioned in quantities exceeding ten kilograms or ten liters and intended for wholesale trade, this information must be stated in the same manner on the package, or failing such package, on the product itself, or on the invoice, shipping bill, or any other document handed in or sent at the time of the delivery. For products delivered per unit of freight exceeding ten kilogram or ten liters, the document of weight and/or measurement must state this information.[1]

The obligation to indicate the nominal quantity rests, depending on the case, with the company which actually prepacks the products or with the company which conditions the products. If the products are imported, this obligation rests with the importer. The final obligation, however, rests with the party who has the products conditioned or prepacked, where this party has informed in writing of this intention, depending on the case, the company which prepacks the products, the company which conditions them, or the importer.[2]

If the nominal quantity is not indicated according to the provisions of Article 8, Paragraph 1, of the Trade Practices and Consumer Protection Act 1991, the seller may offer the products for sale to the consumer only after having indicated the quantity expressed in units of measure, legibly, clearly visible, and unambiguously, on the package or, failing this, on the product itself or on a sign placed near the product. The quantity need not, however, be indicated for those products which are sold loose and are measured or weighed by the customer or in his presence.[3]

1 Trade Practices and Consumer Protection Act 1991, Article 8, Paragraphs 2 and 3.
2 Trade Practices and Consumer Protection Act 1991, Article 9.
3 Trade Practices and Consumer Protection Act 1991, Article 10.

The indications supplied by the measuring instruments with which the quantity of the products which are sold loose is determined also must be legible and clearly visible for the consumer.[1]

For products or categories of products he designates, the King can establish special rules regarding the indication of the quantity, exempt from the obligations imposed by Articles 8-10 of the Trade Practices and Consumer Protection Act 1991 and exempt from indicating the nominal quantity in a unit of measure and prescribe another unit of sale. The King also can determine the permissible differences between the indicated nominal quantity and the real quantity and the way of controlling these differences. He can establish the nominal quantities for the content and/or the recipients of the products which are intended to be placed on the market, and prescribe the number of pieces a prepackage contains and determine the permissible differences between the indicated number and the real number and the way of controlling these differences.[2]

---

1 Trade Practices and Consumer Protection Act 1991, Article 11.
2 Trade Practices and Consumer Protection Act 1991, Article 12.

Section 10

Implementing Consumer Rights

10.1 Information

As stated above, the Consumer Union publishes a monthly consumer magazine, *Test Aankoop/Test-Achats*, which contains comparative test results and a bimonthly magazine, *Budget en Recht/Budget et Droit*, which informs the consumer of his or her rights. Brochures and books on consumer affairs also are published by the Consumer Union.

The other organizations which represent consumer interests, such as the trade unions, the cooperative movements, and the family organization *Bond van Grote en Jonge Gezinnen/Ligue des Familles*, also publish magazines in which consumer-related matters are addressed.

The Research and Information Centre of Consumer Organizations (OIVO/CRIOC) plays an important role in issuing information on consumer affairs.

10.2 Material Incentives

Periodic penalty payments can be imposed in the framework of an action for a cease and desist order. The President of the Commercial Court can impose a periodic penalty payment for every day his order is not respected or for every new act in contravention of his order. The consumer organizations, which can bring an action for a cease and desist order,[1] have seldom taken advantage of this opportunity.

10.3 Class Actions

In Belgian law, class actions do not exist; however, in consumer matters, the right to group actions has been established. Article 98 of the Trade Practices and Consumer Protection Act 1991 grants consumer organizations the right to lodge an action for a cease and desist order. Article 98,

---

1 Trade Practices and Consumer Protection Act 1991, Article 98.

Paragraph 1, states that the action can be initiated at the request of an association for the protection of consumer interests which has legal personality and is represented on the Consumer Council or recognized by the Minister of Economic Affairs. Such an association can stand in court to defend statutorily determined collective interests.

10.4 Streamlined Procedures

Attempts to streamline the procedures in consumer matters have not been successful.

10.5 Technical and Material Support Groups

Arbitration between business and consumers exists in the area of textile cleaning and package holiday tours. These arbitration schemes are organized jointly by a professional organization and one or more consumer organizations.

Note: The authors wish to thank Gert Straetmans, assistant at the University of Leuven, for his assistance in the preparation of this contribution.

Canada

Dale B. Pope
Singleton Urquhart MacDonald
Vancouver, British Columbia, Canada

Canada

Canada

Section 1

Introduction

Pursuant to the provisions of the Constitution Act, 1867, governmental powers in Canada are divided between the federal government and the governments of Canada's ten provinces and two territories. The federal government has power over trade and commerce, while the provincial governments have power over property and civil rights.

The general concept of "consumer protection" can fall within either of these heads of power. Therefore, when considering an issue which falls within this general description, it is important that one determine a more distinct description of that issue in order to determine whether it will fall within the federal or provincial sphere of power.[1]

This means that there will often be an entirely different (although often relatively similar) set of laws, depending on the province one is concerned with. It is, therefore, very important that when one comes to do business in a particular province that one carefully studies the relevant legislation. Since it would be impossible in a survey of this scope to identify and discuss every legislative act of both levels of government, this chapter will focus on general concepts which can be identified throughout Canada and will provide specific examples for illustration.

1.1 Balance between Private Law, Administrative Law, and Self-Regulation

There are a variety of federal and provincial administrative bodies which operate in areas falling within the general description of consumer protection. Canada's Common Law system (with the exception of one province, which operates in part in a Civil Law system) means that there is a body of case law which also falls within this subject area.

1 For a full discussion of the division of powers in Canada, *see* Hogg, *Constitutional Law of Canada*, 3d Ed.

Furthermore, for some services (professions), there is a certain amount of self-regulation which is aimed, in part, at protecting consumers.

It is difficult to assess where the balance between these various forms of regulation lies. However, it is probably accurate to say that outside the area of self-regulation of professions, there is a relatively equal balance between private law and administrative law in consumer protection. In many cases, the various legislatures of the provinces have provided a legislative scheme which will assist a consumer in pursuing his private rights. For example, each province, with the exception of Quebec, has enacted a Sale of Goods Act.[1] These acts are designed to ensure that, in certain types of consumer transactions, a consumer is provided with the correct product for his needs, at a reasonable level of quality. A consumer who finds that this is not the case will be able to pursue a private law remedy on the basis of the breach of the statutory provision.

Even when the parliament of Canada or the legislature of a province has enacted legislation which is designed to regulate an occupation or an industry, a consumer who files a complaint pursuant to such legislation may find that remedy inadequate. For example, an individual who is provided with negligent service by a lawyer may complain to the Law Society of the respective province, and that complaint may result in some form of disciplinary action being taken against the lawyer. However, there is generally no form of financial redress to compensate the complainant for any damages that he or she has suffered. In order to recover in this manner, the complainant will have to be pursue a private law remedy through the court system.

The above example illustrates the difficulty in identifying a balance between these various forms of regulation. In reality, it is possible that a dissatisfied consumer might pursue more than one avenue of redress at the same time, and be provided with different remedies.

1.2 Primary Interest Groups

The primary interest groups in consumer protection in Canada are the consumer, the producer, the retailer, and the government. This is probably no different from any other free-market economy. The consumer,

---

1 Alberta: R.S.A. 1980, c. S-2; British Columbia: R.S.B.C. 1979, c. 370; Manitoba: R.S.M. 1987, c. S-10; New Brunswick: R.S.N.B. 1973, c. S-1; Newfoundland: R.S.N. 1990, c. S-6; Nova Scotia: R.S.N.S. 1989, c. 408; Ontario: R.S.O. 1990, c. S-1; Prince Edward Island: R.S.A.T.P.E.I. 1988, c. S-1; Saskatchewan: R.S. 1978, c. S-1.

of course, is concerned with price, quality, and supply. The producer will want to produce as much of his product as possible at the lowest possible cost. If higher quality means higher cost, then it may be the case that the producer will attempt to produce a product at the lowest possible level of quality without dissatisfying the consumer to the point where consumption is reduced. The retailer is a hybrid, in that he is in one sense a producer, but also a consumer. Finally, there is the government, which is concerned with the economy as a whole and which tries to ensure that there is not an under-supply of goods, causing inflation, or an over-supply, causing deflation and predatory-pricing, or whether some producer is operating in a monopoly.

In recent years, the environmental movement has become involved in these areas. For example, a producer of vegetables might now find that he is faced with higher costs because pressures from environmentalists have led the government to ban certain types of cheap pesticides. A lumber company might find that its costs have risen because environmental pressure has meant that the most efficient forms of logging or wood treatment are no longer acceptable. Motor vehicle producers have been forced to produce cars that cause less air pollution because of global fears regarding the ozone layer. Undoubtedly, the role of the environmental movement will continue to increase in scope and influence in the years to come.

1.3 Administrative Bodies, Public Law Structure

Because of the various governments which legislate within this general area, the existence or non-existence of administrative bodies and a public law structure varies to some degree. In the federal sphere, there are a variety of departments which operate in part to protect consumers. For example, Agriculture Canada is responsible for federal policies, programs, and regulations relating to agriculture and food, and is involved in such activities as grading and inspection, seed certification, regulation of pesticides, feeds, and fertilizers, farm loan guarantees, and so forth. Diagnostic and control programs for animal diseases, market development programs, and market forecasts and reports also come within the jurisdiction of this department. There is also a food production and inspection branch which is responsible for protecting the marketability of agricultural and food products.[1]

---

1 *See Canadian Government Programs and Services Reports*, C.C.H. Canadian Limited.

A further example at the federal level is the Department of Consumer and Corporate Affairs. Its mandate is to promote the fair and efficient operation of the marketplace in Canada. Within that department, the Bureau of Consumer Affairs establishes and enforces regulations and promotes policies to protect, assist, and advocate consumer interests and promote fairness in the market. The Director of the Bureau of Competition promotes competition and efficiency through enforcement and administration of the Competition Act.[1] The department also has a number of other branches which operate within the general description of consumer protection.[2]

At the provincial level, there is a substantial body of public law which is designed to protect consumers. As discussed above, all but one province has a Sale of Goods Act. Several provinces have enacted legislation that provides a set of remedies in cases of misrepresentation, but only in relation to sales of certain goods and services.[3]

In addition, every province has an Act which governs the insurance industry.[4]

Several provinces have legislation which governs contracts for the sale of agricultural machinery[5] and others have legislation which governs residential tenancies.[6]

Again, one must examine the legislative scheme of the relevant province in order to determine what Acts, if any, exist in the particular area with which one is concerned.

1.4 Market Regulatory Systems

There are a variety of regulatory systems in Canada which exist in a relatively diverse group of markets. For example, most provinces have

---

1 R.S.C. 1985, c. C-19.

2 R.S.C. 1985, c. C-19.

3 Ontario: Business Practices Act, R.S.O. 1990, c. B-18; Alberta: Unfair Trade Practices Act, R.S.A. 1980, c. U-3; British Columbia: Trade Practice Act, R.S.B.C. 1979, c. 406.

4 Ontario: R.S.O. 1990, c. I-8, s.234; New Brunswick: R.S.N.B. 1973, c. I-12, s.230; British Columbia: R.S.B.C. 1979, c. 200, s.223; Manitoba: R.S.M. 1987, c. 140, s.58; Nova Scotia: R.S.N.S. 1989, c. 231, s.112; Prince Edward Island: R.S.A.T. P.E.I. 1988, c. I-4, s.220; Alberta: R.S.A. 1980, c. I-5, s.299; Saskatchewan: R.S.S. 1978, c. S-26, s.192; Newfoundland: R.S.N. 1990, c. A-22, s.8.

5 Alberta: S.A. 1982, c. F-4.1; Manitoba: R.S.M. 1987, c. F40; Saskatchewan: R.S.S. 1978, c. A-10; Prince Edward Island: R.S.A.T. P.E.I. 1988, c. 1-4.

6 Ontario: R.S.O. 1990, c. L7, s.82 (1); Prince Edward Island: R.S.A.T. P.E.I. 1988, c. L4, s.96 (3); Newfoundland: R.S.N. 1990, c. R-14, s.15 (2); Saskatchewan: R.S.S. 1978, c. 22, s.30; Nova Scotia: R.S.N.S. 1989, c. 401, s.12 (2); British Columbia: R.S.B.C. 1979, c. 365, s.15.

milk and egg marketing boards, as well as some sort of marketing board relating to chickens, and so on.[1] In addition, the provinces generally have an energy board which is responsible for the regulation of energy supply and prices within the province. At the federal level, the Canadian Radio- Television and Telecommunications Commission (CRTC) is responsible for regulation in the radio and television markets, as well as telecommunications. Again, this body regulates supply and prices within these markets.

In recent years, regulation that was previously seen as being in the public interest, together with publicly owned enterprises which were thought to be serving the public interest, have been seen by some consumer advocates as operating in sheltered and anti-competitive environments that lead to higher prices, poorer quality, and low rates of innovation. Examples, they say, include airlines, trucking, long-distance telecommunications, agricultural supply management schemes, the financial services sector, and certain sectors of the self-governing professions. As a result, Canada has seen a gradual lessening of regulation over the past few years. This is in response not necessarily to alleged monopolistic abuse, but rather to the inefficiencies which some forms of market regulation agruably breed.[2]

---

1 Readers should be aware that, pursuant to the General Agreement on Trade and Tariffs (GATT) negotiations concluded in December 1993, Canada will abandon its system of regulatory bodies insofar as they control market supply and price, but will likely retain some sort of regulatory system pertaining to quality control.

2 Trebilcock, "Taking Stock: Consumerism in the 1990s", *Canadian Business Law Journal*, [1991], Volume 19, at p. 412.

Section 2

Consumer Products and Service Standards

In 1967, the federal government created the Department of Consumer and Corporate Affairs with the aim of protecting consumers by establishing a fair and efficient marketplace through measures designed to reduce any inequality between sellers and buyers, and to provide personal and economic safety by regulating marketplace deception, unfair trade practices, and unsafe products.[1] These measures were supplemented by provincial legislation covering consumer protection, business practices, and the sale of goods. While early regulations focused on the sale of goods, today, services account for approximately fifty per cent of personal consumer expenditures. Hence, both consumer products and consumer services are regulated in Canada by various means, including the requirement of registration and/or licensing as a precondition to the operation of a number of businesses under various federal and provincial statutes.

2.1 General Regime

The perceived requirement for government intervention into the marketplace in order to ensure consumer protection arises from the many and varied causes of consumer vulnerability. In addition to comprehension problems stemming from a general lack of common reading and numerical skills which afflict a large number of Canadians, cultural factors, age factors, and an increasingly complex marketplace all add to consumer vulnerability. New Canadians arriving from countries with different languages, marketplace practices, and customs often face problems that range from not understanding product information, prices, and methods of payments to not knowing how to complain and obtain redress. Children are a particularly vulnerable class, especially with regard to safety problems with household and leisure products. Youths are vulnerable to advertising influences, while seniors are frequently targeted for a

1 "The Market Place in Transition: Changing Roles for Consumers, Business and Governments?", Working Paper, Consumer and Corporate Affairs, Number RG2393/1992E 13.

variety of fraudulent sales schemes. New technologies add to the complexities of the marketplace with the constant introduction of new and improved computerized products.

2.1.1 Source of Rule

To counter the many potential hazards facing consumers in the marketplace, the various governments have implemented a wide variety of consumer protection laws. Indeed, owing to the separation of powers between the federal and provincial governments under the Canadian Constitution, measures have been taken separately by the individual provinces as well as by the central government, in an effort to ensure consumer protection across Canada. Owing to the immense volume of legislation in this area, the rest of this chapter will focus primarily on legislation deriving from the federal government and, where applicable, legislation enacted by the province of British Columbia.

2.1.2 Scope and Application of Rule

It is small wonder that with a regulatory regime as wide as that found in Canada, almost every aspect of consumer product and service standards is regulated, including such aspects as materials, manufacture, packaging, labeling, and distribution. This section considers the general scheme as regards consumer protection legislation, but is equally applicable to the specific schemes that follow, unless otherwise stated.

2.1.2.1 Material

Materials or substances that are or may be poisonous, toxic, flammable, explosive, corrosive, infectious, oxidizing, reactive, or are in some other way dangerous because of their composition are regulated by the Hazardous Products Act,[1] which divides products containing these materials and substances into three categories:

(1) Prohibited products, which are essentially banned from the marketplace;[2]

---

1 R.S.C. 1985, c. H-3.
2 Hazardous Products Act, s.4 (1).

(2) Restricted products, which are permitted in the marketplace under certain prescribed circumstances and conditions;[1] and
(3) Controlled products, which may enter the marketplace only if their supplier meets certain information disclosure requirements.[2]

2.1.2.2 Manufacture

Almost any legislation or policy that regulates the entry of a product into the marketplace also regulates its manufacture. Products falling within the scope of the Hazardous Products Act are either prohibited from manufacture or must be manufactured within specific guidelines so as to meet safety standards.

The manufacturing of goods may be regulated in any number of ways, including by content, method, conditions, or by-product. Buildings in Canada, for instance, may no longer be constructed using urea-formaldehyde-based thermal insulation.

2.1.2.3 Packaging and Labeling

It has been said that the mandatory nature of information disclosure is arguably the most pervasive form of product safety regulation in Canada.[3] Indeed, the Hazardous Products Act, among many others, including the Food and Drugs Act,[4] Textile Labeling Act,[5] Pest Control Products Act,[6] Tobacco Products Control Act,[7] Consumer Packaging and Labeling Act, National Trademark and True Labeling Act,[8] and Precious Metals Marketing Act,[9] and their attendant regulations, prescribe the form, manner, and languages in which products governed by each may be marketed, including the requirement of health and safety warning labels, ingredient labels, fiber content labels, and regulatory standards labels, as applicable.

---

1 Hazardous Products Act s.4 (2).
2 Hazardous Products Act, Part II.
3 Cohen, "Can It Really be Unconstitutional to Regulate Product Safety Information?", 1989, 17 C.B.L.J. 5-4.
4 R.S.C. 1985, CF-27.
5 R.S.C. 1985, c. T-10.
6 R.S.C. 1985, c. P-9.
7 R.S.C. 1985, c. 14 (4th Supp.).
8 R.S.C. 1985, c. N-18.
9 R.S.C. 1985, c. P-19.

2.1.2.4 *Distribution*

In addition to the prohibited, restricted, and controlled products under the Hazardous Products Act discussed above, the distribution of many other products is restricted, regulated, and/or prohibited altogether under various other legislations. Although the primary reason for regulating the distribution of products is health and safety, other factors exist as well. The Food and Drugs Act precludes the distribution of drugs as samples, except to the extent that such distribution is made under prescribed conditions, and only to a limited group of medical practitioners.[1]

The Act also limits and regulates the distribution or sale in Canada, or the offering, exposing, or having in possession for sale in Canada, of any drug or class of drugs manufactured outside Canada as the Governor-In-Council deems necessary for the protection of the public in relation to the safety and quality of any such drug or class of drugs.[2] Another statute authorizing the federal government's regulation of product distribution is the Tobacco Restraint Act , which makes it an offense to sell, give, or provide a person under the age of sixteen years any cigarettes or cigarette papers or other tobacco product for use by that person.[3]

2.1.3 *Standing*

The Minister responsible for the administration of the relevant Act, as the case may be, is vested with enforcement powers which include the appointment of inspectors and analysts to determine if contravention of the Act has occurred. In addition, there are many avenues for dissatisfied consumers to lodge product complaints. Many industries have their own administrative bodies that attempt to establish voluntary standards for their industry and to cooperate with the government in setting regulations.

The Canadian Toy Manufacturers Association is a good example of an industry group which has recognized early on the importance of consumer confidence in the safety of its products, and which aims actively to monitor and improve product safety standards in its industry. Consumer and Corporate Affairs Canada, the Better Business Bureau, and the Consumers Association of Canada keep open files on consumers' product complaints.

---

1 Food and Drugs Act, s.14.
2 Food and Drugs Act, s.30 (1) (b).
3 Tobacco Restraint Act, R.S.C. 1985, c. T-12, s.2.

2.1.4 *Procedures*

Once the Ministry administering the relevant Act becomes aware of a contravention or possible contravention of its legislation, the department responsible may conduct investigations to determine the validity of the allegations. The powers of the inspectors are generally wide, and many of the statutes contain powers of search, seizure and/or forfeiture of the product involved.[1] In addition to government intervention, consumers themselves may seek redress for their complaints directly from their product or service supplier.

In fact, many businesses do welcome consumer feedback, since solving small problems often leads to improved products and services, thereby resulting in improved overall competitiveness and, ultimately, reputation. Problems less amenable to amicable resolution between the business and the consumer may find themselves the subject of mediation, negotiation, adjudication, or litigation.

2.1.5 *Sanctions*

Contravention of any of the Acts discussed in this chapter is quasi-criminal in nature and capable of prosecution by summary conviction or indictment, potentially resulting in monetary liability, imprisonment, or both. Punishments provided for in consumer protection legislation may range from relatively lenient, as in the case of the Tobacco Restraint Act,[2] to very stringent, as in the Hazardous Products Act.[3] Further, where a corporation commits an offense under the Hazardous Products Act, any officer, director, or agent of the corporation who directed, authorized, assented to, acquiesced in, or participated in the commission of the offense is a party to and guilty of the offense, and is liable on

---

1 The Hazardous Products Act, Tobacco Control Act, Tobacco Restraint Act, and Food and Drugs Act, among others.

2 This Act provides for summary conviction only and fines, not imprisonment (a) in the case of a first offense, to an amount not exceeding Cdn. $10; (b) in the case of a second offense, to a fine not exceeding Cdn. $25; and (c) in the case of a third or subsequent offense, to a fine not exceeding Cdn. $100.

3 The Hazardous Products Act, S 28 (1): "Every person who contravenes or fails to comply with any provision of this Act or any regulations made under this Act: (a) is guilty of an offense punishable on summary conviction and liable to a fine not exceeding Cdn. $100,000 or to imprisonment for a term not exceeding six months or to both; or (b) is guilty of an indictable offense and liable to a fine not exceeding Cdn. $1-million or to imprisonment for a term not exceeding two years or to both."

conviction to the punishment provided for the offense, whether or not the corporation itself has been prosecuted or convicted.[1]

In spite of the wide powers of prosecution provided in the various Acts, however, most governmental departments will, in fact, work in cooperation and coordination with industry representatives and individuals, who have a mutual professional and commercial interest in the continued safety and quality of their products. Again, because the applicable legislation involves the criminal law, there is a relatively high standard of proof required in order to secure convictions. Therefore, it is often preferable to establish an environment of informal consultation amenable to the interchange of information and the frank discussion of technical problems.[2]

2.2 Special Regimes

2.2.1 Food

The Food and Drugs Act prohibits the sale of food that contains poisonous or harmful substances, is unfit for human consumption, consists of any filthy, putrid, disgusting, rotten, decomposed or diseased animal or vegetable substance, is adulterated, or is manufactured, prepared, preserved, packaged, or stored under unsanitary conditions.[3] The Act further requires the declaration of all ingredients of prepackaged food products, in their descending order of proportion, on labels affixed to the food packages.

The Governor-in-Council may, by regulation, identify a standard prescribed for a food, or any portion of the standard, as being necessary to prevent injury to the health of the consumer or purchaser of the food.[4] Once a standard has been identified, strict requirements arise for the labeling, packaging, sale, or advertisement of such food item, as well as for its importation into Canada, inter-provincial conveyance, and even possession for the purpose of inter-provincial conveyance preceding sale.

In addition to the Food and Drugs Act, the federal government seeks to guard consumers from hazards to health and from fraud or misleading representations associated with the sale of food by means of the Canada

---

1 Hazardous Products Act, s.28(2).

2 Hirshhorn, "The Administration of the Hazardous Products Act", *The Regulation of Quality: Products, Services, Work Places and the Environment* (ed. Dewees).

3 Food and Drugs Act, s.4.

4 Food and Drugs Act, s.6.1.

Agricultural Products Act,[1] which establishes national standards for agricultural products; the Fish Inspection Act;[2] the Weights and Measures Act,[3] which sets national standards for fair measure in trade for most measured commodities; and the Broadcasting Act,[4] which contains provisions regulating food advertising.

2.2.2 Drugs

Drugs are a highly regulated product in Canada. The Food and Drugs Act imposes strict packaging and labeling requirements on the sale or advertisement of drug products, and draws distinctions between various classes of drugs in Schedules B through H thereof. The later the schedule, the greater the restrictions imposed. Unauthorized possession of and/or trafficking in restricted drugs may give rise to criminal sanctions under the Act resulting in imprisonment for a term not exceeding ten years.[5] "Possession" includes possession of any property or any proceeds of any property obtained or derived from the trafficking, or possession for the purpose of trafficking of a restricted drug.[6]

2.2.3 Motor Vehicles

Pursuant to the provisions of the Motor Vehicle Safety Act, the Governor-In-Council prescribes the safety standards that are to be applicable to a motor vehicle and its components by class. "Safety Standards" means standards regulating the design, identification, construction, or functioning of motor vehicles and their components for the purpose of protecting persons against personal injury, impairment of health, or death.[7] All vehicles manufactured in Canada that meet the prescribed safety standards may have applied to them the words "Canada Motor Vehicle Safety Standard", which is a national trademark. Motor vehicle safety standards may be prescribed for motor vehicles manufactured and used in Canada,

---

1 Canada Agricultural Products Act, R.S.C. 1985, c. 20 (4th Supp.).
2 Fish Inspection Act, R.S.C. 1985, c. F-12.
3 Weights and Measures Act, R.S.C. 1985, c. W-6.
4 Broadcasting Act, S.C. 1991, c. 11.
5 Food and Drugs Act, s.48.
6 Food and Drugs Act, s.50.2.
7 Motor Vehicle Safety Act, R.S.C., c. M-10, s.2 (1).

motor vehicles exported or delivered for export from Canada, as well as motor vehicles imported into Canada.

Manufacturers, distributors, and importers of motor vehicles of a class for which safety standards have been prescribed must give notice of any defect in the construction, design, or functioning of that motor vehicle or its components that affects or is likely to affect the safe operation of that vehicle to the seller of the vehicle, the current registered owner of the vehicle, as well as to the Minister of Transport.[1] In most cases where motor vehicle safety standards regulations or amendments are proposed, they will be published in order to afford a reasonable opportunity for manufacturers, distributors, importers, and other interested persons to make representations to the Minister with respect thereto.

Much like the Motor Vehicle Safety Act, the Motor Vehicle Tire Safety Act[2] prescribes safety standards for motor vehicle tires. The two Acts are virtually identical in their treatment of safety standards, labeling, import and export, notice of defects, and administration. The latter Act, however, does not contain the same provisions with respect to exemption from compliance with safety standards or research and testing as is found in the Motor Vehicle Safety Act.[3]

2.2.4 Electrical Appliances

In British Columbia, the safety of electrical equipment is governed by the Electrical Safety Act.[4] The Electrical Safety Act is in turn administered by the Electrical Safety Branch of British Columbia's Ministry of Municipal Affairs. In addition to the Electrical Safety Act, the following regulations are pertinent: the British Columbia Electrical Code Regulation, which contains safety standards provisions;[5] the Electrical and Communication Transmission and Distribution System Regulation;[6] the Electrical Safety Regulation;[7] and the Television Equipment Installation on Overhead Electric Lines Regulations.[8] Essentially, the Electrical

---

1 Motor Vehicle Safety Act, s.8(1).

2 Motor Vehicle Tire Safety Act, R.S.C. 1985, c. M-11.

3 Motor Vehicle Safety Act, ss.10-12.

4 Electrical Safety Act, R.S.B.C. 1979, c. 104.

5 British Columbia Electrical Code Regulation, B.C. Reg. 452/90.

6 Electrical and Communication Transmission and Distribution System Regulation, B.C. Reg. 453/90.

7 Electrical Safety Regulation, B.C. Reg. 450/90.

8 Television Equipment Installation on Overhead Electric Lines Regulations, B.C.

Safety Regulation requires all electrical equipment sold, offered for sale, or otherwise disposed of to have been approved, and to bear a label signifying such approval.[1]

"Electrical equipment" includes any machinery, plant, works, wires, pipes, poles, conduits, apparatus, appliance, and equipment used or designed or intended for use for or in connection with the generation, transmission, supply, distribution, or use of electrical energy for any purpose. All certification bodies in British Columbia currently must be accredited by the Standards Council of Canada. The oldest certification organization in Canada is the Canadian Standards Association, which is discussed in greater detail in Section 3.

2.2.5 Tools

There is no specific legislation in Canada or in British Columbia dealing with tools *per se*. If tools are manufactured, sold, advertised, or used in British Columbia, they would fall within the scope of the Electrical Safety Act discussed above. If they are simply manual tools, such as screw-drivers, they would not be regulated unless they contained a regulated substance or material, had a dangerous design, or required particular packaging or labeling specifications. Otherwise, their sale would fall within the general sale of goods rules which, in British Columbia, are governed by the Sale of Goods Act.

In fact, every province in Canada, except Quebec, has a Sale of Goods Act modeled after English legislation of the same name. The Act ensures consumer protection with regard to the purchase and sale of goods by imposing, for example, an implied condition of merchantable quality or an implied condition of suitability for a particular purpose. Certain facts, however, must be established before a remedy can be granted under this Act. The Sale of Goods Act is covered in greater detail in Section 5.

2.2.6 Textiles

The Textile Labeling Act requires that information on fiber content and dealer identity be provided on the labels of consumer textile articles,

---

1 Electrical Safety Regulation, B.C. Reg. 450/90, s.3.

while the Canadian Care Labeling Program uses color-coded symbols to provide guidance for the care of textiles.

Further, many products made in whole or in part of textile fibers are tested using the Standard Method of Test for Flammability of Clothing Textiles, a standard of the American Society for Testing and Materials. Potentially dangerous items, such as flammable clothing or bed clothes are regulated by the Hazardous Products Act.

2.2.7 *Toys*

Owing to the relative vulnerability of the product-users in this group, a particular hazard is recognized in the manufacture and design of toys. Particular attention is paid to the composition and design of toys in view of children's tendency to place products into their mouths. Of the forty categories of items prohibited by Part I of Schedule 1 of the Hazardous Products Act, five categories deal exclusively with toys, and one with baby products.

Toys, or other items associated with play or child care, comprise another thirteen categories of restricted items under Part 2 of Schedule I of the Hazardous Products Act.

2.2.8 *Insurance*

The Insurance Act[1] deals specifically with the following classes of insurance:

(1) Life insurance;
(2) Accident and sickness insurance;
(3) Fire insurance;
(4) Automobile insurance; and
(5) Livestock insurance.

The Act contains more than 300 Sections, and it regulates almost every aspect of insurance purchases and sales, including designating the requirements of the contents of insurance policies, specifying the methods by which premiums may be paid or refunded, discussing circumstances

1 Insurance Act, R.S.B.C. 1979, c. 200.

under which a contract of insurance may or may not be rendered affordable, as well as providing for the granting for relief against forfeiture.

2.2.9 *Travel*

Consumer protection in the air travel industry in British Columbia is granted under the Travel Agents Act.[1] All travel agents and travel wholesalers in the province must be registered in compliance with the Act. Under the Act, a fund called the Travel Assurance Fund is established, to which all travel agents and travel wholesalers make payments, and against which claims of direct economic loss can be made by persons suffering by reason of the insolvency or bankruptcy of a travel agent or a travel wholesaler registered under the Act, and in other circumstances where the person should be entitled to repayment of money paid on his or her account for travel service. Claims against the fund are decided by the Travel Assurance Board, also established under the Act, which has exclusive jurisdiction over such rulings.

2.2.10 *Correspondence Courses*

Education, owing to the separation of constitutional powers in Canada, is an area distinctly within the realm of provincial governance. The School Act[2] is the enabling legislation which permits the Minister of Education to regulate correspondence courses within the province of British Columbia.

At the elementary/secondary school level, there are now nine regional correspondence schools in the province of British Columbia. The first of such schools was established in 1986, and by the school year ending 30 June 1993, course enrollment at the secondary level had reached a significant 38,731. The courses for the schools are prepared based on the curriculum existing at the time of drafting, and are developed by the Ministry of Education. They are then delivered by the regional correspondence schools, which provide primarily administrative and instructional marking services. At the post-secondary level, the

1 Travel Agents Act, R.S.B.C. 1979, c. 409.
2 School Act, R.S.B.C. 1979, c. 61, s.182 (2) (h).

Open Learning Agency, which is administered by the Ministry of Advanced Education, oversees the courses.

While both organizations are well publicized, there is no particular mechanism of consumer protection to guard potential enrollees against things such as poorly operated courses, or false or fraudulent course offerings. It is essentially up to the enrollee to confirm the accreditation of their school with the relevant government ministry, or to later seek redress with the institution itself under general trade practice laws or through litigation.

2.2.11 Mail Order

Again, no particular legislation exists to regulate mail-order marketing in itself. Indeed, mail order sales are difficult to regulate because the marketing may originate from different provinces, if not different countries. Fortunately, in Canada there is the Canadian Direct Marketing Association, which was established in 1967 and which has grown from a small twenty-one member group to an organization representing more than 700 companies involved in the 7.86-billion Canadian Dollars direct-marketing industry. Complaints against mail-order suppliers can be lodged with this organization which, albeit in a voluntary capacity, operates an integrity consumer protection program and seeks to enforce a code of ethics and standards of practice on its members. At present, approximately eighty per cent of Canadian direct-marketers are members of CDMA.

In addition to CDMA relief, consumers in British Columbia can have recourse to, where applicable, general consumer protection legislation such as the Sale of Goods Act, the Consumer Protection Act[1] or the Trade Practice Act.[2] Consumers dissatisfied with mail-order goods may be able to obtain compensation under the Trade Practice Act when a deceptive or unconscionable act or practice has occurred. Deceptive acts include any conduct having the capability, tendency, or effect of deceiving or misleading a person, whether such act or practice be oral, written, visual, descriptive, or any other form of representation, including a failure to disclose.[3] Generally, unconscionable acts or practices occur only in situations of extreme inequality.

---

1 Consumer Protection Act, R.S.B.C. 1979, c. 65.

2 Trade Practice Act, R.S.B.C. 1979, c. 406.

3 Trade Practice Act, s.3.

2.2.12 *Other*

As previously mentioned, a large part of consumption in Canada today involves the consumption of services. Services are much more difficult to regulate than products, primarily because of their intangible nature. Damages are difficult to quantify, and are also more difficult to prove. This is so in spite of the extensive regulation of the service sector in Canada. However, regulation in itself may not be sufficient to ensure proper protection of consumers. In the first place, self-regulating bodies may not inspire great confidence in consumers, who often may decide not to pursue a valid claim or complaint where they are under the impression that they will not obtain proper adjudication.

Recently, Canada has witnessed many criminal and/or Civil Law suits brought by patients against their formal medical advisors, some complaining of a lack of response from the College of Physicians and Surgeons, the self-regulating body of the medical profession. Conversely, even where a regulating body may impose strict sanctions on one of its own members, the courts may overturn their ruling and reinstate the professional.

Section 3

Testing

3.1 Voluntary and Mandatory Testing

Many matters relating to consumer protection fall within provincial jurisdictions. The federal government has, however, enacted legislation relating to safety standards and uniform merchandising standards for products, articles, materials, or substances which are subject to interprovincial transportation; these include the Hazardous Products Act and the Motor Vehicle Safety Act, discussed in Section 2.

Legislation has made it mandatory for certain products to undergo testing procedures before these products are released into the marketplace. For example, all electrical products must be tested and approved against fire and shock hazards before they can be introduced and manufacturers of new drugs must make a "new drug submission" under the Food and Drugs Act Regulations,[1] which require detailed testing as to quality control, safety, and clinical effectiveness. Also, the Hazardous Products (Toys) Regulations,[2] detail the specific testing procedures in defining regulatory standards. For the majority of products, however, product testing remains voluntary, even though the applicable regulatory standards may be mandatory.

A number of testing associations and agencies do exist, the most well-known being the Canadian Standards Association (CSA). The CSA is a non-government agency and has no authority to enforce the use of its standards or certification programs. The CSA conducts tests on a voluntary basis to ensure that products meet CSA standards. Products meeting these standards are granted CSA certification. Many municipal, provincial, or federal governments have recognized CSA standards by incorporating or referencing them in their own regulatory standards.

The CSA is also accredited as an "Issuing and Recognizing" National Certification Body (NCB) under the International Electrotechnical Commission Electrical Equipment/Certification Bodies (IECEE/CB) Scheme, which applies to electrical and electronic products. This

---

1 Food and Drugs Act Regulations, C.R.C. 1978, c. 869-871.

2 Hazardous Products (Toys) Regulations, C.R.C. 1978, c. 931 amended by P.C. 1978-1381, P.C. 10980-1105.

accreditation enables the CSA to test a product and issue a Test Certificate and Report for that product; the Certificate and Report may then be accepted by an NCB in a member country without further testing. As an NCB, the CSA also accepts the Certificates and Reports of other NCBs in granting CSA certification in Canada.

3.2 Distribution and Effect of Test Results

The Competition Act provides that a test as to the performance, efficacy, or length of life of a product, if made in a representation to the public, must meet specified requirements regarding the reliability of the test results. Any person contravening the Act is guilty of an offense and is liable on summary conviction or indictment to a fine or imprisonment.[1] Proof of the absence of any testing or inspection system will generally give clear support for a finding of liability in negligence against a manufacturer[2] and the Act provides for good faith defenses to liability.

A manufacturer is not required to perform tests which are commercially unfeasible.[3] The Court will consider whether the procedures for quality control and testing were reasonable in the circumstances.[4] The custom of the industry is always given substantial weight in determining the standard of care, but it is not conclusive. Similarly, where a manufacturer has met a standard of care required by statutory specifications, a plaintiff must adduce evidence establishing that the standards were inappropriate or that testing and inspection procedures were inadequate in order to succeed.[5]

---

1 Competition Act, s.60.

2 Mueller, "Products Liability in Tort", *Torts in the 1980s*, Law Society of Upper Canada, 1983 Special Lectures, at p. 100.

3 *Yachetti* vs. *John Duff & Sons Ltd.* [1942], O.R. 682 (Ont. H.C.) (testing for bacteria in pork was not commercially feasible, and no liability was incurred).

4 *Hart* vs. *Dominion Stores Ltd.* (1968), *1 O.R. 775 (Ont. H.C.)* (method of bottle inspection was inadequate to detect weakened bottles); *MacLenahan* vs. *Dominion Stores Ltd.*, Ont. Dist. Ct., Webb D.C.J., 16 November 1988 (method of bottle inspection inadequate); *Willis* vs. *FMC Machinery and Chemicals Ltd. et al.* (1976), 68 D.L.R. (3rd) 127 (AT P.E.I.S.C.) (defendant negligent in not allowing a longer period of testing of a herbicide); *Western Processing and Cold Storage Ltd. et al.* vs. *Hamilton Construction Co. et al.* (1965), 51 W.W.R. 354 (Man. C.A.) (defendant liable for supplying untested insulation material); and *Lesmesurier* vs. *Union Gas Co.* (1975), 57 D.L.R.(3d) 344 (Ont. H.C.) (utility negligent in supplying defective equipment where testing facility existed).

5 *VISP Construction* vs. *Scepter Mfg. Co.*, Ont. Gen. Divs. Number 26308-88, 14 March 1991 (plaintiff adduced no evidence that standards were inappropriate or that testing and inspection procedures were inadequate, and accordingly, plaintiff failed to prove case).

In order to discharge its duty of care, a manufacturer must ensure that its product is subjected to a system of quality control commensurate with the risk involved. The adequacy of any given system of testing and inspection for latent defects will depend on the nature of the product and the gravity of the risks. In all cases, the suggested system must be practicable, economically feasible in relation to the risk, and apt to reduce the likelihood of damage occurring.[1] Even where an acceptable system of testing and inspection is in place, a manufacturer may still be held liable for the failure of an individual employee to operate the system with a requisite standard of care.

A manufacturer may be liable where a product has been released in a clearly defective state, even though an acceptable system of testing and inspection otherwise ensures quality control. In these instances, the specific facts of the case may permit the application of the maxim *res ipsa loquitur.*[2]

Although the question is unsettled, a retailer may have a duty to carry out independent tests and inspections to discover defects in its retail products.[3] A retailer may be bound to carry out such tests and inspections as are practicable and reasonably necessary having regard to the nature of the product and the size, prestige, and facilities of the retailer. Inquiries as to a manufacturers' systems of quality control and testing

---

1 Miller, *Product Liability* (London, Butterworths, 1977).

2 Arendale vs. *Canada Bread* (1941), 2 D.L.R. 41 (Ont. C.A.) (glass particles in loaf of bread); *Zeppa* vs. *Coca-Cola Ltd.* (1955), 5 D.L.R. 187 (Ont. CA) (glass particles in bottled soft drink); *Mathews* vs. *Coca-Cola Co. of Canada Ltd.*,[1944] 2 D.L.R. 355 (Ont. C.A.) affirmed [1945] 1 D.L.R. 1 (S.C.C.) (dead mouse in bottled soft drink); *Verga* vs. *John Labatt Ltd. et al.* (1956), 6 D.L.R. (2d) 336 (Ont. H.C.) (chlorine in bottled beer); and *Buckley* vs. *Mott* (1919), 50 D.L.R. 408 (N.S.S.C.) (powdered glass in chocolate bar). However, *see Saddlemire* vs. *Coca-Cola Co.* [1941] 4 D.L.R. 614 (Ont. H.C.) (a reasonable possibility of intermediate examination by the consumer was held to insulate the manufacturer from liability for a dead mouse in a soft drink bottle); and *MacLachalan & Mitchell Homes Ltd.* vs. *Frank's Rentals and Sales Ltd.* (1979), 10 C.C.L.T. 306 (Alta. C.A.) (a fire originating from a television set could have been the result of unexplained agencies having intervened, and the court cautioned that the maxim of *res ipsa loquitur* should not be used to secure a covert form of strict liability).

3 *Nernberg* vs. *Shop-Easy Stores Ltd.* (1966), 57 D.L.R. (2d) 741 (Sask. C.A.) (retailer liable for failing to detect external cracks in glass jar which injured plaintiff); and *Kubach* vs. *Hollands*, [1937] 3 All E.R. 907 (K.B.) (retailer liable for distribution of explosive chemicals to plaintiff where ample opportunity existed for examination by retailer).

may satisfy such a requirement. Similarly, a distributor may also have a duty to conduct independent tests and inspections on products which it distributes.[1]

1 *See* Mueller, "Products Liability in Tort", in *Torts in the 80s*, Law Society of Upper Canada, 1983 Special Lectures, at p. 100. *Leitz* vs. *Saskatoon Drug and Stationery Co. Ltd.* (1980), 112 D.L.R. (3d) 106 (Sask. Q.B.) (distributor of sunglasses held liable where it failed to verify advertising claim of "impact-resistant" lenses); *Donsmore* vs. *DeShield* (1977), 80 D.L.R. (3d) 386 (Salk. C.A.) (manufacturer and optometrist held negligent for failing to test whether lenses delivered as "hardex" possessed the impact-resistance claimed); *Watson* vs. *Buckley, Osborne, Garrett & Co. Ltd.* [1940], 1 All E.R. 174 ("old established, important and highly reputable" distributor held liable for not testing hair dye advertised as safe); and *Lesmurier* vs. *Union Gas Co., supra. See*, however, *Castle* vs. *Davenport-Campbell Co.*, [1952] 3 D.L.R. 540 (Ont. C.A.) (an installer was not liable in negligence for a faulty valve in a pump which could not be detected by reasonable examination); *Direct Warehousing & Transfer Ltd.* vs. *John Clouster Ltd.* (1976), 10 Nfld. & AT P.E.I.R. 122 (Nfld. T.D.) (a manufacturer of an oil burner cannot expect a furnace installer to dismantle a burner to inspect for defects); and *Quinton* vs. *Robert & Robert* (1978) Ltd. (1988), 76 Nfld. & AT P.E.I.R. 64 (Nfld. T.D.) (a distributor was under no obligation to inspect windows received from manufacturer prior to installation where there was no reason to suspect a defect existed).

Section 4

Advertising Claims

The very nature of advertising requires a fairly high degree of regulation. The direct communication to the consumer in an attempt to influence buying habits creates a situation which is ripe for abuse, especially with advertisements directed at the more vulnerable elements of society. The regulation of the industry attempts to balance freedom of speech with the consumer's right to useful information and at the same time reflect societal values and norms.

The sources of regulation in Canada range from federal and provincial statutes and regulations to guidelines published by various federal and provincial agencies and industry associations. The scope of this paper does not permit an extensive review of this regulatory framework. However, a brief look at some of the more comprehensive legislation regulating advertising will provide a basis to more effectively analyze the specific issues of comparison advertising, media channels, and target audiences, and how these are regulated in the interest of the consumer.

The Competition Act is a federal statute which, among other things, prohibits misleading advertising in the sale of a product to the public.[1]

Several provinces have enacted legislation aimed at controlling unfair or unethical trade practices.[2] Most include the making of misleading or deceptive representations as an unfair practice. All advertisements, regardless of which media channel is utilized or the subject matter of the message, must comply with these provisions.

The Broadcasting Act empowers the Canadian Radio-Television and Telecommunications Commission (CRTC) to regulate broadcasting in Canada, including the character of advertising and the amount of time broadcasters can devote to advertising. Further, the CRTC can impose conditions on would-be broadcasters before granting a broadcasting license. For example, the CRTC requires compliance with certain advertising industry codes and standards as a condition of granting a broadcasting license.

---

1 Competition Act, s.52 (4).

2 Unfair Trade Practices Act, R.S.A. 1980, c. U-3; Trade Practice Act, R.S.B.C. 1979, c. 406; Trade Practice Act, R.S.N. 1990, c. T-7; Business Practices Act, R.S.O. 1990, c. B-18; Business Practices Act, R.S.A.T.P.E.I. 1988, c. B-7; Consumer Protection Act, R.S.Q., c. P-40.1, as amended, Title II Business Practices; Trade Practices Inquiry Act, R.S.M. 1987, c. T-110.

The Canadian Code of Advertising Standards (CCAS),[1] administered by the Advertising Standards Council, establishes codes of conduct for advertisers, their agencies, and the media. The code itself is supplemented by various other industry codes which are more specific in nature. These codes of conduct are developed by the advertising community and, therefore, voluntary compliance is generally achieved. If the code is contravened, and the advertiser will not take corrective action voluntarily, the Council will advise all media of the contravention, and the media will not accept the message for broadcast in its existing form.[2]

The foregoing gives a very general outline of how advertising is regulated in Canada. The following discussion deals specifically with the regulation of comparative advertising, media channels, and target audiences.

4.1 Comparisons

As a general rule, comparative advertising is an acceptable practice in Canada. The contents of comparative advertisements are subject to the same legal considerations as any other advertisement; that is, whether or not any statement or representation made in the advertisement is false or materially misleading. There is very little legislation regulating comparative advertising specifically. Industry codes of standards provide most of the protection to consumers in this area.

The General Guidelines for Advertising,[3] which is a supplement to the CCAS and is intended to apply to all advertising, regardless of the medium used, includes a section dealing with comparative advertising. The Advertising Standards Council recognizes the legitimacy of utilizing comparisons in advertising as a way of making the information meaningful to consumers, yet at the same time recognizes that this type of advertising is particularly susceptible to abuse by competitors. Suggested guidelines to avoid the unethical use of comparative advertising include using a competitor's name only in the context of a factual comparison, only comparing products that actually compete with one another, only comparing related or similar features, only comparing elements which are measurable and significant in terms of consumer satisfaction, and avoiding the use of selective comparisons to imply

1 *The Source*, Institute of Canadian Advertising, at p. 8550.
2 *The Source*, Institute of Canadian Advertising, at p. 8551.
3 *The Source*, Institute of Canadian Advertising, at p. 8904.

overall superiority. Also, "dangling comparisons" (i.e., utilizing terms like "faster", "better", etc., without comparison to another product) are recognized as being potentially deceptive.[1]

Specific guidelines relating to the use of comparative advertising in food commercials, cosmetics, toiletries, and fragrances also exist.[2]

The nature of comparative advertising requires that the advertiser identify the competitor's product by name or brand. If this name or brand is a trademark, various provisions of the Trademarks Act[3] must be complied with. Section 7 of the Act prohibits any person from:

(1) Making a misleading statement;
(2) Directing public attention to his business in such a way as to cause confusion in Canada; and
(3) Making use of any description that is false in a material respect.

It should be noted that, nationally, under the Broadcast Code for Advertising to Children, comparative toy advertising is specifically prohibited. Likewise, Quebec prohibits all comparative advertising directed at children.[4]

4.2 Media Channels

4.2.1 In General

The distribution or dissemination of commercial messages in various media channels is regulated in Canada in an effort to protect the consumer from excessive exposure to societal problems. Much of this regulation is categorized on the basis of the subject matter of the message itself, rather than comprehensive regulation of any particular media channel from one source.

As noted previously, the jurisdiction to regulate radio and television advertising is found in the Broadcasting Act, which provides for the enactment of regulations "respecting the character of advertising and the amount of time that may be devoted to advertising".

---

1 *See* Black, "A Brief Word About Advertising", *Ottawa Law Review*, Volume 20, Number 3, 1988, at p. 538.

2 "Advertising Code of Standards for Cosmetics, Toiletries and Fragrances", *The Source*, Institute of Canadian Advertising, at p. 8600.

3 Trademarks Act, R.S.C. 1985, c. T-10.

4 Consumer Protection Act, R.S.Q., c. P-40.1, as amended, s.248.

The advertising of alcohol and tobacco products is heavily regulated on both the federal and provincial levels, and throughout the media. There is little perceived societal value to these products. Therefore, advertising restrictions are imposed in an effort to curb society's use of them. There is also significant regulation of the media with respect to advertising food and drugs and hazardous goods.

4.2.2 Alcohol Advertising

The Television Broadcasting Regulations, 1987[1] prohibit the broadcast of commercial advertising of alcoholic beverages unless:

(1) The sponsor of the advertisement is a brewer, winery, ciderhouse, or distiller;
(2) The sponsor is not prohibited under provincial laws from advertising;
(3) The message is not designed to promote general consumption of alcohol;
(4) The advertisement complies with the Code for Broadcast Advertising of Alcoholic Beverages; and
(5) The script has been approved by the CRTC.[2]

Within the regulation itself, reference is made to provincial legislation and industry codes respecting the advertising of alcoholic beverages. All provinces have legislation restricting alcohol advertising generally, with most regulating areas such as the media channels which can be utilized, the message which is conveyed, prohibited target audiences (i.e., children), and limitations on the time of day when advertisements may be aired.

When suppliers are allowed to advertise in accordance with the above provisions, the Code for Broadcast Advertising of Alcoholic Beverages sets out a number of prohibitions with respect to the content of the advertisement itself. These restrictions are aimed at ensuring the product is portrayed in as positive a manner as possible. For example, the message cannot associate consumption with the operation of a motor vehicle; nor can it attempt to establish the product as a necessity of life.

---

1 Television Broadcasting Regulations, 1987, S.O.R./87-49, as amended.
2 Television Broadcasting Regulations, 1987, s.6.

4.2.3 Tobacco Advertising

The Tobacco Products Control Act[1] is designed to prohibit advertising and promotion and restrict sponsorship of tobacco products. Clearly, this legislation is in response to a national public health problem. The Act prohibits advertising of tobacco or tobacco products in any media in Canada, including advertising in any media originating outside of Canada for the purpose of promoting the product in Canada.[2]

Sponsorship by manufacturers of tobacco products is restricted to utilizing the company's full name in representations to the public which promote cultural or sporting events.[3] The Act also requires that packaging of tobacco products be in accordance with the regulations, including requisite health warnings.[4]

The tobacco industry itself has established an advertising code of conduct, with the imposition of sanctions against the offending party for non-compliance.[5]

4.2.4 Food and Drugs

The Broadcasting Act and regulations thereto require that any commercial for a food, drug, cosmetic, or device to which the Food and Drugs Act applies, or any commercial which contains a recommendation for the treatment of a disease or ailment, must have the script pre-approved to ensure compliance with the Food and Drugs Act, the Narcotics Control Act,[6] the Consumer Packaging and Labeling Act, and any regulations thereto.[7]

The Food and Drugs Act prohibits advertising products governed by the Act in a false, misleading, or deceptive way, or so as to create an erroneous impression regarding their character, value, quantity, composition,

---

1 Tobacco Products Control Act, R.S.C. 1985, c. 14 (4th Supp.); Tobacco Products Control Act, S.C. 1988, c. 20.

2 Tobacco Products Control Act, ss.1, 2, and 4.

3 Tabacco Products Control Act, s.6.

4 Tobacco Products Control Act, s.9; Tobacco Products Control Regulations, S.O.R./89-21, as amended.

5 "Cigarette and Cigarette Tobacco Advertising and Promotion Code of the Canadian Tobacco Manufacturers' Counsel", *The Source*, Institute of Canadian Advertising, at p. 8560.

6 Narcotics Control Act, R.S.C. 1985, c. N-1.

7 Television Broadcasting Regulations, 1987, S.O.R./87-49, as amended, s.7; Radio Regulations, 1986, S.O.R./86-982, as amended, s.5.

merit, or safety.[1] The regulations to the Act prescribe standards for those products, and those standards must be met in order to advertise the product as a food, drug, device, or cosmetic.[2]

4.2.5 Hazardous Products

Federal legislation prohibits entirely the advertising and sale of certain hazardous products, while allowing for the advertisement and sale of other hazardous products in accordance with regulations enacted under the Act.[3] Many of the regulations relate to labeling requirements and do not restrict the choice of media channel used in the advertisement.

4.2.6 Regulation of Alternate Media Channels

Each of Canada's provinces has enacted statutes which regulate the location of signboards, billboards, and other forms of outdoor advertising. These statutes do not regulate the content of the advertisement, but merely its location. The regulation of the content is governed by the sources previously discussed.

The labeling of specific products could be described as a separate media channel used to advertise products. The numerous regulations imposing specific requirements on labeling are discussed in Section 2.

4.2.7 Target Audiences

The only major target audience which is subjected to special regulation in Canada is children. The legislation and codes of conduct recognize the special characteristics of such an audience, and attempt to eliminate the potential abuse of that audience.

The Broadcast Code for Advertising to Children sets out clear and comprehensive guidelines with respect to what can and cannot be utilized in commercial messages aimed at children under twelve years of age. The Code includes, among other provisions, guidelines aimed at avoiding undue pressure on parents, establishing scheduling

---

1 Food and Drugs Act, ss.5, 9, and 20.
2 Food and Drugs Act, ss.6, 10, 17, and 21.
3 Hazardous Products Act, R.S.C. 1985, c. 24 (3rd Supp.).

prohibitions, and prohibiting promotions by characters, as well as the depiction of products in an unsafe manner.

Further, the advertisement may not be inconsistent with ethical or legal standards in contemporary Canadian society, and if claims are made regarding specific product qualities, the advertiser must be prepared to provide evidence supporting such a claim. As additional assurance of compliance with the Code, all advertisements directed at children must be pre-approved by the Advertising Standards Council.

In Quebec, the Consumer Protection Act specifically prohibits advertising directed at children under thirteen years of age, except in certain limited circumstances.[1] Division II, Chapter VII of the Regulations deals with advertising directed at children. Specifically, advertising is only allowed if it appears in a children's magazine which is for sale and not published more than once every three months, if it is to announce a child's program or show, or if the advertisement consists of a store window, display, container, or wrapper. All of these exemptions are subject to regulations which prohibit, *inter alia*, exaggeration of the character, performance, or duration of the goods, use of superlatives, use of comparisons, directly inciting a child to buy, the portrayal of reprehensible family lifestyles or a person acting in an imprudent manner, portrayal of a product in a dangerous manner, or the use of animated cartoons or comic strips.[2]

As noted previously, there are prohibitions against directing comparative advertisements at children. In addition, many of the codes and legislation that restrict advertising of specific products prohibit messages directed at children.

1 Consumer Protection Act, s.248.

2 Regulations under the Consumer Protection Act, R.R.Q., 1981, c. P-40.1, r. 1, as amended, ss.88-90.

Section 5

Standard Terms (Adhesive Contracts)

There are no statutes which specifically address standard term contracts. However, each province's Sale of Goods Act[1] contains provisions which are relevant to most of the sub-headings below.

5.1 Delivery and Payment Terms

The question of where goods shall be delivered is determined by the terms of the contract. Normally, the place of delivery is the seller's business address. However, in the case of specific goods which are located elsewhere, delivery will be at such other place. If time is not fixed by the terms of the contract, then the goods must be delivered within a reasonable time.[2]

Delivery by installments will be binding on the buyer only if agreed to in the contract. If delivery by installments is agreed to, then non-delivery or non-payment of one of these installments may or may not lead to a repudiation of the whole contact, depending on the specific terms.[3]

If a seller is ready, willing, and able to deliver goods and so informs the buyer, and the buyer does not take delivery within a reasonable length of time, the buyer will be liable to the seller for any damages suffered, together with a reasonable charge for care and custody of the goods.[4]

---

1 For a full discussion of these Acts, *see Canadian Commercial Law Guide*, C.C.H. Canadian Limited.

2 Alberta: R.S.A. 1980, c. S-2, s.30; British Columbia: R.S.B.C. 1979, c. 370, s.33; Manitoba: R.S.M. 1987, c. S10, s.31; New Brunswick: R.S.N.B. 1973, c. S-1, s.27; Newfoundland: R.S.N. 1990, c. S-5, s.31; Nova Scotia: R.S.N.S. 1989, c. 408, s.31; Ontario: R.S.O. 1990, c. S 1, s.28; Prince Edward Island: R.S.P.E.I. 1988, c. S-l, s.29; Saskatchewan: R.S.S. 1978, c. S-1, s.29.

3 Alberta: s.32; British Columbia: s.35; Manitoba: s.33; New Brunswick: s.29; Newfoundland: s.33; Nova Scotia: s.32; Ontario: s.30; Prince Edward Island: s.31; Saskatchewan: s.31.

4 Alberta: s.36; British Columbia: s.41; Manitoba: s.39; New Brunswick: s.35; Newfoundland: s.39; Nova Scotia: s.39; Ontario: s.36; Prince Edward Island: s.37; Saskatchewan: s.37.

5.2 Risk

Contractual terms regarding risk are generally known as exclusion or exemption clauses in Canada. The provinces have legislation designed to prevent the exclusion of sellers' obligations in consumer sales pursuant to each province's Sale of Goods Act.

Several provinces have enacted legislation which provides for an outright ban on exemption clauses in consumer sales transactions.[1] In addition, some provincial legislation deals with unfair business practices and, as an incident thereto, provides control over some kinds of exemption clauses. These include, but are not limited to, the Business Practices Act in Ontario,[2] the Unfair Trade Practices Act in Alberta,[3] and the Trade Practice Act in British Columbia.[4] The legislation varies between provinces and should be carefully studied in each case.

As to transfer of risk, goods will remain at the seller's risk until the property in the goods passes to the buyer. Where the property in the goods is transferred to the buyer, the goods are at the buyer's risk whether or not delivery has occurred. If delivery is delayed, the risk in the goods will lie with the party who is at fault.[5]

5.3 Title

A buyer who purchases goods from a seller who is not the owner of the goods and who does not have the authority or consent of the owner to sell those goods, acquires no better title to the goods than the seller had. In some cases, the owner of the goods may be precluded by virtue of his conduct from denying the seller's authority to sell. If the seller has a voidable title which has not been avoided at the time of the sale, the buyer acquires good title to goods bought in good faith and without notice of the defect in title.[6]

---

1 Ontario: R.S.O. 1990, c. C-31, s.34; Manitoba: R.S.M. 1987, c. C-200, s.58; Nova Scotia: R.S.N.S. 1989, c. 92, ss.26, 27; British Columbia: R.S.B.C. 1979, c. 370, s.20.

2 R.S.O. 1990, c. B-18.

3 R.S.A. 1980, c. U-3.

4 R.S.B.C. 1979, c. 406.

5 Alberta: s.23; British Columbia: s.25; Manitoba: s.22; New Brunswick: s.21; Newfoundland: s.22; Nova Scotia: s.23; Ontario: s.21; Prince Edward Island: s.22; Saskatchewan: s.22.

6 Alberta: ss.24, 25; British Columbia: ss.26, 28; Manitoba: ss.23, 24; New Brunswick: ss.22, 23; Newfoundland: ss.23-25; Nova Scotia: ss.24-26; Ontario: ss.22, 24; Prince Edward Island: ss.23-25; Saskatchewan: ss.22, 24.

5.4 Conformity

Each province's Sale of Goods Act provides that, when there is a contract for the sale of goods by description, there is an implied condition that the goods shall correspond with the description. If the sale is by sample, as well as by description, it is not sufficient that the bulk of the goods correspond with the sample if the goods do not also correspond with the description.[1]

5.5 Rejection

When goods are sold by description, if goods of a different description are delivered and accepted in the belief that they accord with the terms of the contract, the buyer will not be in a position to return the goods after having accepted them. However, he may treat the breach of the condition as if it were a breach of warranty and then sue for damages.

If goods are delivered in a lesser quantity than contracted for, the buyer will be in a position to reject the goods. If goods are delivered in a quantity greater than contracted for, the buyer may accept the goods in the amount set out in the contract and reject the balance, or he may reject the whole. When goods contracted for are delivered with goods of a different description and not contracted for, the buyer may accept the goods contracted for and reject the balance, or he may reject the whole. These provisions may be altered by agreement.[2]

5.6 Replacement

The question of whether a dissatisfied buyer will be entitled to have defective goods replaced will depend on the terms of the contract.

---

1 Alberta: s.16; British Columbia: ss.17, 20 (2); Manitoba: s.15; New Brunswick: s.14; Newfoundland: s.15; Nova Scotia: ss.16, 17; Ontario: s.14; Prince Edward Island: s.15; Saskatchewan: s.15.

2 Alberta: s.31; British Columbia: s.34; Manitoba: s.32; New Brunswick: s.28; Newfoundland: s.31; Nova Scotia: s.32; Ontario: s.29; Prince Edward Island: s.30; Saskatchewan: s.30.

5.7 Refund

Again, this will depend on the terms of the contract. Of particular relevance is the Common Law regarding conditions and warranties.[1]

5.8 Warranty

There is no statutory requirement for warranties *per se*. This will generally depend on the terms of each contract. However, in the case of sale of goods, each province's Sale of Goods Act holds that when the buyer expressly or impliedly advises the seller of the purpose for which the goods are required and indicates that he is relying on the seller's skill and judgment, and when the goods in question normally are supplied in the seller's ordinary course of business, there will be an implied condition that the goods are fit for their particular purpose.[2]

5.9 Service

This is a matter of private contract law, and thus will depend on the terms of each specific contract.

1 For a full discussion of this topic, *see Canadian Commercial Law Guide*, C.C.H. Canadian Limited, at pp. 231-235.

2 Alberta: s.17; British Columbia: ss.18, 20 (2); Manitoba: s.16; New Brunswick: s.15; Newfoundland: s.16; Nova Scotia: s.17; Ontario: s.15; Prince Edward Island: s.16; Saskatchewan: s.16.

Section 6

Price Controls

This topic is addressed in more depth in Section 10, Implementing Consumer Rights. Examined herein are the checks and balances generally available in Canada.

6.1 Price Information

In Canada, there is legislation in place (for example, the Competition Act) to ensure that products and services are not dominated by a particular firm or organization that has unilateral market power. The possibility of anti-competitive acts by any one corporation depends on the demand and supply conditions in the market for the industry in question. Similarly, anti-dumping provisions and predatory pricing restraints prevent the ability of one supplier to discriminate against others and thereby lessen competition. The anti-dumping provisions have the effect of the protection and preservation of domestic competitors to some extent, while the predatory pricing laws simply proscribe the activity.

Minimum and maximum prices for natural products are often affected by national or provincial marketing boards.

6.2 Residual Controls against Exorbitant Prices

Canada is primarily a market-based economy *vis-à-vis* consumer products and services and, therefore, prices are generally market-driven except where anti-competitive acts are concerned, the latter being regulated and/or proscribed by statute. In addition, other businesses such as financial institutions, utilities, and natural products are regulated by government control or government agencies through legislation, regulatory boards, and marketing boards. Public interest advocacy groups are welcome to participate in hearings before these types of tribunals in order to ensure that consumer interests are voiced and that prices set are fair and reasonable.

6.3 Competition Law

The competition laws of Canada are designed to prevent monopolies, predatory pricing, and discriminatory pricing, and to encourage the development of competitive markets in all goods and services. Therefore, the marketplace with the assistance of government regulation will dictate the price of products which, in a perfect market-driven environment, would ensure fair consumer prices.

Typically, the interests of consumers are represented at the hearing level by organizations such as the Consumers Association of Canada and other consumer groups which are often funded (due to statutory requirement) by the proponent of the increased price.

However, public interest advocacy in Canada before the courts (as opposed to the regulatory tribunals) is weaker than in the United States, due in part to the lack of legislation providing for treble damage lawsuits and the inability of the private citizen to have access to the competition tribunal (*see* comments regarding class actions in Section 10).

The Director of the Bureau of Competition is aggressively prosecuting anti-competitive acts of corporations and their individual officers and directors to ensure compliance with Canada's anti-competitive laws.

Section 7

Installment Payments and Consumer Credit

7.1 Rates

In Canada, the rates at which consumers may borrow small amounts are governed by the Interest Act.[1] Unless otherwise legislated, the Interest Act generally provides that there is no restriction on the rate of interest or discount which may be agreed on by the parties to a contract.[2] There are, however, two provisions which have an impact on consumer transactions.

First, whenever any interest is payable by the agreement of the parties or by law, and no rate is fixed by the agreement or by law, the Act fixes the rate of interest at five per cent per annum.[3]

Second, if, by the terms of any written contract, any interest is payable at a rate or percentage for any period less than one year, no interest in excess of five per cent per annum is chargeable unless the contract contains an express statement of the equivalent yearly rate or yearly percentage of interest.[4] The Criminal Code of Canada also prescribes sanctions for the charging of a criminal interest rate, which is an effective annual rate which exceeds sixty per cent on the credit advanced.[5]

7.2 Disclosure

Consumer credit legislation in Canada provides for the disclosure of credit charges to consumers before they enter into a borrowing transaction.

1 R.S.C. 1985, c. I-18.
2 Interest Act, s.2.
3 Interest Act, s.3.
4 Interest Act, s.4.
5 Criminal Code, R.S.C. 1985, c. C-34, s.477.

Each of the provinces has enacted legislation requiring lenders in consumer transactions to disclose to consumers the full cost of the credit extended.[1]

Credit may be extended to consumers in three ways: in the sale of goods or services, by loan agreements, or by the extension of variable credit.

A lender who extends credit, with the exception of variable credit, is required to provide the borrower with a written disclosure statement before advancing the credit. In the statement, the full cost of borrowing must be expressed as one sum in dollars and cents and also as a yearly percentage rate. The written statement also must include, among other things:

(1) The amount to be received in cash by the borrower;
(2) The cash price of the goods or services received by the borrower;
(3) Any amount to be credited to the borrower as a down payment or for a trade-in; and
(4) The amount charged for insurance or other fees.

As the disclosure requirements vary between the provinces, the applicable provincial legislation should be consulted in each case.

Variable credit refers to credit which is made available to the borrower for the purchase of goods or services, but is to be used at the borrower's option. Variable credit generally includes revolving credit, budget and cyclical accounts, and deferred payment plans.

Before extending variable credit, a lender must provide the borrower with a written statement showing the full cost of borrowing with respect to the outstanding balances. The cost of borrowing must be expressed as a yearly percentage rate, or as a scale of percentages that the borrower

---

1 British Columbia: Consumer Protection Act, R.S.B.C. 1979, c. 65; Alberta: Consumer Credit Transactions Act, S.A. 1985, c. C-22.5; Saskatchewan: Cost of Credit Disclosure Act, R.S.S. 1978, c. C-41; Manitoba: Consumer Protection Act, R.S.M. 1987, c. C-200; Ontario: Consumer Protection Act, R.S.O. 1990, c. C-31; Quebec: Consumer Protection Act, R.S.Q. 1978, c. P-40.1; New Brunswick: Cost of Credit Disclosure Act, R.S.N.B. 1973, c. C-28; Newfoundland: Consumer Protection Act, R.S.Nfld. 1990, c. C-31; Nova Scotia: Consumer Protection Act, R.S.N.S. 1989, c. 92; Prince Edward Island: Consumer Protection Act, R.S.P.E.I. 1988, c. C-19. *See,* generally, Clark and Belanger, "Consumer Protection and Product Liability", in *Doing Business in Canada*, Stikeman and Elliot, Volume 3, Linton, ed. (Matthew Bender, Toronto, 1991), at S25.01[3][a]; and *Canadian Commercial Law Guide*, C.C.H. Canadian Ltd., North York, Ontario, 1993, at Paragraph 15-080.

is required to pay monthly or periodically on the unpaid balances and the minimum dollars and cents charge, if any.

The cost of borrowing also must be stated in dollars and cents in a schedule of outstanding balances showing the corresponding charges for the cost of borrowing. During the period in which credit is extended, the lender also must periodically provide the borrower with a written statement setting out the status of the account and the ongoing cost of borrowing. This statement must be provided every four to five weeks during the period that credit is extended. The written statement may include:

(1) The initial and final outstanding balances for the period;
(2) The cost of borrowing charged during the period;
(3) The amount credited to the account during the period; and
(4) The cost of borrowing with respect to unpaid balances.

The applicable legislation should be consulted for the specific disclosure requirements of each province.

It should be noted that the provinces have exempted certain types of transactions from their consumer protection legislation.[1] While the legislation differs in each province, the following are representative of the transactions exempted:

(1) Sales involving relatively small dollar values;
(2) Contracts for the sale of goods which are purchased for resale;
(3) Loans secured by mortgages on real estate;
(4) Credit extended for business purposes;
(5) Loans made by credit unions to their members; and
(6) Loans from life insurance companies to policyholders solely on the security of the cash surrender value of their policies.

---

1 British Columbia: Consumer Protection Act, R.S.B.C. 1979, c. 65, s.26 (2), B.C. Reg. 62/87, s.12; Alberta: Consumer Credit Transactions Act, S.A. 1985, c. C-22.5, ss.2, 3, and 20; Saskatchewan: Cost of Credit Disclosure Act, R.S.S. 1978, c. C-41, s.2 (2); Manitoba: Consumer Protection Act, R.S.M. 1987, c. C-200, ss.3, 4 (1), and 13 (1); Ontario: Consumer Protection Act, R.S.O. 1990, c. C-31, ss.1, 2; Quebec: Consumer Protection Act, R.S.Q. 1980, c. P-40.1, ss.2, 5, 5.1, 6, 6.1, 88-89, and 100; New Brunswick: Cost of Credit Disclosure Act, R.S.N.B. 1973, c. C-28, s.1. Newfoundland: Consumer Protection Act, R.S.Nfld. 1990, c. C- 31, s.2; Nova Scotia: Consumer Protection Act, R.S.N.S. 1989, c. 92, s.1; and Prince Edward Island: Consumer Protection Act, R.S.P.E.I. 1988, c. C-19, s.1.

Additionally, each province has enacted legislation which regulates the manner in which the cost of credit may be advertised.[1]

Generally, a lender may not advertise his charge for credit in any manner unless that advertisement includes the cost of borrowing expressed as a yearly percentage rate and in the same manner as is required for the written disclosure statement provided to the borrower. It should be noted, however, that Quebec has specific requirements regarding the use of certain terms in the advertising of credit.

7.3 Cancellation

In Quebec, a consumer may cancel a contract for credit or the loan of money at his or her discretion, without charge, within two days of the time that both parties are in possession of a copy of the contract.[2]

Each of the provinces provides that a consumer may prepay the amount owing on the principal and credit charges before the due date. In most cases, the lender may not charge a penalty for pre-payment and is required to provide a partial rebate to the borrower of the cost of borrowing.

1 British Columbia: Consumer Protection Act, R.S.B.C. 1979, c. 65, s.30, B.C. Reg. 62178, s.8; Alberta: Consumer Credit Transactions Act, S.A. 1985, c. C-22.5, ss.15, 16; Saskatchewan: Cost of Credit Disclosure Act, R.S.S. 1978, c. C-41, s.12; Manitoba: Consumer Protection Act, R.S.M. 1987, c. C-200, ss.26, 27; Ontario: Consumer Protection Act, R.S.O. 1990, c. C-31, s.29; Quebec: Consumer Protection Act, ss.244-247, 311, 312, and 316; New Brunswick: Cost of Credit Disclosure Act, R.S.N.B. 1973, c. C-28, ss.13, 18; Newfoundland: Consumer Protection Act, R.S.Nfld. 1990, c. C-31, ss.15, 19; Nova Scotia: Consumer Protection Act, ss.16, 20; and Prince Edward Island: Consumer Protection Act, R.S.P.E.I. 1988, c. C-19, ss.14, 20.

2 Consumer Protection Act, R.S.Q. 1980, c. P-40.1, ss.73-79.

Section 8

Trade Descriptions and Occupational Licensing

8.1 Scope and Application

Every province in Canada has legislation which requires the registration or licensing of various persons who are engaged in occupations which deal with the public. Licensing may be aimed at maintaining the standards of the profession or occupation, which in itself indirectly protects consumers, or it may be directly aimed at protecting consumers. Dishonest or unscrupulous individuals may be denied registration under the relevant acts and, therefore, at least in theory, are restrained from engaging in those occupations.[1]

The regulation of professions and occupations generally takes the form of restrictions on entry coupled with rules of conduct, which often include fee-setting and administration by a governing body. This regulation comes within the provincial power over property and civil rights.[2]

Businesses which require registration include collection agents, real estate agents and salespeople, motor vehicle dealers and salespeople, mortgage brokers, consumer reporting agencies, lenders, dealers, and vendors of farm implements, travel agents, and individuals engaged in funeral services. It should be remembered that not all of these occupations will be regulated in all of the provinces. Legislation relevant to the particular province should be examined.

8.2 Sanctions

As mentioned above, the various professions are self-regulated in their respective provinces. Sanctions for those who are found to be in violation of the governing statutes or bylaws of the professions include fines, suspension or revocation of membership, as well as exposure to liability for costs of any disciplinary proceedings.

---

1 For a full discussion of regulation of trades throughout the various provinces, *see Canadian Commercial Law Guide*, C.C.H. Canadian Limited, at p. 3025.

2 Hogg, *Constitutional Law of Canada*, 3rd ed., at p. 546.

The same is generally true for occupations other than the professions, except that the proceeding will be taken by some governmental body outside the occupation. The grounds on which registration or licenses may be cancelled, suspended, or refused will vary according to each act and each province.

Section 9

Merchandise Classes as Applied to Bulk Products

The classification of bulk products into various merchandise classes is a widespread practice in Canada, due largely to the country's agriculture and resource-based economy. While there is comprehensive legislation governing the packaging and labeling of pre-packaged products, the source of regulation for the classification of bulk products is very diverse. Federal and provincial statutes legislate on quality standards and the requisite compliance with those standards before the bulk product is graded accordingly.

The legislation is generally industry or product specific, and the scope of this paper does not permit a review of all the legislative schemes for classifying bulk products. Federally, feeds, fish, livestock, meat, seeds, timber, and wheat are examples of types of bulk products which are classified prior to sale or trade. Similarly, most provinces legislate the classification of dairy products, fish, livestock, and meat. The actual mechanisms for establishing and enforcing various merchandising classes will vary from province to province and also will depend on the nature of the product.

Reference should be made to federal legislation and the appropriate provincial legislation to determine the grading scheme and regulations with respect to labeling, selling, or advertising the product based on its classification.

There is one piece of federal legislation which is applicable to all bulk product classifications. The National Trade Mark and True Labeling Act[1] regulates the labeling of any commodity, package, or container regarding the material content or quality of the product. The National Research Council, at the request of the Minister of Consumer and Corporate Affairs, will advise on commodity standards and specifications for certain grades of products, as well as analyze any commodity for its content and qualities to determine if it complies with prescribed standards.

The protection afforded to the consumer by the classification of bulk products appears to be self-evident. Grading will provide the consumer with otherwise unavailable information regarding that product's quality

1 R.S.C. 1985, c. N-16.

and characteristics. The value of that information is only as good as the consumer's confidence in the grading process. The fact that grading is done by independent government agencies would appear to increase consumer confidence in this information.

Section 10

Implementing Consumer Rights

Although there are many remedies available to consumers, statistics show that only a minority take action of any kind.[1] Even then, disgruntled customers frequently begin and end the complaint process with a complaint to the seller.[2]

10.1 Information

While, as noted throughout this chapter, many useful statutes have been enacted to assist and support the consumer in situations involving violations of the marketplace rules and ethics, it can be concluded that, for some statutory schemes, the consumer faces difficulty assessing the information and then processing the complaint. However, active agencies regularly face regulatory tribunals and vigorously represent consumer interests.

10.2 Material Incentives

As discussed in Section 5, each province's Sale of Goods Act contains an implied condition of fitness for the purpose and a condition that goods shall be of merchantable quality. Further, the British Columbia Act prohibits sellers from excluding their obligations in the case of a "retail sale".

Protection can also be assured in those provinces that have enacted a Personal Property Security Act (P.P.S.A.).[3] Of central importance to the consumer in the personal property security scheme is the "seize or sue"

---

1 Best and Andreasen, "Consumer Response to Unsatisfactory Purchases: A Survey of Perceiving Defects, Voicing Complaints, and Obtaining Redress" (1976-77), 11 *Law and Society* R701.

2 Ramsay, "Consumer Redress Mechanisms for Poor Quality and Defective Products" (1981), 31 *University of Toronto Law Journal* 117.

3 Alberta: S.A. 1988, c. P-4.05; British Columbia: S.B.C. 1989, c. 36; Manitoba: R.S.M. 1987, c. P-35; Saskatchewan: S.S. 1979-80, c. P-6.1; Ontario: R.S.O. 1990, c. P-10.1.

election provision, which protects debtors in default in situations where the secured party is about to enforce its security interest in "consumer goods". A recent amendment to the British Columbia Personal Property Security Act prevents corporations from taking advantage of this provision.[1]

The British Columbia Consumer Protection Act and Trade Practice Act and their equivalents in other provinces present parallel and occasionally overlapping regimes for the implementation of consumer rights. A "deceptive act or practice" is defined in the Trade Practice Act,[2] and a non-inclusive list of examples is set out. A body of law has developed around this definition, so that a deceptive act will be one that tends to lead a person into making an error of judgment.[3]

The courts have noted that a deceptive act "does not necessarily involve deliberate intention to deceive", and have held that a supplier owes a positive duty of candor to the consumer. This duty embraces telling the consumer any material fact known to the supplier. What is a material fact will depend on the circumstances. "Puffery" will not excuse the giving of an unqualified opinion when the supplier has factual knowledge indicating that the opinion may in an important respect be wrong.[4]

The doctrine of unconscionability is a burgeoning area in Canadian law. Generally, in order to establish a claim of Common Law unconscionability, a party must establish, firstly, that there was an inequality in the position of the parties and, secondly, that the bargain was substantially unfair.[5] The British Columbia Trade Practice Act provides a statutory, non-inclusive definition of how a court is to decide whether or not "an act or practice is unconscionable",[6] while the Consumer Protection Act deals with unconscionability in the realm of mortgage transactions. The latter provision provides a list of "indicia of unconscionability",[7] largely drawn from the Common Law. Examples include "undue pressure by the lender" and situations where "the terms or conditions ... are so harsh or adverse to the debtor as to be inequitable".

---

1 Personal Property Security Act, s.55 (2.1.).

2 Trade Practice Act, s.5.

3 *British Columbia (Director of Trade Practices)* vs. *Household Finance Corp.* (1991), 59 B.C.L.R. (2d) 250, at p. 257.

4 *Rushak* vs. *Henneken* (1989), 35 B.C.L.R. (2d) 145.

5 *Principal Investments Ltd.* vs. *Thiele Estate* (1987), 12 B.C.L.R. (2d) 258, at p. 263 (C.A.).

6 Trade Practice Act, s.4.

7 Consumer Protection Act, s.43.

Punitive damages are available in Canada at Common Law but may only be awarded in respect of conduct which is deserving of punishment because of its harsh, vindictive, reprehensible, and malicious nature. Although usually awarded in tort actions, punitive damages also may be awarded in respect of a breach of contract.

Some provincial Acts include sections which contemplate an award of damages akin to Common Law punitive damages. Indeed, the British Columbia Consumer Protection Act contemplates an award for treble damages[1] when a seller fails to comply with some of the Act's previous sections, as outlined above, while the Trade Practice Act allows the court to award the plaintiff consumer damages, including punitive or exemplary damages, when the court has found a deceptive or unconscionable act or practice.[2]

10.3 Class Actions

The rules governing when a class action may be instituted arise by virtue of the interaction between each province's rules of court and the Common Law. Generally, where numerous persons have the same interest in a proceeding, the proceeding may be commenced and, unless the court otherwise orders, continued by or against one or more of them as representing all or as representing one or more of them.[3]

In determining whether to allow a class action, the court will ask whether the purported class is capable of clear and finite definition, whether the principal issues of fact and law are essentially the same as regards all members, and whether, assuming liability, there is a single measure of damages applicable to all the members.[4]

10.4 Streamlined Procedures

The term "streamlined" is not a term of art in Canadian law. Essentially, the provisions in both statutory and Common Law discussed above which allow class actions represent "streamlined" procedures to redress consumer complaints.

---

1 Consumer Protection Act, s.18.
2 Trade Practice Act, s.22.
3 *See*, for example, the British Columbia Rules of Court, R5 (11).
4 *Kripps et al.* vs. *Touche Ross and Company et al.* (1987), 7 B.C.L.R. (2d) 105 (S.C.).

In addition to class actions, in British Columbia, both the Trade Practice Act and the Consumer Protection Act contain separate provisions allowing for a variety of investigations to be conducted by the Director and for the use of force, if necessary, in the conduct of searches of persons suspected of having contravened those Acts.[1]

10.5 Technical and Material Support Groups

There are a variety of groups of this nature in Canada. They include, for example, the Consumers Association of Canada, the Better Business Bureau, the National Anti-Poverty Association, and the various professional associations discussed in Section 5.

Note: Co-authored by Dale B. Pope, David A. Goult, Nancy E. Fish, Neal S. Steinman, Charmaine H. Hung, Patricia Courtney, and Ronald S. Chin.

1 Trade Practice Act, s.10 (4); Consumer Protection Act, s.48 (1).

GPSR Compliance

The European Union's (EU) General Product Safety Regulation (GPSR) is a set of rules that requires consumer products to be safe and our obligations to ensure this.

If you have any concerns about our products, you can contact us on ProductSafety@springernature.com

In case Publisher is established outside the EU, the EU authorized representative is:

Springer Nature Customer Service Center GmbH
Europaplatz 3
69115 Heidelberg, Germany

Batch number: 10830943

Printed by Printforce, the Netherlands